Comic Book Culture

Fanboys and True Believers

Comic Book

Studies in Popular Culture
M. Thomas Inge, General Editor

Fanboys and True Believers

Culture

Matthew Pustz

University Press of Mississippi / Jackson

www.upress.state.ms.us

Copyright © 1999 by the University Press of Mississippi
All rights reserved
Printed in Canada

07 06 05 04 03 02 01 00 99   4 3 2 1

∞

Library of Congress Cataloging-in-Publication Data

Pustz, Matthew J., 1968–
    Comic book culture : fanboys and true believers / Matthew J.
Pustz.
        p.   cm. — (Studies in popular culture)
    Includes bibliographical references and index.
    ISBN 1-57806-200-4 (cloth : alk. paper). — ISBN 1-57806-201-2
(pbk. : alk. paper)
    1. Comic books, strips, etc. — United States — History and
criticism.   2. Books and reading — United States — History — 20th
century.   3. Comic book fans — United States — History — 20th
century.   4. Popular culture — United States — History — 20th century.
I. Title.   II. Series: Studies in popular culture (Jackson, Miss.)
PN6725.P87   1999
741.5'973'0904 — dc21   99-31140
                                                            CIP

British Library Cataloging-in-Publication Data available

To Mom and Dad, for giving me the inspiration to start this project. And to Jen, for giving me the inspiration to finish.

Contents

Introduction

American cultural diversity comes from more than just race and ethnicity. It is also born out of groups of people whose expressive lives center on particular interests or activities. Being involved in a culture based on popular media is central to the lives of many Americans, allowing them to identify themselves as fans. Like the media fans described by Henry Jenkins in *Textual Poachers: Television Fans and Participatory Culture,* American comic book readers and fans have also created a distinctive culture with its own language, knowledge, and practices—all based on their favorite texts. Most Americans may not be familiar with this comic book culture, but it is well known to those participating in it and to those creating the texts for it. As a result, depictions of fans and other comic book readers are common in the comics themselves.

One recent example accurately captures the idea that this group of people constitutes a unique culture. In *Simpsons Comics* #39, Homer and the Comic Book Guy, owner of Springfield's comic book shop, are put on trial for possessing and selling obscene comic books. Acting on behalf of himself and Homer, the Comic Book Guy's opening statement, filled with references to comics and science fiction films, so confuses the jury that the court needs a group of fans to translate. This situation gives Bart an idea for a defense. The next day, he takes over as the pair's lawyer and begins by telling the jury that he's a comic book reader. The translators are comic book readers, he explains, and so are Homer and the shop owner. But the members of the jury are not. "Did any of you even know comic books were still published when you became jurors? Have any of you been into a comic book store? Members of the jury, do you even know who ol' Bolthead is? How about Abin-Sur? Brother Voodoo?" he asks.

The point, Bart explains, turning to the judge, is that none of the jury are peers of the defendants. "They are not comic geeks. They aren't even sci-fi fans. They, your honor, are bland civilians!" His argument convinces the judge to fill the jury with members of the local fan community, pimple-faced young men and women with comic book slogans on their colorful T-shirts. The jury eventually finds the two men innocent of obscenity charges but guilty of other crimes, including "cover crinkling, price gouging, using highly acidic boards, selling comics soiled by burrito drippings, [and] ruining the ending to 'The Death of Superman'" (*Simpsons Comics* #39 [1998]: 17–21).

As the story in *Simpsons Comics* #39 suggests, comic book fans can be very different from ordinary (or nonfan) Americans. But the fans depicted in this story, devoted to superhero stories and fascinated by sci-fi television and movies, are not the only comic book readers. Acting almost as a separate culture within the larger one are people who enjoy what are called alternative comics. Working in opposition to their mainstream counterparts, alternative comics are aimed at an educated adult audience that is willing to read what are often very realistic stories in a medium normally devoted to heroic fantasy. These comics are often political, criticizing social mores, cultural trends, and political issues. Others merely offer a skewed view of the world or give voice to non- or even anticorporate stories.

Mainstream and alternative readers and the conflict between them are at the center of this work. By analyzing these and other reading communities involved with American comic books, this book will demonstrate that these groups function not just as separate entities, with different goals, preferences, and practices regarding their favored texts, but also as a broader (albeit not entirely unified) culture. This work characterizes these readers' worlds, illuminating heretofore ignored aspects of a generally maligned form of popular culture, and then examines how the comic books themselves contribute to the construction of these fan cultures. The book ends with an analysis of the sites of comic book culture: conventions, fanzines and magazines, letters pages, and various forms of electronic interaction.

The most important site, though, is the comic book store. Unknown to most nonreaders, comic shops serve as a kind of cultural clubhouse where fans can spend time being themselves among their friends and other like-minded individuals. Born out of changes in the ways in which comic books are distributed, the shops began to become common parts of the American retail landscape in the early 1980s. By the beginning of the 1990s, perhaps as many as 85 percent of all comics were purchased at these shops. Fans now often make weekly trips to their favorite shops to get the newest editions and to search for back issues to complete their collections. Most comic shops also sell collecting equipment (such as special bags, boards, and boxes to protect comics), comic-related T-shirts and toys, and other items of interest to fans, such as collectible card games and *Star Wars* action figures. Despite all the shops have to offer, many regulars find that the real reason for patronizing these establishments is interaction with the people there, including other customers and employees. In this way, the comic book store is a site for culture as well as commerce.

Of course, comic book culture began long before comic book specialty shops came into existence. Beginning in the 1940s, when as many as 95 percent of all American children were reading comics, the medium had a very distinctive audience. Many publishers were actively trying to get their youthful audience to identify with the characters, leading to the creation of young sidekicks for heroes such as Batman and the Human Torch as well as groups of urban boys banded together to fight for themselves and against the Nazis and Japanese. Comic books were popular with many soldiers as well as children. As soldiers began to return home after the end of the war, publishers shifted the comics' subject matter, moving from superheroes to more realistic genres, such as romance and crime, to appeal to this audience. Many of these comics were openly aimed at adults, even announcing their targets on the cover. Other companies, such as EC Comics, were consolidating their younger audience by creating a sense of cooperation between readers and creators. Letters pages in EC titles such as *Vault of Horror* and *Weird Science* allowed fans to interact with each other and, in the company's horror comics, with the titles' hosts.

Both of these trends of the late 1940s and early 1950s came to an end in large part because of the controversy over comics (fueled by Fredric Wertham's *Seduction of the Innocent*) and the eventual passage of the Comics Code. This list of what could and could not be depicted in comics helped to bring about a sharp decline in comic sales, and many companies were forced out of business. Others, such as DC, shifted their emphasis back to the superheroes who had been so successful during World War II. This revival helped to create comic fandom, as older readers who enjoyed both the original heroes and their new counterparts began to contact and meet with each other. The early Marvel comics of the 1960s appealed to these fans, too, but the company solidified its audience even further by following the example of EC and creating a rhetoric of cooperation between its fans and creators. By doing this, Marvel created a group of "true believers" who thought that they were reading cutting-edge literature that made them superior to people reading the comics of other companies as well as to those who did not read comics at all.

The world of contemporary comic book readers is still filled with people devoted to Marvel and its characters. Superheroes are still the dominant genre, now making up the majority of mainstream comics published in the United States. Most of the people reading these comics are young males from approximately ten to twenty-one years of age. There are also older readers, still devoted to the comics of their childhood, and a few women. Readers often have very different reasons for buying comics, though. Some are overt speculators, buying comics as an investment and hoping to sell them as they increase in value. Some of these speculators buy rare comics from the 1940s that can be worth tens of thousands of dollars, but others merely purchase multiple copies of current comics, hoping to catch a popular trend or character. The term *fanboy* originates in this phenomenon: many other readers use the term derisively to describe young adolescents buying comics according to the dictates of magazines such as *Wizard* that tell their readers which characters and creators are "hot." Many of these fanboys do not even read their comics, instead putting them into sealed plastic bags to insure that they stay in mint condition and thereby insuring maximum resale value. Other mainstream readers have recaptured the term *fanboy,* using it to describe reading comics of any kind with a sense of fun and fascination, but the term remains controversial within comic book culture.

The alternative comics audience has much greater diversity. Including older, often more literary-minded readers and more women, this segment of comic culture can make generalization difficult. Politically and culturally, they are more liberal than their mainstream counterparts, and many are also involved with various forms of alternative music. The comics they enjoy can range widely, from DC's Vertigo imprint, including titles such as *Sandman* and *Preacher,* which offer mythological/theological speculation and moody stories, to independent comics produced by individuals through small, non-corporate companies, to truly alternative comics that offer challenges to the political and social status quo. Other alternative readers, including some academics, have become comics snobs, focusing their reading on European comics or the most obscure, hard to find minicomics.

Despite this conflict, comic book culture is still somewhat unified, if only by the comics themselves. Mainstream and alternative readers are all devoted to the comics medium and are united by their knowledge and expertise in comics literacy. At its most basic level, this literacy includes fluency in the language of comics. Different from straight prose or film, comics uses a unique language that demands training and experience for full understanding. Scott McCloud explains this language in *Understanding Comics: The*

Invisible Art, but most readers have already internalized it through their experience with comics. Comics literacy is manifest in other places as well: in comics that violate the rules of the medium, allude to and parody various events and figures in its history, and discuss comics creators and fans. All these literacy-based comics limit and define the audience for comic books to those people who already have the knowledge necessary to understand them. These limitations — often knowingly put there by the creators themselves — work to form one of the most essential boundaries between comic book culture and the outside world.

This culture has been constructed in other ways as well. Comic book conventions, held annually throughout the United States, give fans a physical place to gather. There, they can buy comics from a wide variety of dealers and meet and get advice from comic book professionals. Various meetings are held during the conventions to allow fans to talk about their favorite comics and characters. Fan groups often plan their own gatherings that allow members to meet old friends. Other activities include trivia contests, seminars for prospective creators, and masquerade balls. Fans also gather in the comic books themselves, as letters pages provide a textual meeting site. On these pages, readers can interact with each other (through debates), the creators of their favorite titles (through letters of praise and criticism), and the content of the comic book (through interpretations of stories). Other fans gather in magazines and fanzines where they discuss broader issues in comic book culture. In fanzines especially, readers have offered their own interpretations of comics and other issues without the interference of magazine or letters-page editors. These kinds of opinions can also be found in various forms of electronic interaction, thereby giving fans a virtual site for their gatherings. Many of the interactions that occur in fanzines also take place on web pages, but other forms of computer-aided communication — such as chat rooms and Internet role-playing games called MUDs — allow comic fans to interact with each other in real time.

All these different forms of interaction have helped to form comic book culture. Just as Bart Simpson argued, comic book fans differ from other Americans. They have different interests, different experiences, and even a different language. This culture is important, however, because of the centrality of participation in it. Nearly every member of comics culture — nearly every reader of comic books — is an active participant, not just a consumer. Whether participation occurs at comic book conventions or the comic shop, in letters pages or fanzines, on web pages or in the imaginations of readers dreaming of one day becoming professional writers or artists, it is more widespread than in any other culture centered around popular media. This book will show how this culture can serve as an important example of how culture in general is created through participation and boundaries.

A note about methodology: much of the research for this book was conducted through interviews with comic book fans. Some of these interviews were conducted in person from October 1995 to August 1996. Many of the fans that I interviewed were employees at Daydreams, an Iowa City comic book shop, while others were people who were involved in a graduate-student comic book–reading group that was active approximately from the spring of 1995 through the fall of 1997. A few of the people interviewed were regular Daydreams customers who had filled out a survey I distributed there in the fall of 1995. Other interviews were done through the mail with people who had responded to a questionnaire I mailed in late May 1996 to fans who had written to the *Comic Buyers' Guide.* These responses (many of them quite detailed and very forthright) were received over the following three months. All of the quotations that are not otherwise attributed come from these interviews.

I owe a debt of thanks to a number of people who, sometimes unknowingly, helped in the creation of this book. First, I am grateful to the people at Daydreams Comics and Cards for always being helpful and happy to answer any of my questions. Paul Tobin at Daydreams deserves a special thanks for his willingness to be interviewed for an earlier project that got me interested in comic books again, both as a reader and as an academic. I also thank the special collections librarians at Michigan State University, popular culture librarians at Bowling Green State University, and workers in the interlibrary loan department of the University of Iowa's library, without whom the research for this work would have proved impossible. I am grateful to the comics creators who agreed to have their work included in my book and to my dissertation adviser, Brooks Landon, whose praise gave me the encouragement to keep going. Finally, I thank Jen, my wife, for reading all this and for always believing in me. I could not have written this book without her.

Comic Book Culture

Fanboys and True Believers

1

Discovering Comic Book Culture

A pedestrian mall cuts through the middle of downtown Iowa City, providing University of Iowa students and other residents with a variety of bars, restaurants, and stores. There is a lot of foot traffic, especially when the weather is nice, as workers and students on their lunch hours escape their offices and classrooms to get a little air and sun. Others rush past the businesses on their way to class or an important meeting, only vaguely aware of what is inside each storefront.

"Daydreams Comics and Cards," says one of the windows. For the people who walk by it without going in, it is just a comic book shop. If they were to go in, though, they would find an alien world of bright colors and strange images. Displays of T-shirts and posters greet visitors with icons well known to the store's regulars. On either side are trade paperbacks—comic books and strips collected into hardcover and paperback books. Above them begins a series of color photocopies of especially rare comic books, from *Action Comics* to *X-Men*, arranged like wallpaper to show the shop's prized inventory. Farther in sits the counter, behind which are boxes of comics reserved for the shop's pull-list customers. On the counter itself are magazines devoted to comic books, action figures, and cult television and movies. Inside the glass case are more expensive items: statues, figurines, watches, and cigarette lighters, among other things. Opposite the counter is an alcove filled with classic comics collections, especially DC's Archives series, which republishes the earliest adventures of Superman, Batman, and others.

A replica of the head of Chewbacca the Wookie (from *Star Wars*) directs visitors around the corner and into a special room within the shop filled with toys of special interest to comics fans. Old action figures, from original versions of *Star Trek* heroes Kirk and Spock to Marvel supervillains in their original packages, are found here, but the bulk of the toys come from the *Star Wars* universe. Casual visitors to the store will stop here for a time and marvel at the cost of these toys from the 1970s and 1980s. "I had one of those land-speeders," someone will inevitably say. "I always wanted one of those Millennium Falcons," another moans. Occasionally one of these visitors will buy an old toy for the sake of nostalgia, but most of the display is aimed at collectors searching for particular figures to complete their collections.

Leaving the action-figure room, visitors find a large display of Japanese comics, or *manga,* which are becoming a more important part of the shop every day. Ranging from children's stories to near pornography, Daydreams' *manga* collection includes both English and original Japanese versions of many of the works that are considered classics in the field. Running along most of the east wall past the toy room is a display of *anime* videotapes — feature-length Japanese animated films — available for purchase or rent. And if visitors are lucky and smile at the right employee, they might even get to borrow a dubbed copy of a particularly hard-to-find video — at no cost.

Once visitors to Daydreams have gotten past all of these sections, the comic books finally appear. Racks of new comics fill the west wall of the shop past the counter all the way to the north wall. Above the comics are plastic sleeves housing the newest issues to help regular customers wade through material that has already been in the shop a couple of weeks. The racks of comics begin with a set of recommended reading — three or four titles from all of the Daydreams employees, highlighting their individual tastes and inspiring new purchases from regular customers who trust the workers' judgment. The long row displays recent issues of comics from virtually every publisher in the United States and Canada. Behind them are long boxes filled with the store's back stock — the collectors' treasure trove.

For some visitors, the part of the shop with comic books may not be very important. Many Americans — especially males — have read comics, with varying levels of involvement, as children and hence have some vague familiarity with the medium. Some people read or looked at a friend's or relative's comics, some received comics as gifts, and some even bought comics. A few people were even seriously involved with comics for a time. Most of these readers, though, abandon comic books at some point, deciding that they are not interesting (or, more likely, not cool), too expensive, or too juvenile. To these people, the display shelves of new comics can be a bit disconcerting. At a shop such as Daydreams, such visitors would find different kinds of comics with a wide variety of styles of images. Some of the titles, such as *Batman* or *Archie,* might be familiar, but most will be totally foreign to these patrons' previous experience with comics.

If the visitors glance at something that strikes a nostalgic chord, they might be a bit shocked by what is inside. Styles of art have changed, paper quality has improved, and coloring techniques have been upgraded. More important, though, the kinds of stories — and the ways of telling them — have changed. A woman who read *Detective Comics* in the early 1960s would be surprised by current stories' violence and grim and gritty focus. Even more recent comic book readers would be surprised. Some might be shocked to open a copy of *Hepcats* and find two anthropomorphic animals having sex; others might be appalled while paging through *Lady Death,* one of the many "bad girl" comics that feature powerful women with gravity-defying breasts doing horrific things to victims. A man who read *Uncanny X-Men* in the early 1980s would certainly be confused by the new situations and plethora of new characters if he picked up a new issue of one of the many X-titles.

Most regular customers will not even notice this confusion, since they will be busy picking out new comics, talking with employees, gossiping with friends about the new artist on *Wonder Woman,* or just silently counting the money in their wallets, trying to figure out if there is enough to buy an expensive back issue of *Green Lantern.* Most regulars are male (female patrons usually come in to get what they want and leave quickly, even though Daydreams is more female friendly than most comic book shops) and relatively young, usually around high school or college age. Some of these regulars pick out a stack of magazines that will become their weekly purchase; others retrieve the comics the shop has set aside for them from the week's shipment.[1] Both groups, though, always return to the racks of new comics to search for something they may have missed.

The bowels of the shop — with boxes of hundreds of thousands of carefully stored old comics and with racks of new issues of hundreds of titles — can easily overwhelm visitors new to the environment. Although arranged in alphabetical order, the back issues are not displayed for easy browsing. To find something, fans need to know the exact title and the specific issue number. There are no indexes and generally no genre or publisher categories. Regular comic shop patrons, however, have no trouble finding their way around the back issues and certainly are not afraid to dig around in the boxes. Here, fans, collectors, and speculators might be able to find a long-sought-after prize, a rare issue, a first appearance, or a special creative pairing. At the far end of the shop, another display counter houses role-playing games and equipment. Flyers are often posted to advertise the beginning of a new campaign, sometimes in a brand-new game, sometimes in an old favorite. As with the rest of the shop, most of this section be very strange to newcomers. After finishing this quick tour, visitors probably will not linger, because, for them, Daydreams can truly be an alien world. For regulars, though, Daydreams is something very different.

For comic book aficionados, comic shops are gold mines, places to find buried treasure, catch up with old friends, make new acquaintances with like-minded souls. Daydreams is no different. Fans get many benefits from being regulars at comic shops. Before these stores came into existence, fans had no place where they were guaranteed to find their favorite titles. Comic book professional Peter David explained, "People ask me if I knew I wanted to write comics when I was a kid. Write them? Most of the time my dreams were limited just to being able to find them" (31). Comic book readers before the 1980s, when comic shops became widespread, had to search out local newsstands, drugstores, and occasionally bookstores to find favorite titles. Fans could subscribe to publications, but the comics often arrived in mailboxes damaged by weather or folded to fit into envelopes.[2] Finding back issues was even more difficult; for most readers, flea markets and secondhand bookstores were virtually the only sources and were never very reliable. Today, though, fans can have favorite titles reserved so that they do not have to worry about missing an issue.

Fans also find a supportive environment at their local comic shop. American society simply does not respect comic book reading, and most people consider it a childish activity. Comic book fans who might otherwise be afraid to talk about their hobby for fear of ridicule can go to a comic book shop and find themselves reaffirmed. At the comic shop, reading comics is normal: it is what everyone there does. The shop is a place where fans can use all the knowledge that they have accumulated over the years without being ashamed. It is one place where fans can truly be themselves. The people who work there are usually friends or at least friendly. At Daydreams, it is not uncommon to find employees having long conversations with customers about what is good to read, the silliness of Marvel's latest crossover story line, or the pleasures of reading old issues of *Superboy and the Legion of Super-Heroes*. Finding fellowship at comic shops is an important element of their popularity and success. "Sometimes I think I come here just to talk to my friends instead of to buy comics," one of Daydreams' regular customers said about the store.

As far as comic book stores go, Daydreams is relatively successful. When Michael Zeadow opened the store in 1986, it was located in a ten-by-ten-foot room in the Hall Mall, a 1960s throwback full of vaguely disreputable countercultural shops of the sort frequently found in college towns. In 1992 Daydreams moved to College Street, where the shop had four times as much space in which to display its products. Since then, Zeadow has removed a wall and made other physical changes to the space to make better use of the new location. He has also added employees. In 1991 he only had one other person working for him; by 1996 he had five full-time workers. Early that year, he even began renting the shop next door, which he operates as a traditional-style newsstand, in part to have even more space for expansion. Still, like most independent comic shop owners, Zeadow is not making a profit from selling comics, or so he claims publicly. "I opened up this business to be a service to people and supply them with what they want," he told a reporter (Schoenberg 2A).

Daydreams's continued expansion is remarkable for comic shops in the mid-1990s, and the fact that it is not the only such establishment in Iowa City—a college town of approximately sixty thousand full-time residents—makes it even more amazing. The other shop, Iguana's Comic Book Cafe, opened its doors in 1992 and since then has catered to a generally younger and even more predominantly male clientele than Daydreams. Local comics fans generally agree that Iguana's customer base is limited to high-school-aged fanboys, while Daydreams's patrons include a wider variety of ages and reading interests. As a result, Iguana's focuses on superhero comics and other genres that are supposed to be "hot" in its target market. Its back stock is much more limited than that of Daydreams, and "mature" titles have their own section of the store instead of being integrated with the other comics. Since 1996, however, Iguana's has expanded its trade paperback section and has been actively pushing such mild alternative comics as Strangers in Paradise in an attempt to broaden its market share. The fact of the matter, though, is that Iguana's still relies on fanboys and other speculators in collectibles for its survival. During the brief comics market crisis of 1994–95, Iguana's remained in business by selling large quantities of single cards for "Magic: The Gathering," a collectible fantasy card game that has become popular among comic book readers. In recent years, the store has catered to buyers of whatever is the latest collectible trend, whether it is Star Wars toys or Beanie Babies.

The success of Daydreams through this period came, in large part, from its being a full-service comic book store. Daydreams sells virtually everything related to comic books, including almost the complete spectrum of comic books from those published by the major companies, Marvel and DC, to smaller publishers such as Drawn and Quarterly, Fantagraphics, and Dark Horse, to self-published comics such as Dave Sim's *Cerebus.* The newest issues of all of these comics are displayed together—alternative next to mainstream, adult next to general audience, superhero next to autobiography. All publications are also housed together in the back-issue bins. This variety has helped to establish a broad customer base for Daydreams. Unlike many comic shops, these customers include a fairly substantial number of women. Both female employees and a relative lack of posters featuring women with unbelievable amounts of cleavage help to make Daydreams relatively hospitable to female customers. For a time, the shop even placed small signs next to titles deemed "girl friendly."

Unfortunately, most comic shops are different. In most cases, women who enter stores quickly hurry out. Although they may have heard that interesting things are going on in the industry or may have read a friend's comics, women are turned off by comic shops' atmosphere. Female visitors commonly become uncomfortable or feel unwelcome as a result of the gazes of male patrons who are surprised to see women in that setting or by posters that frequently objectify women and/or glorify violence. Comic book shops also frequently sell soft-core pornography, such as *Playboy* magazine or Betty Page pinups. Other women are simply turned off by the fact that there do not seem to be any comics interesting to female readers.

Most comic book shops also simply lack the variety of Daydreams. These stores frequently sell only the most mainstream of comics—that is, those published by corporate giants Marvel and DC and a few other companies. Even if more alternative titles are sold, they are often separated from the rest of the comics. The "for mature audiences" label on many of these comics may be responsible for this kind of ghettoization but does not account for many shops' placement of such comics a distance away from the rest and, more significantly, away from the flow of traffic within the shop. Many of the people who run such shops—and shops that call themselves comic shops but really specialize in something else, such as role-playing games, trading cards, or sports memorabilia—simply know little about alternative comics and certainly do not know enough to recommend a new title or to give a customer a plot synopsis.

Other aspects of Daydreams generally typify comic book shops, particularly the store's relationship to its customers, both regular and potential. Regular customers are treated well — their books are set aside for them, they get discounts on new comics and back issues, and employees know their names and their likes and dislikes. Comic book fans visiting Iowa City may not get quite this treatment, but they do walk into an environment that is familiar and comforting. With some occasional exceptions (especially at the beginning of the school year), new customers are not wooed by coupons or newspaper advertisements. Although the shop's window displays (changed on a regular basis by the employees) feature a wide variety of comic book and occasionally comic strip material, Zeadow simply does not appear to be interested in attracting non–comic book fans to Daydreams. Most retail establishments actively try to attract new customers, but comic book shops are not like most other stores. They are more than retail establishments aimed at making profits. Like Zeadow, many owners are not in it for the money (although that certainly is part of their motivation) but instead are interested in opening a shop where they and their friends can meet, find their favorite titles and occasional back issues, talk about comics, and perhaps organize (or even play, on a slow afternoon) the next session of a role-playing game. The comic book shop is a meeting place, like the clubhouse at a country club or a small-town barbershop. It is a place for commerce, but, more importantly, it is a place for culture.

To begin to understand this culture, it is necessary to understand something about comic books. Most people think they know what comic books are: brightly colored pamphlets, about six and a half inches wide and about ten inches tall, printed on cheap paper, featuring superhero stories enjoyed primarily by children. To some extent, this view is correct. Superman is still starring in *Action Comics* (the first superhero publication, started in 1938), Batman is still starring in *Detective Comics,* and their stories are still enjoyed by large numbers of children, especially boys. But to really understand this storytelling format, it is necessary to comprehend the tremendous (and often unheralded) diversity among comic books. Quite simply, comic books are not now — and really never have been — merely Superman and Archie. The comics medium — defined as "juxtaposed pictorial and other images in delib-

erate sequence, intended to convey information and/or to produce an aesthetic response in the viewer" (McCloud, *Understanding* 9) — is a mode of
communication that can do or be anything, from telling stories of all kinds
to making academic-style arguments.

One of the first aspects of the diversity within the comics industry involves
the difference between mainstream and alternative comics. Mainstream
comics include either those published by Marvel and DC (the two largest
publishers in the 1990s) or by smaller companies that mimic the themes
and topics of the big two's products. Historically, mainstream comics tell
whatever kind of story, whatever genre, will sell the best (or that publishers
think will sell the best) at any given time. Today, most mainstream comics
feature fantastic adventure stories, usually starring superheroes, but this category would also include contemporary Disney and Archie comics. In the
past, mainstream comics have included a wide variety of genres: war, horror,
romance, Westerns, comedy, science fiction, mystery, and crime stories. It is
important to remember that the mainstream comic book industry — like
all entertainment industries — is profoundly imitative: if some particular
kind of story is popular at a particular time (Westerns, for example), then
the comic book industry will publish a lot of those kind of stories. Starting
in the early 1960s, when superhero stories came to dominate the mainstream,
other genres began to fulfill a secondary role in the market.

Another important aspect of mainstream comics is that both they and
the characters featured therein are corporately owned. Superman's copyright,
for instance, is owned by DC Comics and its parent company, Time Warner,
not by the men who created him. Also, most mainstream comics have been
created by an assembly-line process in which one person writes the story,
another does the basic art, a third inks the pages, a fourth puts in the lettering,
and a fifth does the colors and then an editor (who answers to an editor-in-
chief and ultimately a publisher) decides whether the product is acceptable.
Because of this process, most mainstream comics are corporate products in
more ways than one. Companies such as Image, where characters are owned
by their creators, are changing this scheme somewhat, but most of their titles
still focus on superheroes in the same way that Marvel and DC comics do.

Alternative comics, the second category of comic books, often work in
opposition to their mainstream counterparts (see fig. 1). Although it is hard
to generalize, most alternative comics tell stories that are more aimed at
adults: these publications deal with real situations, realistic characters, and

Fig. 1 Alternative comics often challenge both the stories and the visuals of their mainstream superhero counterparts by telling realistic stories through a wider variety of artistic styles, ranging from the representational to the exaggerated. Top: Harvey Pekar agonizes about his life ("Awaking to the Terror of the New Day," *American Splendor* #3 [1978]: 10; by Harvey Pekar, Greg Budgett, and Gary Dumm, © Harvey Pekar); bottom: Buddy Bradley has a brainstorm (*Hate* #8 [spring 1992]: 22; © Peter Bagge).

realistic emotions. Most are in black and white and come more directly out of the creators' personal visions. These comics are usually produced by a single person who has total control over what happens to the characters. Because of this artistic freedom, alternative comics can be very political. They also include much more diversity of content than one would find in the mainstream. Alternative comics can be realistic fiction, fantasy-based fables, autobiography, political journalism, graphic essays, comedy, cultural criticism, or anthologies featuring a combination of all of these genres. The bottom line is that alternative comics run the entire gamut of communication, from pleasant stories that both adults and children could enjoy, such as Jeff Smith's Tolkienesque *Bone,* to offensive, angry rants, such as Mike Diana's bloody, misogynistic *Boiled Angel* (which resulted in its author's imprisonment on obscenity charges), that only the strongest of stomach could read without being disgusted.

Despite the variety and quality that can be found in alternative comics, they are generally much less popular than mainstream comics. In 1998, a typical successful mainstream comic sold one hundred thousand copies; a wildly successful alternative comic might sell ten thousand, and most rarely sell more than three thousand copies. Harvey Pekar's *American Splendor* barely sold ten thousand copies per issue when he was self-publishing it in the 1980s, and Martin Wagner was lucky to sell five thousand copies of his well-known anthropomorphic series *Hepcats* in the early 1990s—and these were prominent series during times of relatively good health for the industry. As a result, deciding to do alternative comics is rarely a lucrative career move. Many creators, in fact, start out publishing their own comics, often as minicomics such as Adrian Tomine's *Optic Nerve.* Minicomics are usually written, drawn, printed, and even stapled by a single creator. Most are done on copying machines, with the 8½-by-11 inch pages folded and cut into small booklets. Although sometimes available at comic shops, most minicomics are obtained through direct communication with the authors, either at comic book conventions or through the mail. Other comic creators self-publish their comics in traditional formats. Some, such as *Cerebus,* have achieved long-term success, carving out a market (and cultural) niche for themselves; most, though, end up losing money, forcing creators to take day jobs to make ends meet. Others, such as *Optic Nerve,* are picked up by publishing companies (a development that will occasionally anger fans worried about the artists selling out).

One reason for alternative creators' economic problems is these comics' very different audience from that of mainstream publications. About 90 percent of mainstream readers are adolescent males ranging in age from about twelve to twenty. According to Paul Tobin and other Daydreams employees, alternative readers include roughly 40 percent females and are generally older, usually college age and a bit beyond. Many readers of alternative comics have come to them from alternative culture: these people listen to alternative music (a category as diverse as that of alternative comics), have nonconformist ideas regarding lifestyle, clothing, and personal appearance, and practice more liberal politics than most Americans. Most important, though, is that most alternative-comics readers set themselves up in opposition to traditional mainstream American culture and to mainstream comic books. Aside from picking up a copy of *X-Men* for a few laughs or buying an old issue of DC's *Superboy and the Legion of Super-Heroes* for its nostalgic value, most alternative-comics fans would not be caught dead reading mainstream comics. And, for that matter, most mainstream readers do not like alternative comics. Consequently, there has been little crossover between these two groups. However, there are certainly more readers of mainstream comics. Estimates suggest that there might have been as many as two million comic book readers in the United States in 1995, maybe one hundred thousand of them readers of alternative comics (John Jackson Miller 61–63). In recent years, DC Comics has tried to bridge the gap between these two groups with its Vertigo line, including titles such as *Sandman, Preacher,* and *Invisibles* that meld an alternative attitude with mainstream marketing. DC's efforts have been fairly successful (especially in attracting female readers), and Vertigo has established a niche somewhere around the middle of the mainstream-alternative spectrum.

While these alternative fans might visit Daydreams on an irregular or even monthly basis, mainstream readers are much more obsessive about getting their favorite comics. Many will visit the shop weekly to make sure they get the first issue of the next big series or the complete run of the newest "important" miniseries. Many of these fans are very serious about comics, almost religiously buying up any appearance of their favorite characters and sometimes buying multiple copies when they believe that an issue will become a collector's item and hence increase in value. So, in 1991, when Marvel began a second X-Men title, this time without the "uncanny" prefix, the publisher knew it had a hot property on its hands. To make it even hotter, Marvel published the first issue with five different covers. Many fans bought all five for the investment potential and simply to have a complete set. The result was that *X-Men* #1 sold seven million copies, none of which currently has much resale value.

Publishers use other gimmicks to attract the attention of collectors and speculators. The most popular is the gimmick cover, for example, the thin foil used on the first issue of *Generation X* (yet another X-Men spin-off). Other such novelty covers include holograms and cardboard cut out into special designs. Publishers also do many special crossover series, such as DC's 1985–86 *Crisis on Infinite Earths,* that compel readers to buy connecting issues of other series to completely understand the larger story. More insidious might be the prebagged comics. The resale value of an old comic is based in part on its condition: to get the highest price, the comic must be in mint condition. Many fans believe that the only way to get true mint condition is to never read the comic; hence, they seal it in a plastic bag to protect it from any kind of damage. Other fans argue that reading an issue once — very carefully — will probably not noticeably affect its condition.[3] In recent years, comics publishers have taken to prebagging special issues, meaning that maximum value will only result if the bag is sealed. The publishers hope that people interested in the story will buy two copies, one to read and one to save. Sometimes, the bags even contain extra goodies. For example, buyers of the issue of *Superman* featuring his much-hyped death (v2 #75 [January 1993]) received not only the comic but also a full-color poster, four stickers, a mock obituary from the *Daily Planet,* a trading card, and a special black mourning armband. Of course, collectors might never see these goodies without purchasing a second copy.

Appealing to collectors and speculators helped the industry grow in the early 1990s, when comic books increasingly became commodities. Although there is a history of comics as collectors' items, the extreme commodification of the hobby is fairly recent. In the golden age of comics, comic books were ephemera. A kid would read a copy of *Marvel Mystery Comics* and then trade it for a copy of *All-Star Comics.* The new owner would then trade the issue for *Detective Comics,* and the third kid would trade it for something else. This process would continue until all of a group of friends had read the comic or until the comic fell apart. Because comic books were printed on cheap paper and bound together with weak staples, the books did not last a long time. Publishers would often use coupons and contests to encourage kids to destroy their comics. Many comics from the 1940s were certainly recycled during paper drives for the war effort. For all of these reasons, comic books from the first two decades of the format's history can sell for as much as hundreds of thousands of dollars.

Comics became collectible — that is, sought after for preservation by fans of the medium — for the first time in the early 1960s. To be sure, comics were previously saved by handfuls of devoted readers as far back as the 1940s. These fans, though, were few and far between, searching out used bookstores and flea markets for stashes of old comics. People selling these back issues usually had almost no idea that people would actually want the comics, so fans commonly paid pennies for comics that today would fetch hundreds and thousands of dollars from collectors. The rise of comics fandom in the 1960s began to increase the demand for these old comics, resulting in savvy dealers beginning to charge more substantial amounts of money for back issues. By 1964 fans were suggesting that there was a need for a guide to standardize the often divergent prices for old comics. Around this time, some bookstores even began to specialize in old comics, and the increasing numbers of collectors began to attract attention from the news media, bringing new fans to comics. After the ranks had been swelled by the success of the *Batman* television program in the late 1960s, Robert Overstreet finally published a comic book price guide in 1970. Although most fans had their complaints about the *Overstreet Comic Book Price Guide,* it was an important step for comics culture. "Without a responsible and credible price guide," writes fan historian Bill Schelly, "comics could never become a legitimate collectible" (*Golden Age* 122).

Truly collectible comics, especially those from the 1940s, have become commodities much in the same way as works of art. A collector might pay sixty-five thousand dollars for an early issue of *Batman,* but it is not being purchased to be read. Instead, it is an investment, a work of art or an antique that is put away, usually in some sort of vault, to appreciate in value. This high-end collectors' market has existed since the 1960s, but the collectors' market for contemporary comics is a relatively recent development. Because many speculators do not read their comics, publishers do not have to bother with quality stories or artistic coherence. Covers have always been important to comic books — serving as self-contained advertising, the art and paper have almost always been better on the covers than inside the comics—but comics' shift from entertainment to commodity has increased the covers' significance.

Increasingly, the comic books themselves are becoming less important even to the publishing companies. Today, Marvel and DC can make more money from the licensing of their characters than they can from the apparently finite number of comic books they can sell. For DC and its corporate owners, much more money can be made from the film *Batman and Robin* (1997) than from *Detective Comics;* Marvel can make more money from the toys and other products generated from the X-Men animated series than it can from the comic books. In the late 1970s Marvel created characters, including She-Hulk and Spider-Woman, to copyright the names and images for possible use in television projects (Sullivan, "Marvel" 35). In 1995 fans who worried about decreasing sales of X-Men comics cynically speculated that Marvel would always publish them as long as money can be made from the products featuring the characters, the Saturday morning cartoon, and a perpetually rumored film.

The bottom line is that comic book publishing—even for alternative comics—is an industry governed by economic forces that have perhaps damaged the medium's artistic potential. At the same time, though, these economic forces have also worked to help create comic book culture. This culture may be based in comic book shops like Daydreams, but these shops would not exist without the direct market. In the past, a distributor for the direct market would be able to send a shop virtually every comic book published during a given week. This system, however, is changing. In early 1995 Marvel purchased Heroes World, a major comic book distributor, and announced that the company would exclusively distribute Marvel Comics. Later, DC responded by signing an exclusive deal with Diamond Distributors. Under these new arrangements, it became more difficult for comic shop owners to tailor their inventory to their clientele. Both Marvel/Heroes World and DC/Diamond required that shops order a minimum number of titles and copies to get the traditional discounts that are necessary for shops to make a small profit on the books they sell. Meanwhile, smaller publishers have been concerned about how this shift is going to affect their sales. At the 1995 Pro/Con (a convention for comic book professionals), Dark Horse editor Bob Schreck compared the situation to musical chairs: "The music is still going," he explained, "and we don't know how many seats there will be or who the players will be in the next four to six months" (Eric Reynolds 1). By 1996 independent publishers had become much more confident, believing that the superhero market had been saturated and that the independents' more-diverse products were where the industry would have to grow in the next few years. Much of this confidence had disappeared by 1997 and 1998, as the number of comic shops nationwide and overall sales of comics continued to dwindle. The *Comics Journal* even ran a special section on the "comic book crisis" in October 1997.

Many comic book professionals — and many fans — are very concerned about the effect of all these changes in the comic book marketplace. Although some commentators seem to think that this current crisis (including the bankruptcy and related financial problems of Marvel) might weaken or even destroy the industry, at least in terms of how it has functioned for the past fifteen years, others are actually optimistic. During a panel discussion at the 1995 Chicago Comicon, Colleen Doran, the writer, artist, and (at that time) publisher of *A Distant Soil*, predicted that the changing distribution networks would result in a division of retail outlets for comics, with some specializing in mainstream comics and others in alternative comics. Economic necessity might demand that publishers find new outlets for comics, including bookstores and record stores. In the long run, Doran explained, this separation would benefit the medium as an art form, as alternative comics would finally have a chance to truly distance themselves from their mainstream counterparts.

This change, of course, would have important implications for comic book culture. At this moment, the diversity among comic book readers is unified into a single culture, if only by their shared need for what the comic book shop can offer them. A full-service comic book shop such as Daydreams offers mainstream readers a chance to expand their literary horizons, a chance to go from *Daredevil* to *Stray Bullets*. Alternative readers at Daydreams can browse through new issues of old favorites while buying the latest issue of *Hate* or *Eightball*. Allowing people to both grow intellectually and appreciate their childhood pleasures at the same time is one of the important advantages of full-service comics shops. If the market — and the culture — were divided in two, this process could not take place. It is likely that alternative comics would become even further ghettoized. Today, they are hard to find, but in the future they might available only in a few limited outlets in major cities and college towns. Comic book shop owners in small and medium-sized towns, faced with the choice between Marvel and DC comics that they know will sell and alternative comics that traditionally have not sold well, will choose the products of the mainstream companies. For most shop owners—who may not be in it for the money but certainly are not in it for bankruptcy—there will not even be a choice. For the comic book industry—and for the culture it has helped to create—now is an important moment. A comic book culture still thrives in the late 1990s. Made up of a variety of different reading communities, this culture may be filled with conflict, but there is a shared background, a foundation of commonality, a devotion to the comic book medium that brings people together. This culture, though, may not be able to survive the economic conflict within the comic book marketplace that many have been predicting.

Comic book culture may be vulnerable because, more than other cultures surrounding popular texts, this culture is truly one of consumption and commodity. Media fans such as those described by Henry Jenkins in *Textual Poachers: Television Fans and Participatory Culture* and Camille Bacon-Smith in *Enterprising Women: Television Fandom and the Creation of Popular Myth,* whose leisure cultures revolve around television shows, need only to watch them. Although fans of *Star Trek* and other shows do buy related artifacts, the core texts are broadcast and require only regular purchases of videotapes. One of the main activities of the fans described by Jenkins and Bacon-Smith involves the creation of fan fiction that requires knowledge of the relevant programs and universes but not necessarily the purchase of special texts. Sport fandoms work similarly. Although fans often buy tickets to professional games, doing so is not a requirement for becoming a sports fan. Instead, someone who follows a particular basketball or baseball team can watch the events on television or listen on the radio. No special purchases are needed to gain the knowledge necessary to be this kind of fan.

The closest similarity to comics culture and comic book collecting is the sports-card market. There, the value of a card is based on its condition and scarcity and the quality of the player depicted. As with comic books, truly valuable cards combine all three, with serious investors looking for rookie and other rare cards of such Hall of Famers as Mickey Mantle and Willie Mays. Average collectors, most often young people, lack the money for those kinds of cards, though. Instead, these collectors' speculate based on their estimates of the future importance or quality of certain players. As with comic book shops, card shops rarely make money. In researching his 1991 dissertation, "Cardboard Images of the Past: Baseball Card Collecting and the Politics of Sport," John Douglas Bloom spent a great deal of time at these shops. His primary location for research, he explains, was "operated as a sort of 'hang-out' for local boys who would buy cards, and then play games by comparing the cards they received in packages they had opened" (144). For Bloom's informants, children as well as adults, collecting baseball cards is more about recapturing a personal (and national) innocence or finding joy in the game and in knowing about players than about making a profit (155, 197).

The price of comic books and the frequency with which they are published often make it difficult for those interested in the simple pleasures of reading. Comic books, in the mainstream retail market, need to be purchased and collected to have any impact on fans. Darcy Sullivan suggests that "comics are so object-based, in fact, that the most vital way of interacting with them is to engage their function as objects, rather than as narrative vehicles; that is, to buy them. . . . Buying comics (or 'collecting' them, to use the industry's aggrandizing jargon) is more important than reading them." Comic books are like potato chips—fans cannot have just one. "We want more comics not because they satisfy us so much, but because each one satisfies us so little" ("More" 4). They are the perfect consumer products. Most mainstream titles today are published monthly, with stories that sometimes continue for more than a year, so fans "need" to buy every part of the series and "need" to go to the shop regularly for new issues. This cycle never stops, creating an almost infinite stream of comic books. The American economy too is seemingly based on endlessly getting what is "new and improved"—the computer with the most memory and the fastest processor, the crunchier, tastier brand of cereal. The mainstream comic book industry takes this planned obsolescence to new heights, with products only good for a single month, if that.

Of course, not everyone involved in the culture of comic books buys into this system. There is much more variety among comic book readers—just as there is more variety in comic books—than most Americans realize. The core readership is still adolescent males—the fanboy stereotype—some of whom read comics just because they are cool but many of whom seem to be involved for speculation's sake, at least to some extent. Some older readers buy to speculate, but many are also looking for the feeling of nostalgia they can gain from reading and owning the comics they read as children. Many fans of alternative comics are former fanboys who remain committed to the medium but now are looking for more realistic or mature stories.

There are also fairly specialized readership groups: gay and lesbian readers, fans of war comics, readers of pornographic comics, academic readers, and so on.

These distinct groups have different standards, reading histories, and knowledge regarding comics. As a result, each group constitutes its own distinct reading community. In *Is There A Text In This Class?: The Authority of Interpretative Communities* (1980), Stanley Fish suggests that readers with similar reading competency—the "backlog of language experience which determines probability of choice and therefore of response" (44) and the internalized system of rules of a language or a literature—function as an interpretative community, meaning that its members will have uniform responses to particular texts. Although the uniformity of response within one of these interpretative communities is doubtful, groups of fan consumers do share similar reading competencies. Jenkins suggests that media fans "debate the protocols of reading, the formation of canons, and the ethical dimensions of their relationship to primary textual producers almost as much as they discuss the merits and significances of individual program episodes," thereby constituting "a particular interpretive community" ("Strangers" 210–11). The same practices would certainly apply to different groups of comic book readers. It is not uncommon, for example, to hear mainstream comic book fans debating which Batman graphic novels fit into the official DC continuity or discussing the personalities of their favorite creators.

Being part of a particular reading community allows readers to identify themselves as fans. This identification, of course, marks these people as separate from the rest of the "mundane" (nonfan) population. Reading as a fan, Jenkins argues, is "a distinctive mode of reception" that often involves reviewing or rereading and translation into other cultural and social activities. "Fan reception can not and does not exist in isolation, but is always shaped through input from other fans" ("Strangers" 210). Fans both set themselves apart from and are set apart by the rest of the cultural world. They may be marginalized and ridiculed by mainstream society, but identifying as a fan can also give an individual a certain amount of "collective identity" through which "to forge an alliance with a community of others in defense of tastes which, as a result, cannot be read as totally aberrant or idiosyncratic" (Jenkins, *Poachers* 23). For its members, according to Jenkins, fandom "offers ... a community not defined in traditional terms of race, religion, gender, region, politics, or profession, but rather a community of consumers defined through their common relationship with shared texts" ("Strangers" 213).

As Jenkins suggests, fans are not a community in a traditional sense. Comic book reading communities—like other fan communities—are not based on living together in a geographical locality like a neighborhood or a town. Fans certainly are not consistent with the classic American notion of community advocated in Robert Bellah et al.'s *Habits of the Heart: Individualism and Commitment in American Life* (1985). These authors see an ideal community as "an inclusive whole, celebrating the interdependence of public and private life and of the different callings of all" (72). Comic book reading communities, in fact, are more consistent with Bellah et al.'s "lifestyle enclave," a group segmented from the rest of American society by choices of leisure and patterns of consumption. More importantly, the lifestyle enclave "celebrates the narcissism of similarity" (72) by joining together people of similar cultural or economic backgrounds. Unlike a true community, where the energies of individuals and groups are channeled to serve the common good, lifestyle enclaves encourage a degree of separatism by making outsiders irrelevant or invisible, thereby robbing them of the moral benefits of community: learning and growing as a result of the participation of diverse individuals. Although Bellah and his colleagues do not view lifestyle enclaves as a positive cultural development, they argue that the they are perhaps an appropriate "form of collective support in an otherwise radically individualizing society" (73). In this way, they are more a symptom than a cause of a larger problem in American society.

Bellah and his coauthors fail to see that there are people who, for whatever reason, do not particularly want to be part of the American public life that is the focus of *Habits of the Heart*. Deadheads, Generation X-ers, radical homosexual activists, and those interested in alternative culture might simply receive more from interactions with their own community than from participating in a society that they see as unjust, superficial, immoral, or artificial. The same is also true of dedicated fans of popular culture and popular media. Writing about the social networks that have evolved in and through multiuser dungeons (MUDs, on-line computer games where players can immerse themselves, along with others from all over the country, in fantasy worlds), Howard Rheingold suggests, "The phenomenon of fandom is evidence that not everyone can have a life as 'having a life' is defined by the mainstream, and some people just go out and try to build an alternate life" (167).

Rheingold's idea of community is, in many ways, different than the traditional one that most Americans imagine when they think of the word. Community, for Rheingold, is not a physical place. Rather, it is a feeling born out of communication and cooperation. In this way, it certainly can be found in an actual space, like a neighborhood where the residents know each other and help solve the area's problems. But it can also be a virtual space, a location in cyberspace where people can communicate freely and receive information, aid, and support from their fellow participants. For Rheingold, a community is any cooperative group of people and, according to him, "every cooperative group of people exists in the face of a competitive world because that group of people recognizes there is something valuable that they can gain only by banding together. Looking for a group's collective goods is a way of looking for the elements that bind isolated individuals into a community" (13).

One of the aims of this book is to examine the collective goods that are defined by the wide variety of comic book–reading communities. These different communities' different values bring them into conflict. Distinct comic book–reading communities have very particular visions of what comic books should be, who should be reading them, how comic book shops should attract customers, and in what direction the industry is heading. These different communities have different favorite texts; different standards for art, story, and overall value; different needs from comic book shops and conventions. Strong boundaries separate mainstream and alternative comic book fans, but these barriers are not as strong as the border between readers and nonreaders, between fans and those in the ordinary world. Each group of comics readers maintains its own integrity, to some degree or another, but they all still share more in common than some of their members would like to admit. What they share is a culture, a body of knowledge and information, an appreciation of a medium that most Americans have dismissed as hopelessly juvenile and essentially worthless.

This book focuses primarily on how this culture functions in light of the conflict among its members. This conflict makes comic book culture different from the media fan cultures studied by Jenkins and Bacon-Smith, the romance novel readers examined by Janice Radway in *Reading the Romance: Women, Patriarchy, and Popular Literature* (1984), and the role-playing gamers analyzed by Gary Alan Fine in *Shared Fantasy: Role-Playing Games as Social Worlds* (1983). This conflict makes comic book culture a useful laboratory for studying Americans' relationship to popular culture and for studying the ways in which cultures in general evolve out of— or perhaps into— states of conflict.

Beyond this conflict, there are important boundaries between all comic book readers and outsiders, the tens of millions of Americans who do not read comics. This limited access promotes insularity and, to go along with it, a certain amount of postmodern self-referentiality that is the source of part of readers' pleasure in comic books. Regular readers enjoy a miniseries such as *Radioactive Man* because it is filled with insider jokes, parody, and allusions to comic book history, a history about which most nonreaders simply do not know. Readers enjoy a graphic novel such as *Watchmen* in part for what Alan Moore and Dave Gibbons do to bring the superhero into the realm of adult literature. Readers get pleasure out of reading *Acme Novelty Library* and seeing how Chris Ware's art style challenges and expands the formal, traditional rules of comic book storytelling. For most noncomics readers, though, these pleasures will be unachievable, thereby further alienating them from the medium and eventually making the comic book world even more impenetrable for the casual reader.

The comic book shop itself is another way in which this culture is closed off to most Americans. Although the shop may function like a clubhouse for regular readers, for others it is so intimidating that new readers, especially women, can find it difficult to become involved. Literary readers might also be turned off by the clubbish nature of the shop and the large quantity of superhero comics there. For longtime readers, the environment is normal and sometimes even comforting. Being able to see — and buy — the comics one enjoyed as a child gives these readers a sense of nostalgia that can contribute to them feeling at home. Sullivan even suggests that the comic book shop is a "fundamental part of the way in which [fans] interact with the medium" ("More" 4). That shops' clientele is often limited to a very exclusive group of people is a double-edged sword. This limiting of consumers makes the comic book shop a cultural place in a way that a store aimed at a general audience can never be, but at the same time this exclusivity prevents people who might otherwise be interested in the medium from taking part.

American culture may be heading in this direction. Magazines seem to be aimed at increasingly specific audiences, and Internet newsgroups are very self-selective and exclusive, focusing on narrow interests. Movies, television programs, and even networks seem to have particular target audiences. The same type of segmentation also seems to be occurring in music. In "Notes on the Life and Death and Incandescent Banality of Rock 'n' Roll," Greil Marcus suggests that rock as a single genre of music no longer exists, that it has been divided up into separate, distinct sounds and audiences. "There is an overwhelming sense of separation, isolation: segregation," Marcus writes. No longer does rock speak to all of its fans in the same language — because there is no single rock. "There is no central figure to define the music or against whom the music could be defined, no one everybody feels compelled to love or hate, nobody everyone wants to argue about (what is pop music if not an argument anyone can join?), unless it's the undead Elvis Presley" (68–69).

For Marcus, this kind of musical segmentation is a problem because it robs rock and roll of its potential for cultural impact. If Americans no longer speak the same cultural language, then it is no longer possible for a single song or a single text of any kind to make people think, to transform individuals and society. This, of course, is the same reason that Bellah and his co-authors criticized lifestyle enclaves: the individuals involved close themselves off from the rest of the society and cease speaking America's common cultural language. The trouble with both Bellah et al.'s and Marcus's vision is that all Americans probably never spoke a common cultural language. Some people have always been denied access to this language, and some people have always found alternative languages more to their liking. The segmentation of rock music, for example, has allowed these other languages — like grunge and rap, which perhaps would not have been heard if there was a single rock music — to grow and develop. Specific, closed cultures like that surrounding comic books have allowed voices to be heard that might not have been audible in a world in which all cultural texts speak the same common language.

To be sure, though, America would be a better place if these voices could be heard in forums that were more accepting of outsiders. Howard Cruse might have important things to say about the development of a gay-rights movement in his graphic novel *Stuck Rubber Baby*, but if no one outside comic book culture reads his work, it will not have the impact that it should. Joe Sacco might have a new interpretation of the Israeli-Palestinian controversy, but no one on the outside is going to see *Palestine* if the work cannot transcend comic book culture. The same is certainly true of other media that also seem to have become more exclusive. The truth is, we as a country need both a common (although diverse) cultural language that is used in a public forum in which everyone can participate and specific cultural sites where quirky, nonmainstream tastes and views can be allowed to grow and develop. Whether this situation exists anywhere in the United States is too large a question for this work. Instead, this book focuses on examining how comic book culture exists and functions within this schema at this particular moment in time.

In *The Great Good Place* (1989), Ray Oldenburg argues that people need places they can go to escape both work and domestic life and to be a part of an informal community. These sites are sources of comfort, conversation, and companionship that do not get involved too deeply in private lives. These places are attractive not because of the beauty of the building or the quality of the management but rather because of the other regulars there and the playful, relaxing atmosphere. These places offer homes away from home where there are a congenial environment and people with similar concerns and beliefs. For most Americans, these places are barbershops, beauty parlors, bars, community centers, corner hangouts, or coffee shops (Oldenburg 3–62). For comic book readers, though, a shop such as Daydreams is a meeting place, a forum, a Mecca, the "great good place" its patrons need to lead a complete life.

2

EC Fan-Addicts and Marvel Zombies

Historical Comic Book–Reading Communities

The history of comic books in America can be written any number of ways. Some scholars have analyzed the aesthetic trends of comic books; others have examined particular genres, characters, or creators. But another important way of writing the history of comic books is to focus on the people reading them. The problem, though, is getting to these men, women, and children. There are no reading diaries and very few organized meetings of these fans. Many are dead, and others have come so far from their comic book–reading pasts that their memories would be spotty at best. Because of this problem, this chapter will describe these people's world more than engaging them in any kind of dialogue. This chapter examines comics readers from the 1940s into the first half of the 1980s, including the ways in which comic book publishers (especially EC in the early 1950s and Marvel in the 1960s and early 1970s) tried to create and increase their readerships.

Comic books began in the early to mid-1930s as reprint collections of newspaper strips that were read by male and female Americans of all ages. In 1937 the first issue of *Detective Comics* was published. Filled with mystery stories of various types, it was one of the first genre-based comic books. As more comics began to focus on detective stories, Westerns, or other genres, they began to attract more specific audiences. As the superhero comic book began to dominate the industry after the success of Superman in *Action Comics* in the late 1930s and early 1940s, the average age of readers began to fall (Sabin, *Adult Comics* 146). Publishers found that they could make the most money with stories of mystery men fighting crime and battling spies rather than stories of funny animals or adaptations of literary classics.

And most of the publishers were making a lot of money, or at least selling a lot of comic books. According to a survey done by the Market Research Company of America and reported in the December 27, 1943, issue of *News-*

week, 95 percent of all children ages eight to eleven read comic books regularly, as did 84 percent of those from twelve to seventeen years old. Readership declined in the eighteen-to-thirty age group, but 35 percent of these people were still regular readers ("Escapist" 55). In 1943, even with paper shortages because of the war, approximately twenty-five million comic books were sold each month, with sales for the year reaching thirty million dollars. In 1945 comics were selling at a rate of 102 percent, meaning that even damaged copies were being purchased by consumers. DC Comics alone sold more than twenty million comics in the first quarter of 1945 and more than twenty-six million in the first quarter of 1946 (Benton, *Golden Age* 53). Most of the people buying these comics were children, and many of the issues would be read repeatedly by friends who swapped copies until they were virtually destroyed.

Many of the stories appealed to these children through very direct identification. Kids may have been attracted to Superman because of his colorful costume or his amazing feats of strength, but his unassuming secret identity as Clark Kent helped make the Jerry Siegel and Joe Shuster creation into, in the words of comics historian Jim Steranko, "the graphic representation of the ultimate childhood dream-self" (1:40). It certainly was not hard for mild-mannered boys and girls reading *Action Comics* and later *Superman* to imagine that their calm, everyday existence was merely a lie hiding a heroic, adventurous, powerful interior. This kind of identification probably was even stronger in the case of Fawcett Publications's Captain Marvel. This hero was, in reality, Billy Batson, an orphaned newspaper boy. Given a magic word by a mysterious wizard hiding deep in the subway tunnels of New York, Billy could, at a moment's notice, could become the mighty (and adult) Captain Marvel. As a result, Marvel was a natural for children's play. As Steranko explains, "You started out as second banana Billy Batson and—SHAZAM!— you said the magic word and suddenly you were an adult capable of righting any wrongs inflicted upon you. In short, the ultimate childhood fantasy" (2:9). As a result, Captain Marvel was, for a time, more popular than Superman and had spin-off characters (Captain Marvel Jr. and Mary Marvel, among others) and a movie serial (1941's *Adventures of Captain Marvel*).

Other comic book stars were, in fact, children. Beginning with Batman's Robin, introduced in 1940, many prominent superheroes took on young sidekicks. Captain America had Bucky, Human Torch had Toro, the Sandman had Sandy, and so on. Editors must have thought that these characters would attract readers who would identify with Bucky or Robin instead of Captain America or Batman. Whether such was actually the case is another matter entirely. In *The Great Comic Book Heroes* (1965), cartoonist Jules Feiffer remembers, "I couldn't stand boy companions. If the theory behind [them] was to give young readers a character with whom to identify it failed dismally in my case. The super *grownups* were the ones I identified with. They were versions of me in the future. There was still time to prepare. But Robin the Boy Wonder was my own age. One need only look at him to see he could fight better, swing from a rope better, play ball better, eat better, and live better [than I could]" (42–43). Steranko explains, "Didn't [the writers and editors] know that no kid wanted to be Bucky if he could be Captain America instead? Robin was a second choice, a bit player, when young imaginations became their favorite heroes" (2:9).

Other young characters were more independent and hence might have been more successful in attracting reader identification. In 1941 Joe Simon and Jack Kirby created the Young Allies, a diverse group of boys (including Bucky, Toro, a Brooklyn-born bruiser named Knuckles, a rich boy inventor named Jefferson Worthington Sandervilt, a fat "circus escapee" named Tubby, and a harmonica-playing, watermelon-eating African American named Whitewash Jones) dedicated to fighting spies and "practicing war maneuvers against invasion" (*Young Allies* #1 [summer 1941]: 9). By the end of their first adventure, the group had circumnavigated the globe, met Joseph Stalin, tricked Adolf Hitler, and evaded the entire Japanese navy. In the end, the Young Allies had to be rescued by Captain America and the Human Torch, but for most of the adventure, the boys were on their own.

A year later, while at DC Comics, Simon and Kirby created two other kid gangs: the Newsboy Legion (in the pages of *Star-Spangled Comics*) and the Boy Commandos (in *Detective Comics*). The Newsboy Legion was a group of boys from the Suicide Slum (an area clearly reminiscent of Kirby's own childhood in the ghettos of New York City) who were saved from reform school by policeman Jim Harper, who was secretly the mystery man named Guardian. Clearly reminiscent of the Dead End Kids that were so popular in films of the late 1930s, Kirby's Newsboy Legion stories were also filled with urban dialects and dialect-based humor with which he was probably familiar from reading Horatio Alger and assorted dime novels as a child. With the Boy Commandos, Simon and Kirby took the gang concept to Europe, where an international group (the British Alfy, the French Andre, the

Dutch Jan, and the American Brooklyn, complete with a strong New York accent) took on the Axis powers with the help of Captain Rip Hunter. The Boy Commandos were so popular that they received their own title from late 1942 until 1949. Many other kid gangs appeared during the early 1940s, including the Young Defenders, Boyville Brigadiers, Boy Soldiers, and Little Wise Guys (Steranko 1:79–83). Young readers could easily imagine themselves and their friends in the place of any of these groups, either fighting for friends on familiar city streets or battling Nazis and Japanese soldiers and spies far from home.

Comics represented one way in which young readers could feel involved in the war effort. Patriotic heroes such as Captain America were common. He was introduced in the first issue of *Captain America Comics,* cover dated March 1941, and publishers saw how quickly that issue sold out, spawning literally dozens of imitators, including the American Crusader, the American Eagle, the Fightin' Yank, Mr. Liberty, the Liberator, Spirit of '76, Uncle Sam, the Flag, Liberty Belle, Miss America, and Captain Freedom. And not only were heroes with patriotic names fighting the Germans and the Japanese. In the pages of *Military Comics,* Will Eisner helped to create the Blackhawks, an international group of aviators that used only fists, courage, piloting skill, and advanced planes to fight the Axis powers. In *Action Comics* and his own title, Superman fought the enemy at home and abroad. (In one memorable episode of the animated series produced by the Max Fleischer Studios, Superman even brought the war directly to Tokyo, years before it happened in real life.) Other heroes, from Captain Marvel to the Spy Smasher, fought the enemy whenever and wherever they could as U.S. enemies provided easy models for villains. As propaganda, the effect of Captain America and the other heroes was "awesome," argues Steranko: "If nothing else, comics taught their readers who the enemy was and what they stood for" (1:52, 55). These readers could then go on and imagine themselves as their heroes, fighting the Nazis and the Japanese in the same way that their neighbors, older brothers, uncles, and fathers might have been doing, thereby allowing the children to feel part of the war effort.

Even before the war, young fans could not get enough comics and were interacting with them in a number of ways. The first issue of *Action Comics,* for instance, included a contest. One of the stories, "Chuck Dawson," a Western, was printed in black and white. The contest asked readers to color the first page of the story with crayons and send it to the publisher. The twenty-five best pages would receive a cash prize of one dollar. Other comic books urged readers to join fan clubs devoted to their favorite heroes. In 1944 Harvey Zorbaugh reported that the Captain Marvel Club had 573,119 members ("Comics" 200). Fans of the Justice Society of America, from DC's *All-Star Comics*, could become members of the Junior Justice Society, thereby receiving a variety of collectibles from the publisher. Captain America fans could become Sentinels of Liberty, the hero's "great army of spy-smashers." By sending a dime to Timely Comics, prospective members could receive a membership card and an official badge "made of the same metal used in police and firemen badges" (*Captain America Comics* #2 [April 1941]: 16). Later, when metal became scarce because of its importance to the war effort, Cap urged fans not to send their dimes. Bucky suggested they use the money for a war savings stamp instead (Steranko, 1:55).

Science fiction fandom began to notice comic books around this time. In the late 1920s and 1930s, pulp magazines such as *Amazing Stories* began to publish letters from readers that included their authors' names and addresses, thereby allowing fans of the genre to find and meet others with similar interests, first via the mail and later in person. Organizations devoted to science fiction quickly developed, and these organizations spawned amateur magazines — "fanzines" — and conventions. People interested in science fiction began to discuss comic books in these fanzines. James V. Taurasi's fanzines *Fantasy News* and *Fantasy Times* were among the first to prominently feature comic book news. Bill Schelly, a historian of comic book fandom, argues that although "comic books received little more respect from SF fans than from the general public," interest on the part of some readers in both science fiction and comics — so-called "double fans" — "characterized the embryonic stages of comicdom's evolution" (1995, 12, 13). The first fanzine devoted entirely to comic books and strips was *Comic Collectors' News,* published by Malcolm Willits and Jim Bradley in October 1947. Their publication was one of the first places where "comic book collectors could advertise for their favorite titles and communicate with other collectors" (Weist A104).

These developments suggest a post–World War II growth in adult readership for comics. In fact, there had been a sizable number of adult readers in the first half of the 1940s: servicemen. According to Benton, two-thirds of all soldiers read comic books at least occasionally during the war years. On military bases, comic books outsold *Saturday Evening Post, Life,* and *Reader's Digest* combined by a ratio of ten to one (*Golden Age* 53). In *Adult*

Comics: An Introduction, Roger Sabin reports that "comics were sent out to the troops in much the same way as other supplies. They were considered lightweight entertainment for men with other things on their minds" (147). As these soldiers began to return to the States, as publishers became more aware of their adult audience—and surveys done in 1947 showed that 41 percent of men and 28 percent of women were regular readers—comic books began to change (Muhlen 81). Some publishers began to infuse their titles with more sex. Some heroes—such as Captain America—lost their boy side-kicks and took on new, curvaceous female partners. Female heroes in general began to appear more often, some of them drawn in the style of what has come to be known as "good girl art"—scantily clad women in classic pinup poses or compromising positions, sometimes involving bondage. Despite these innovations, superhero comics became much less popular as readers became more interested in other genres.

The first of these genres to succeed was the crime comic book. Introduced in 1942 in *Crime Does Not Pay,* the genre failed to really take off until after the war. By 1948, the peak of the crime genre, it constituted 15 percent of all comic sales, and *Crime Does Not Pay* alone was selling 1.5 million copies an issue, comparable to the most popular magazines of the day. Critics suggested that these comics, often based on true stories, glorified crime, turning the criminals into heroes. This accusation and the fact that the crime comics were more violent than anything the medium had seen before prompted much of the controversy that would end in the passage of the Comics Code in 1954 (discussed further later in this chapter). To avoid some of this criticism, many publishers began to label their comics as "for adults only." And many readers were adults. A 1948 survey showed that 57 percent of the readers of *Crime Does Not Pay* were over twenty-one (Server 9–10).

Many adult readers were probably switching to comics from pulp fiction, a very popular form of cheap literature throughout the first half of the twentieth century. At their peak, these magazines, seven inches wide and ten inches high with brightly colored covers—often featuring barely clothed women menaced by some villain or ghoul—and pages made of cheap paper and filled with stories of almost any imaginable genre, reached an audience of tens of millions of Americans per month (Server 136). By the 1940s, the pulps were beginning a decline, brought on in part by the popularity of comic books. Paperback books also became common in the 1940s, and both of these new formats began to squeeze the pulp magazines off the newsstand racks.

By the end of the decade, reports Lee Server, author of *Danger Is My Business: An Illustrated History of the Fabulous Pulp Magazines* (1993), "Nearly all the remaining publications were detective, science fiction, or Western" (137). And by the middle of the 1950s, all that remained was a handful of pulps devoted to science fiction stories (Tebbel and Zuckerman 341). Many pulp readers no doubt simply stopped reading and began to watch television, but others must have switched to comic books. It is not hard to imagine a fan of *Spicy Detective Stories* picking up an issue of *Crime Does Not Pay* or a fan of *Weird Tales* being interested in *Vault of Horror*. Many comics even had sensationalistic covers like the pulps.

There were, of course, also pulp magazines filled with romance stories, first introduced in 1921. The success of the genre spawned eighteen different magazines with a combined circulation of more than three million per month (Howell 2). Romance readers could also read these kinds of stories in magazines such as *True Confessions* and various "women's" magazines. But beginning in 1947, they could also read romance in comic books. Developed in 1947 by Simon and Kirby, *Young Romance* and its cousins tapped into the substantial female audience and attracted adult readers of both genders. Like the crime comics, some of the romance titles were actually advertised as being for older readers. The covers of *Young Romance,* for example, said under the title that the publication was "designed for the more **adult** readers of **comics.**" The first issue of *Young Romance* sold 92 percent of its print run. By the third issue, the print order had tripled. By 1949, 120 romance titles appeared on the newsstands (Sabin, *Adult Comics* 151–52). The Simon and Kirby stories especially mixed sensationalism, realistic settings, contemporary concerns, and a high moral tone. For example, "Different" (*Young Romance* v4 #6 [June 1950]), told the story of Irma, the daughter of immigrant (probably Jewish) parents. Her family moves from the city to a small town, where everything is going well until the townspeople discover that the family is not "good American stock." Irma's father's business is boycotted, and the family generally is hated by the rest of the town. The one exception is Gil, Irma's boyfriend, who sticks by her and her family despite his parents' prejudice. The story ends with the local millionaire declaring his respect and support for the immigrant family, but Irma remains skeptical about ever being truly accepted by the townspeople.

One result of the expanded audience was that publishers were selling more comic books than ever before. Based on a number of different sources, one estimate shows that monthly circulation of comics was 45.6 million in 1950 and 59.8 million in 1952 (Parsons 68). Other estimates have suggested eighty million comic books a month in 1952, or nearly one billion for the entire year (Inge A-99). Of course, with this increase in sales and the large numbers of comic book readers in the United States, critics became even more concerned about — and academics more interested in — a medium that had been attacked by some since the early 1940s.

One of the first academic examinations of comics was an in-depth study of children's comic book–reading habits compiled and written by Katherine M. Wolf and Marjorie Fiske, two social psychologists from the Columbia University Bureau of Applied Social Research. The 1949 study "The Children Talk about Comics" was published in *Communications Research* 1948–1949 along with articles on radio programming, newspaper and magazine reading, and Soviet broadcasting networks. Wolf and Fiske justified their work by arguing that the relatively new medium "now reaches probably at least as many children as are exposed to motion pictures and radio." They sought simply to interview a group of children about "the motives for and effects of comic book reading" (3). Much of the information Wolf and Fiske developed seems rather elementary (children divide comics into three main groups: funny animal, adventure, and educational; most children read superhero comics to identify with the characters and boost their self-esteem), but their comments about different types of readers demand more analysis. Wolf and Fiske argue that there are three main types of young comic book readers: fans (37 percent of the sample), moderate readers (48 percent), and those who were indifferent or hostile to comics (15 percent).

According to Wolf and Fiske, fans were nearly pathological in their attachment to comic books, "children whose interest in comics is patently violent and excessive. They prefer comic reading to all other activities and if left to their own devices would apparently do nothing else.... Once in possession of a comic book, the fan cannot stop reading.... And after the comic book is read, it remains a treasured possession.... Even in front of an observer in a new situation, the fan reading a comic becomes so absorbed that the rest of the world is forgotten" (22–23). Moderate readers, Wolf and Fiske argue, read comics for fun or information or to identify with a powerful, charismatic hero. The vast majority of fans — 82 percent — read comics to "satisfy the invincible hero need" (25). These authors contend that although fandom is just one of children's three phases of comic book reading, most fans have their literary development arrested at this point. For fans, the "invincible hero need" is even different than for "normal" moderate readers who read about Superman and other characters to boost their ego. Instead of identification, fans find an object of worship in the superhero. According to Wolf and Fiske, "the fan is apparently a child whose peace and security have been in some way so undermined that he needs not merely an invincible hero with which to identify, but rather a god, a being wholly different from men, a creature of unalterable perfection, dedicated to the protection of the otherwise insecure child" (27).

Being a comic book fan, Wolf and Fiske argue, is both a symptom of a larger problem and a cause of other behavioral problems. That larger problem usually involves self-confidence or personal power. The authors report that 52 percent of children short for their ages had become fans, with only 16 percent of those tall for their ages becoming fans or hostile to comics: "the physically weaker children, barred from achieving status in physical competition with their contemporaries, turn hopelessly away from identification with a physically superior human, and seek solace instead in the worship of a distant and omnipotent personal protector" (28). Wolf and Fiske also found that children of professional parents were very unlikely to become fans, while 54 percent of children of nonprofessionals did so (43). Fans were also unable to tell coherent stories, were dissatisfied with traditional text-based books, and used comic books to judge (and eventually reject) reality.

For Wolf and Fiske, the bottom line is that comic books are not entirely bad things if read in moderation and at the proper level of development. In fact, the authors argued that comics met the needs of "normal" children "more effectively than did the literature available to the last generation" (20). Comics could also relieve maladjusted readers of their neuroses. The problem was, however, that these readers became fans and hence were addicted to comic books. But this development "can no more be blamed upon the comics, than morphine can itself be blamed when a person becomes a drug addict" (35). Although Wolf and Fiske's work in many ways reads like a blueprint for stereotypes of fans as psychologically weak individuals whose main sin seems to be taking something normal and using it to excess, most other academics writing about the medium focused more on direct, sociological effects of comic book reading, namely crime and juvenile delinquency.

School and public librarians had been worried about comic books since the early 1940s. By the end of the decade (and as a result of the larger controversy), some were even becoming desperate. In December 1948, the *Library Journal* published an article entitled "Youth's Librarians Can Defeat Comics," written by former children's librarian Jean Gray Harker. She argued that comic books were among the most profound and important cultural threats of the day. "If we were to set out deliberately to undermine the future of our country, to rob our future generations of the ability to think, to talk, to read, to act with intelligence," she wrote, "we could have no more effective weapon than the comic book" (1705). An editorial a few months later in the same journal called for self-censorship of comic books prompted by consumer boycotts ("What Is the Solution" 180). The *Wilson Library Bulletin* even published the transcript of an anticomics speech given by psychiatrist Fredric Wertham at the Philadelphia Free Library Festival (Wertham, "Reading").

Wertham was the most famous of the comics critics from the late 1940s and early 1950s. He first began criticizing comic books in 1948 with the publication of his article "The Comics... Very Funny!" in the *Saturday Review of Literature*. There, he introduced his arguments about comic books' ability to turn otherwise well-behaved American children into rampaging packs of juvenile delinquents and sex fiends. Wertham wrote, "You cannot understand present-day juvenile delinquency if you do not take into account the pathogenic and pathoplastic influence of the comic books, that is, the way in which they cause trouble or determine the form that trouble takes." His reasoning was a simple causality: violence and juvenile delinquency have risen "hand in hand" with the increasing sales of comic books (28).

Some academics attacked the work of Wertham and other critics for lacking in evidence and violating criminological traditions about the complex causes of such behavior.[1] Nevertheless, many adults had reservations about comic books as acceptable reading material for children. The results of a survey compiled by Harvey Zorbaugh, chairman of the department of educational sociology at New York University, and published in 1949 showed that approximately 50 percent of the American public was concerned about comics, with half of those people considering all comic books unsuitable for children and the other half believing only some such publications to be unsuitable. Although much of this concern centered on dangers to children's "character and mental health," worries about comics' effects on children's cultural development were also important ("What Adults Think" 226). Zorbaugh found that opposition to comics varied with age, gender, education, and the adults' own experiences with comics. "More men than women consider them suitable," he reported, "more younger persons than older persons, more of the less educated than the more highly educated, more parents than non-parents" ("What Adults Think" 231). College-educated critics tended to focus equally on comics' effects on cultural development and on children's behavior, while less-educated critics were much more concerned about behavior. Only 36 percent of adults, according to Zorbaugh, had no reservations about supporting comic books as reading material for children ("What Adults Think" 234). However, this opposition to comics certainly did not seem to stop people from reading them: as mentioned earlier, circulation rates climbed during the early 1950s.

The most important comics of that period, and those with the most interesting relationship to their readers, were those published by EC Comics. William Gaines took over the company (originally called Educational Comics) in 1949 after his father, comics pioneer Max Gaines, was killed in a boating accident. At that point, the company was publishing the typical genre fare of the period. Beginning in 1950, though, with the help of editor and artist Al Feldstein, EC (now Entertaining Comics) launched its New Trend titles, including innovative horror (*Vault of Horror* and *Crypt of Terror*), science fiction (*Weird Science*), crime (*Shock SuspenStories*), and war comics (*Two-Fisted Tales*). By 1952, the company was also producing the highly successful satire *Mad,* which sold five hundred thousand copies by its sixth issue. Not all of EC's comics were big sellers, but Gaines's dedication to quality meant that the successful books, like the horror titles, would help support the war and science fiction comics.

This stability meant that readers knew what they were getting when they purchased an EC title. The science fiction and crime comics almost always ended with some surprise, O. Henry–esque ending, while the war comics were filled with enough realism to constantly remind readers that no war, as fought by actual soldiers, was glorious or heroic. The stories in the horror comics, introduced by fictional hosts such as the Crypt-Keeper and the Old Witch, generally opened with someone committing a crime, doing some evil deed, or simply doing something vaguely wrong or dishonest. Eventually, though, justice would be meted out to the villain — sometimes through some mysterious force that was an almost-personified spirit of vengeance — almost always through something related to the original crime or wrongdoing. Thus readers did not need to figure out if justice would be done but rather to ascertain how.

A perfect example of this pattern is William Gaines and Graham Ingels's story, "Dying to Lose Weight!" (*Vault of Horror* #18 [April–May 1951]: 23–30), where the retribution is double. A group of people in a small town want to lose weight but are not willing to give up their candy or start exercising to do so. (This is the first guilty act.) One day, a Doctor Perdo sets up shop in the town and begins advertising a method of losing weight without dieting or exercise. The people take a pill and lose weight. Unfortunately, they cannot stop losing weight, no matter how much they eat, and they eventually all die. (Their murder is the second guilty act and also the first act of retribution, if one that seems out of proportion.) The local doctor performs an autopsy and discovers the cause of the deaths, but it is not revealed to the reader. Months later, Doctor Perdo is driving through the town and stops to get gas. The attendant recognizes the evil doctor, and the townspeople quickly begin chasing him. In desperation, Perdo runs into the cemetery and decides to hide in an open mausoleum that belongs to one of the people he killed. He hears a rustling sound from the casket and, curious, opens it. He screams, and the townspeople are soon able to find him — or at least, what is left of him. We soon learn that Perdo had been eaten by an enormous tapeworm that came out of the casket, the same tapeworm that had killed one of his patients (see fig. 2). As in all of the EC horror stories, justice is done in the end.

Sometimes the punishment would far outweigh the evil of the crime. For example, in William Gaines and George Evans's "An Ample Sample" (*Vault of Horror* #32 [August–September 1953]: 17–22), a woman guilty of using too much of her husband's salary to buy chocolates is eventually killed, dismembered, and put into an oversized sampler box by her crazed husband. At other times, the retribution would be almost funny. Always, though, the host would end the story with an awful pun. (In the summer and fall of 1953, readers of *Tales from the Crypt* were encouraged to contribute puns that could be used for future story titles. Some of the puns were published on the letters' page.) This sense of humor was central to the comics' appeal. Although stories could be very grim, the puns gave readers the idea that nothing should be taken too seriously, that they were involved in a secret, inside joke that nonreaders or those not devoted to EC Comics simply could not understand. Of course,

Fig. 2 The stories in EC's horror comics almost always fit a pattern of guilt and retribution. Here, the evil Dr. Perdo is killed by the same tapeworm that he used to kill a handful of townspeople who wanted only to lose weight ("Dying to Lose Weight," *Vault of Horror* #18 [April–May 1951]: 7; by William Gaines and Graham Ingels, © William M. Gaines, Agent, Inc.).

many of these outsiders were the parents of adolescent readers, and the fact that these adults generally did not understand the comics and sometimes actively opposed them undoubtedly increased their appeal.

William Gaines and his writers/editors Al Feldstein and Harvey Kurtzman occasionally produced stories that readers not familiar with EC Comics could not appreciate. The early issues of *Mad* focused on parodies of EC's own comic books. Feldstein and Wally Wood's "EC Confidential" (*Weird Science* #21 [September–October 1953]: 1–8) featured the entire EC staff and revealed that the writers and artists were actually a group of beings from Venus sent to warn humans of the dangers posed by belligerent Martians. It is not hard to imagine that a die-hard fan would love the kind of inside knowledge it would take to tell this story with wit and personality. This insiderism — making readers feel like they were part of an exclusive group — typified EC's relationship to its readers. It was one of the first companies to give credit to creators, sometimes including extended biographies of writers and artists, providing readers a sense that there were real people behind the stories. EC's letters pages were filled with comments from readers and responses from the horror comics' fictional hosts and the editors.

Letters also occasionally included readers' invitations to become pen pals or join fan clubs. One issue of *Tales from the Crypt* featured a letter from Bob Oravec of Johnstown, Pennsylvania, that invited his fellow readers to join his new EC fan club (*Tales from the Crypt* #35 [April–May 1953]: 18). In 1953 *Weird Science* included a letter from Bobby Stewart of Kirbyville, Texas, announcing the publication of a new fanzine, "EC Fan Bulletin" (*Weird Science* #20 [July–August 1953]: 18). The company also had its own organization, the EC Fan-Addict Club, announced in its December 1952–January 1953 publications (see fig. 3). Membership included a certificate, an identification card, a shoulder patch, a pin, and a subscription to the EC Fan-Addict Club Bulletin. According to Robert Warshow, whose son, Paul, joined the club, the bulletin "publishes chitchat about the writers, artists, and editors, releases trial balloons on ideas for new comic books, lists members' requests for back numbers and in general tries to foster in the membership a sense of identification with this particular publishing company and its staff" (596).

William Gaines and EC would try to use this sense of identification with the company when the controversy over comic books heated up in 1953 and 1954. Perhaps because of its sometimes gruesome material, its realistic portrayal of warfare, and its relationship with its fans, EC seemed to come under

Fig. 3 An advertisement for the EC Fan–Addict Club epitomizes the company's sense of humor and its relationship to its fans (*Vault of Horror* #38 [August–September 1954]: 17; by Jack Davis, © William M. Gaines, Agent, Inc.)

special attack from Wertham and other comics critics. In an era when American culture had been "politicized," as historian Stephen J. Whitfield put it (10), these characteristics could have made the EC titles seem very subversive to conservative commentators and others not familiar with comic books. Gaines was also one of the few people in the industry who was willing to stand up in the face of such criticism. Gaines appeared before a congressional subcommittee studying the effects of comic books on children, especially their role as a possible cause of juvenile delinquency, and his company encouraged its readers to get involved. An editorial, "Are You a Red Dupe?" done in the style of EC's *Mad* satires, suggested that attempts to censor or ban comic books took place in the same spirit as limitations on a free press in the Soviet Union (*Vault of Horror* #38 [August–September 1954]: inside front cover).

Two issues later, the situation had become so desperate that Gaines and his editors abandoned their usual sense of humor to deliver a serious "Special Editorial" in *Vault of Horror* (#40 [December 1954–January 1955]: inside front cover) and other comics. The editorial blamed the controversy over comic books on "a psychiatrist who has made a lucrative career of attacking comic magazines [i.e., Wertham], certain publishing companies who do not publish comics and would benefit by their demise, many groups of adults who would like to blame their lack of ability as responsible parents on comic mags instead of on themselves, and various headline hunters." EC urged its fans to write to the Senate Subcommittee on Juvenile Delinquency to convey what real comic book fans think about what they read. "Unless you act now, the pressure from this minority [opposing comic books] may force comics from the American scene. It is members of this minority who threaten the local retailers, who threaten the local wholesalers, who have sent letters to the Senate Subcommittee on Juvenile Delinquency (now investigating the comic industry). IT IS TIME THAT THE MAJORITY'S VOICE BE HEARD! It is time that the Senate Subcommittee hears from YOU . . . *each and every one of you!*" (inside front cover). Of course, there are no letters (or any kind of testimony) from actual comic book readers in the more than two hundred pages of the report that the hearings produced (U.S. Senate).

By 1954 Wertham, through his various articles and his book *Seduction of the Innocent,* and other critics had finally pressured (sometimes through vague threats of political action) the comic book industry into creating the Comics Code, strict censorship standards that the industry itself would enforce. Publishers would send pages to the Comics Code Authority, which would review them and approve them (bestowing the Code seal), send them back for modification, or reject them. Because distributors refused to handle most material without the Code seal, publishers had to join the organization and have books approved before they could be mailed or purchased. Without the seal, publications would not be distributed. As the EC editors explained in a page devoted to their canceled comics, "Magazines that do not get onto the newsstands do not sell well" (*Tales from the Crypt* #46 [February–March 1955]: inside front cover).

Gaines and the editors at EC tried to continue in light of this important change. Ending its New Trend titles, the company began following a "New Direction" through comics that attempted new genres (*Piracy, Extra! Psychoanalysis,* and *MD*) and presented cleaner versions of adventure comics (*Valor* and *Impact*). At first, Gaines thought that distributors would handle the books without the approval seal of the Comics Code, but he was wrong. Beginning with the second issues of these new titles, he regretfully began sending his material to the Comics Code Authority for its approval. In 1955, after five issues of most of the New Direction titles (and after the Code Authority demanded that sweat beads on an African American astronaut in the story "Judgement Day" be eliminated), Gaines decided it was no longer worth being involved in the comic book industry. He and Kurtzman had already converted *Mad* into a standard-size magazine, so there was nothing holding him back. The company tried to do the same with its other comic books, reprinting classic stories in new magazine-sized titles advertised as "picto-fiction" (Reidelbach 32–35).

The loss of Gaines and EC Comics was only the first of many repercussions the passage of the Comics Code and the controversy that spawned it would have on the industry. The entire medium was, in effect, devalued, as publishers de facto admitted that comic books were indeed harmful, creating disreputable associations that persist to this day. The Code and its enforcers essentially demanded that all comic books published in the United States and distributed to established outlets be aimed at an audience of children. The adult audience for comics that had been growing during the late 1940s and early 1950s had been instantly destroyed. Sales figures bear out this loss of audience. In 1952, before the Code, 630 different comic book titles were published. After the Code, in 1956, there were only 250 titles (Sabin, *Adult Comics* 163). In 1956 34.6 million comic books were sold per month, a sharp drop from the nearly 60 million copies per month recorded in 1952 (Parsons 68). Although the increasing popularity of television certainly contributed to the decline, the Comics Code undoubtedly constituted an important element in the bankruptcy of many publishers, the change in subject matter, and the redefinition of the comic book audience toward younger readers.

Despite this change, some adults remained interested in comics. Many of these readers had begun with superhero comic books as children and simply never stopped enjoying comics. Although organized groups of fans surrounded the EC comics of the 1950s, historians such as Bill Schelly, author of *The Golden Age of Comic Fandom* (1995), argue that devotees of the superhero comics of the 1940s represented the beginnings of comic book fandom. Schelly specifically points to the 1960 World Science Fiction Convention in Pittsburgh as a crucial event in this chronology. There, Dick and Pat Lupoff presented the first issue of their fanzine *Xero*. In it was the first installment of a column focusing on comic books, "All in Color for a Dime." The first topic was the special appeal of Captain Marvel, and the Lupoffs came to the convention's masquerade dressed as the hero and Mary Marvel. Also at the convention were Don Thompson and Maggie Curtis, who in 1961 produced a fanzine called *Comic Art* that advocated the development of a specialized comics fandom (Schelly, *Golden Age* 19–21).

A number of factors began to attract people to this new movement. Some of the appeal was nostalgia, and some was a desire to simply share a hobby with like-minded people, especially in light of the attacks on the medium during the 1950s. Also important was DC Comics' slow revival of its Golden Age characters, albeit in new, updated forms. Starting in 1956, the Flash and other characters received updated costumes and enemies, while the new Green Lantern and Hawkman, among others, had origins rooted in science rather than magic. Reviving these old names in new heroes attracted a new generation of readers ready for the adventures of superheroes while establishing a sense of continuity with the fans of the original versions, who were beginning to establish the new comics fandom. As these older fans' imagination became engaged, they got more involved in these revivals, even coming up with (and suggesting to the DC editors) some of their own, including the Atom, the Spectre, and Dr. Fate (Schelly, *Golden Age* 24, 27).

At the beginning of 1960, DC introduced comic book fans to the Justice League of America, an updated version of the 1940s Justice Society that included the company's core characters, including Superman, Batman, Wonder Woman, the Flash, Green Lantern, Aquaman, and the Martian Manhunter. This revival thoroughly energized older readers who had grown up reading about the Justice Society's adventures in *All-Star Comics*. The new Justice League inspired Jerry Bails, an assistant professor of natural science at Wayne State University, to think of "ways to support and encourage this exciting development" (Schelly, *Golden Age* 23). A twenty-year-old fan named Roy Thomas also began corresponding with Bails, and in March 1961 the two men published the first issue of their fanzine *Alter-Ego*. According to Schelly, "the Golden Age of comic fandom had begun" as a result of Bails's organizational skills and enthusiasm for comic books (*Golden Age* 23–29).

One element that was crucial to the success of *Alter-Ego* and to the growth of comic book fandom itself was the increasing popularity of letters pages. In 1958, editor Mort Weisinger began printing regular letters pages in DC's Superman titles. This development was important, write Will Jacobs and Gerard Jones in *Comic Book Heroes from the Silver Age to the Present* (1985), because, "after twenty years of costumed heroes, someone was finally asking the people who bought the comics what they wanted to read." As a former editor of science fiction pulp magazines, Weisinger was generally receptive to the desires of the readers and sometimes made changes based on their suggestions, for example, the introduction of Superman's cousin, Supergirl, in 1959 (Jacobs and Jones 25). In 1961 in DC's *Brave and Bold*, editor Julius Schwartz began including correspondents' complete addresses along with their letters (Schelly, *Golden Age* 24). This policy was as important for comics fandom as it had been for the growth of science fiction fandom: it gave readers a chance to correspond with and meet in person other aficionados of their favorite comics. It also gave Bails a ready-made mailing list of potential readers for his new fanzine.

Editors of fanzines also attracted new readers through the pages of the comics themselves. Thomas, for example, wrote a letter, printed in *Justice League of America* (#8 [January 1962]), plugging *Alter-Ego*. According to Schelly, there were "so many responses that demand for the fanzine now exceeded [the] supply" that could be produced on Bails's portable spirit duplicator. Schelly estimates that by the end of 1961 there were as many as five hundred people actively involved in comic fandom (*Golden Age* 33). Many of these fans began to publish their own fanzines using ditto and mimeograph machines. "As the decade progressed," writes Schelly, "it seemed as if new fanzines were sprouting up at every turn. A teenage comic fan would see his or her first fanzine, and instantly become seized with the compulsion to publish." Many such publications were clearly amateurish and hence short-lived, but the most respected fanzines, including *Alter-Ego, Comicollector, Rocket's Blast,* and *Fantasy Illustrated,* became important additions to a fan's regular reading. Editors slowly began moving to photo-offset printing and expanded distribution. Schelly reports that eight to ten thousand copies of *Alter-Ego* issues 4–9 were distributed (*Golden Age* 99, 91).

Typically, these fanzines had very similar content. Many early publications focused especially on delineating the history of comic books and indexing specific titles. Later, contemporary comics news and gossip became more important, as did reviews of the latest issues of *Brave and Bold* or *Justice League of America.* Most fanzines also included amateur comic strips, many of which featured characters clearly reminiscent of the Golden Age super-heroes with which so many of the artists and editors had grown up. Some — such as Thomas's "Bestest League of America" (*Alter-Ego* #1 [spring 1961]: 17–21) — were parodies of existing strips or books, but others were original, serious characters created by writers and artists hoping to someday become professionals. (For these fan-produced comics, see Schelly, *Labors of Love;* Schelly, *Labors of Love* 2; Schelly, *Fandom's Finest Comics.*) Another important element of the early fanzines was information on collecting. Many fanzines were filled with ads from eager fans listing issues missing from their collec-tions and other comics they were willing to sell or trade. "Collectors were positively scintillating with excitement over the possibilities of making con-nections with their counterparts from around the country," writes Schelly. Some fanzines, in fact, came to specialize in these ads, the first being *Comi-collector* beginning in September 1961. The fanzines also contained infor-mation about the fans themselves: their likes and dislikes, their lives outside of comic books, their meetings with other fans (Schelly, *Golden Age* 37, 33).

Fanzines quickly became a place where readers and collectors of comic books could have a dialogue about their hobby. In 1963 Bails proposed the formation of the Academy of Comic Book Fans and Collectors in the eigh-teenth issue of his fanzine, *Comic Reader.* The academy's charter was mailed to ninety-two fans and quickly ratified. It said that the academy would con-duct an annual award program, publish *Comic Reader,* endorse a code for the selling and trading of comics, publish a fan directory, assist in the plan-ning of a future comic book convention, and encourage the involvement of industry professionals, among other things. The first comic book convention, attended by well-known fans, dealers, and even representatives from a new publisher called Marvel Comics, would take place a year later in New York City (Schelly, *Golden Age* 58, 74).

By 1965 the academy had grown to 1,200 members, including both fans and professional writers, artists, and editors. Fandom had gone beyond simply influencing the work of those in the industry. The fans were beginning to become professionals themselves, led by Thomas. After briefly working at DC, Marvel Comics hired Thomas as an assistant editor and part-time writer (Schelly, *Golden Age* 77). There, he succeeded Stan Lee, writing many of the company's most prominent books, including *Avengers, X-Men,* and *Fantastic Four.* In 1970 Thomas introduced the comics world to Robert E. Howard's *Conan the Barbarian,* starting a sword-and-sorcery craze that would see dozens of imitators during that decade. Beginning in 1975 he also spearheaded the revival of Marvel's 1940s characters in *Invaders.* When Thomas returned to DC in the early 1980s, he did the same for that company's Golden Age heroes in *All-Star Squadron.* Throughout the late 1960s and 1970s, many other fans also moved from the amateur to the professional ranks.

Comic fandom and collecting also began to receive attention from the mainstream press in 1965. After articles in the *New York Times* about the increasing costs of collectible comics appeared late in 1964, other media outlets quickly jumped on the bandwagon. In fandom, the February 15, 1965, *Newsweek* article entitled "Superfans and Batmaniacs" was among the most infamous. The article opens with the shocking information (for nonfans) that the first issue of *Action Comics* was selling for a hundred dollars among "comic-book fanatics." The tone of the article is clearly mocking, as the writer emphasized the silliness of the comics from the 1940s while pointing out the seriousness with which fans — or "cultists," as the article calls them — read the books. Other articles in *Time* and the *New Yorker* were a bit more respectful, but all emphasized the possibilities of making money by selling old comics. As a result, fans noticed increasing prices for old comics and most realized that "the days of Golden Age comics [selling] for a few dollars each would soon be gone forever" (Schelly, *Golden Age* 81). People with no knowledge of or love for comic books increasingly began to see them as possible investments.

This development of course affected fans' collecting practices. Schelly suggests that the rise of the "capitalist spirit" in fandom "provided the last element necessary in ensuring that comic book collecting would be more than a fad." The 1966 premiere of the Batman television program further attracted "a whole new breed of investment-minded collector." The next key event in the growth of the collecting aspect of comics culture was the publication of the first comic book price guide in 1970, which Schelly also sees as a crucial moment for the growth in popularity of comic books: "without a responsible and credible price guide, comics could never become a legitimate collectible." Other fans were less positive about the new price guide. For Bails, "It meant a loss of innocence for fandom. Speculators with no interest in the comics themselves came out of the woodwork, and prices started soaring" (Schelly, *Golden Age* 87, 93, 122).

The price guide created one of the first divisions within comic book culture. Longtime fans such as Bails, interested primarily in the stories and the feeling of nostalgia gained from reading them, were on one side, while on the other were those fans interested in comic books as popular-culture artifacts that could be bought, sold, and traded in the same way as paintings, movie posters, or stamps. This division certainly has survived to the present, with vigorous differences of opinion between readers and collectors or speculators. In 1996, for example, issues of *Comics Buyers Guide* were rarely published without a letter or two complaining about or praising the presence of price/investment guides in the publication.

Another important change for fandom in the early 1970s was the growth of "pro-zines," magazines about comics published by industry professionals. Art or stories by established professionals would guarantee increased sales for a publication, and many editors — professional and fan — needed those sales to counter the rising costs of photo-offset printing. As fans increasingly favored the pro-zines, there came to be fewer and fewer articles about "fannish" concerns. Quite simply, fewer people seemed interested in the comings and goings of the fans themselves, and more people seemed interested in the gossip surrounding the lives and work of established writers and artists (Schelly, *Golden Age* 114–17). Fandom had become less personal, less about fans getting together with other fans to enjoy their hobby and company. Fandom seemed to have become more about appreciation of the art form, the work of established professionals, and the value of comic books themselves to fans and collectors. Although fanzines continue to be published, and although fans do still enjoy the company of other comic book fans, the changes between 1970 and 1972 were so significant that Schelly ends his history of the Golden Age of comic fandom at this point.

One of this period's enduring legacies was the establishment of Marvel Comics as an industry leader. From early in the company's history, beginning with the 1961 publication of the first issue of *Fantastic Four,* Lee and Marvel's other editors courted the fan audience, sending thank you notes for fanzines the company received and printing complete addresses of correspondents with their letters (Schelly, *Golden Age* 95). Lee's style of answering these letters "was one of easygoing, hip familiarity. He wanted to impress his readers with this honesty and self-efffacement." The Marvel practice of crediting everyone involved with the creation of a particular story — complete with nicknames — was done "with the intention of creating a sense of family" (Jacobs and Jones 70). Creators would often become part of the narrative. Lee and artist Jack Kirby's conspicuous appearance on the cover of the tenth issue of *Fantastic Four* became an event. The copy reads, "In this epic issue: surprise follows surprise as you actually meet LEE and KIRBY in the story!!" (see fig. 4). These elements created a unique philosophy and a mass of devoted fans, "Marvel zombies" who would brag about buying every issue of every comic book the company published. For these readers, the philosophy of a comics creating/comics reading brotherhood or club was very seductive, and inclusion in the Marvel family often began with Lee's hyperbole-filled prose, which was displayed in credit boxes, letter pages, and "Bullpen Bulletins," a regular feature filled with gossip about writers, artists,

Fig. 4 Marvel readers met Stan Lee and Jack Kirby early in the company's history (*Fantastic Four* #10 [January 1963]: 5; by Stan Lee, Jack Kirby, and Dick Ayers, © Marvel Comics).

and new titles, all of which, according to Lee, were the greatest thing to come along since the debut of Spider-Man. Until the early 1980s Lee also regularly contributed editorials to the bulletins, discussing new projects and explaining key points of the company's philosophy.

In *The Origins of Marvel Comics* (1974), a volume that collected the earliest adventures of many of the company's oldest characters, Lee became even more enthusiastic with his praise. Writing about correspondence responding to the company's first success, *Fantastic Four*, Lee explains, "After a while I began to feel I wasn't even the editor; I was just following orders — orders which came in the mail" (73). In the book's frontispiece, he made Marvel's creation an event of virtually biblical importance.

In the beginning Marvel created the Bullpen and the Style.
And the Bullpen was without form, and was void; and
    darkness was upon the face of the Artists.
And the Spirit of Marvel moved
    upon the face of the Writers.
And Marvel said, Let there be The Fantastic Four.
And there was the Fantastic Four.
And Marvel saw The Fantastic Four. And it was good (Lee 7).

In the course of introducing the stories in *Origins*, Lee portrays himself as the sole creator. In the Marvel Comics universe, then, Lee is even more important than God.

Although the creation of characters such as Spider-Man and the Fantastic Four is a matter of intense dispute among comics fans and scholars, most would agree that Lee was the central figure in the creation of the Marvel philosophy, much in the same way that Hugh Hefner was the central figure in the creation of *Playboy*. The first part of the Marvel philosophy is simply the company's concept of heroism (or superheroism, as the case may be). Marvel's central heroes may have been filled with angst and self-doubt, but they knew that they had an obligation to fight evil and try to right the world's wrongs. These superheroes seemed to learn collectively of this duty through the example of Spider-Man, created by Lee and artist Steve Ditko. Spider-Man's first adventure tells the story of a teenage science whiz — a social outcast in his high school — who receives amazing powers from the bite of a radioactive spider. His first actions, though, are selfish — he appears on television and generally tries to make as much money as possible from his new

Fig. 5 Spider–Man finally defeats his uncle's killer and learns that he bears responsibility for his uncle's death ("Spider-Man!" *Amazing Fantasy* #15 [August 1962]: 11; by Stan Lee and Steve Ditko, © Marvel Comics).

powers. After the death of his beloved Uncle Ben (see fig. 5), Spider-Man learns that "with great power there must also come — great responsibility!" (Lee and Ditko 11). The heroes of the countless subsequent Marvel comics would learn the same lesson: the powerful have an obligation to help the powerless and battle those who would take advantage of them.

Despite this noble sentiment, Marvel heroism also concerned self-actualization and personal status. Many of its heroes — including, at times, Spider-Man — seemed to have great fun putting on costumes and fighting villains. At other times, Marvel heroes seemed to be radical individualists, dedicated to the benefits of macho vigor that come from standing up for oneself against apparently insurmountable odds. A perfect example of this philosophy came in the middle of Lee and Kirby's "... To Wake the Mangog!" (*Thor* #154 [July 1968]). In this story, Thor — a Norse god who comes to value humanity after being taught a lesson in humility by his father, Odin — is searching New York for his archenemy, Loki. Suddenly, Thor encounters a group of hippies and asks for their help, but they refuse, explaining that they have dropped out of society. On the spot, Thor decides to lecture them on their mistakes:

"Though thou be truly pure of heart — in thine innocence, thou art fair misguided. The true guru thou seekest doth lie within thyselves! Heed you now these words — 'tis not by dropping out — but by plugging in — into the maelstrom of life itself — that thou shalt find thy wisdom! There be causes to espouse!! There be battles to be won! There be glory and grandeur all about thee — if thou wilt but see! Aye, there be time enow for thee to disavow thy heritage — yea, thou mayest drop out fore'er — once Hela herself doth come for thee! But, so long as life endures — thou must live it to the full! Else, thou be unworthy of the title — man!" As the confused hippies walk away, Thor thinks to himself, "Verily, they have eyes, but seeth not! When life doth seem too much to bear — 'tis not the time to renounce the struggle! The ostrich hides — the jackal flees — but man — and god — do persevere!" (23, 26).

In many ways, this exchange ran counter to another part of the Marvel philosophy, the company's claims of being hip during the 1960s. Many factors made Marvel comics seem cool during that decade. In comparison to DC, most of its characters were brand-new and, unlike Superman, Batman, and Wonder Woman, lacked the cultural baggage of having survived the Comics Code. Spider-Man, the Fantastic Four, and other Marvel characters were new and exciting, making for comics that were fresh and unpredictable, at least in ways that Superman stories could never be. The fact that many of the Marvel heroes had Cold War origins helped make the stories seem like they were pulled from contemporary headlines. The Fantastic Four gained their powers trying to beat the Russians into space, the Hulk was created in a nuclear weapons test, and Iron Man began his career after being captured by the enemy in Vietnam. A well-developed sense of humor also added to the sense of Marvel Comics being hip, as did the occasional countercultural allusion. Artists Jim Steranko and Neal Adams were well known in the late 1960s for their unique visual styles filled with strange angles, odd layouts, and bright, psychedelic colors. Earlier in the decade, the company even called itself Marvel Pop-Art Productions in an attempt to cash in on associations with certain movements in contemporary art.

The final part of the Marvel philosophy was realism, or at least what Lee and his writers and artists saw as realism. A central part of the appeal of characters such as Spider-Man and the Fantastic Four was that they were real in ways that DC stars such as Superman and Batman never were. Where the members of the Justice League were blandly polite to each other, Marvel's group bickered like a family. The Thing was always sensitive about his appearance and constantly sought ways to regain his humanity. The Human Torch experienced mood swings and crushes much like any other teenager. Reed Richards was a bit overprotective of his wife, the Invisible Girl (later the Invisible Woman). Spider-Man seemed to spend most of his time agonizing over his personal life, something that Batman would have never done.

Marvel realism also involved the company's reliance on continuity, on how the stories about the Fantastic Four, Spider-Man, and all the rest fit into a single narrative that had a past, present, and future. By the 1970s Marvel was publishing comics set in all three of these periods, requiring fans have knowledge of hundreds of years of events to completely appreciate the Marvel universe and its continuity-based realism. This narrative required that characters' powers remain consistent, both in and of themselves and in relation to other characters, which resulted in frequent debates in letters pages about the relative strengths and abilities of various Marvel heroes and villains. Fans wanted rational and sometimes even scientific explanations for superpowers. In letters pages and elsewhere, fans would try to explain how the Human Torch flew or how Spider-Man stuck to walls.

While encouraging this sort of discussion, Marvel also claimed that its comic books were traditionally realistic by reflecting the world in which the creators and readers lived. Like DC, Marvel published some stories that were clearly meant to be relevant to current events. Spider-Man's friend, Harry Osborn, became addicted to pills of some sort, giving the hero a chance to deliver a handful of moving speeches about the dangers of drug abuse (*Amazing Spider-Man* #96–98 [June–August 1971]). Emboldened by the fact that the Department of Health, Education, and Welfare had requested that the company do a story on the subject, Marvel decided to publish and sell the issues without the Comics Code Association seal of approval. Although the Code would soon be revised, Marvel's decision only added to its mystique of relevance and taking risks. Writing directly to Lee, fan Ron Sorrells of Medford, Oregon, gushed, "My congratulations on defiance of the Comics Code, but more important on doing something that will cut a little out of your pocketbooks, but will also help in the improvement of mankind. You are showing the mettle of the man that took a chance in 1961, a chance that changed the course of the superhero comic book. And this latest achievement proves you still have it" (*Amazing Spider-Man* #101 [October 1971]: 31). Another fan, Guy Houghton of the Bronx, praised Marvel for the inclusion of African American characters such as the Black Panther, thereby "actually easing the tension of our times" and emphasizing "the obvious superiority of Marvel" over its competition (*Fantastic Four* #61 [April 1967]: 31).

Marvel frequently turned this praise around, suggesting that the company could produce mature, relevant stories only because of the intelligence and wisdom of its devoted readers, its "true believers." On the "Bullpen Bulletins" page of its April 1971 comics, Lee wrote that he and the rest of the Marvel staff quickly "realized that our readership was far more mature, far wiser than anyone had suspected" and that the company could therefore "touch upon real issues, real problems that confront this woebegone world of ours" (*Avengers* #87 [April 1971]: 28). In fact, praising the audience was another part of the Marvel philosophy. Lee and other editors constantly made the point of telling the company's readers how smart and hip they were. In response to a letter from Jeff Pierce of Stanford, California, an editor wrote, "[Y]our laudatory letter again proves that *SHIELD* readers are among the *most literate* in the comic world! The profound perceptions you've penned reflect precisely the reactions we had hoped for! Take our word for it, as long as fans like you feel this way, we'll do the best job we can to bring depth and realism to *SHIELD*" (*Nick Fury, Agent of SHIELD* #5 [October 1968]: 23).

This intelligence was an important way in which Marvel could differentiate its readers from those of DC and other companies. In a 1967 "Bullpen Bulletins," Lee explained why he would not respond to attacks on Marvel in the letters pages of some DC comics: "Actually, they're not competition! You see, they obviously aim for a totally different type of reader than we do. We don't cater to any special age group, but we do cater to a special intellectual level. Our rollickin' readers, no matter what their age, have proven to be bright, imaginative, informal, and sophisticated! ... So let them continue catering to the bubble-gum brigade — and more power to 'em. The public needs *some* sort of pablum 'til it's grown up to Marvel! Nuff said?" (*Thor* #146 [November 1967]: 23). Many Marvel zombies internalized these statements and saw themselves as superior to people who read other comic books or who did not read comic books at all. Belonging to this in-group was so important that some fans even began to develop loyalty tests. Mark Thomas of Cincinnati had a simple one: "A true Marvelite likes anything you guys put out, unless they are ex-Marvelites" (*Fantastic Four* #61 [April 1967]: 30).

Others tests were based on participation in the Marvel universe. The easiest way to do so was to read religiously "Bullpen Bulletins," which appeared in every Marvel comic from 1966 into the mid-1990s. Along with "Stan's Soap-box," "Bullpen Bulletins" included a number of items that would interest only devoted fans of Marvel comics. The November 1967 bulletins, for example, included "Stan's Soapbox," the "Mighty Marvel Checklist" (including infor-mation on thirteen different upcoming comics that are variously described as "dynamite," a "landmark," a "real mind-snapper," and "groovesville!"), and nine miscellaneous items including the celebration of Jack and Roz Kirby's twenty-fifth wedding anniversary and the announcement of a new art team for *Sgt. Fury and His Howling Commandos* (*Thor* #146 [November 1967]: 23).

That edition of "Bullpen Bulletins" also included a list of honorary titles for different levels of Marvel readers. By the late 1960s, the entire list of titles for the "Hallowed Ranks of Marveldom" was regularly published on letters pages:

RFO (Real Frantic One): a buyer of at least 3 Marvel mags a month

TTB (Titanic True Believer): a divinely-inspired "No-Prize" winner

QNS (Quite Nuff Sayer): a fortunate Frantic One who's had a letter printed

KOF (Keeper of the Flame): one who recruits a newcomer to Marvel's rol-lickin' ranks

PMM (Permanent Marvelite Maximus): anyone possessing all four of the other titles

FFF (Fearless Front Facer): an honorary title bestowed for devotion to Mar-vel above and beyond the call of duty (*Amazing Spider-Man* #68 [January 1969]: 24).

Of course, holding these ranks—or even simply being a Marvel fan—was even better when everyone knew about it, and the best way for fans to adver-tise their status was to purchase some of the Marvel products sold as early as 1965. An advertisement in the February 1966 *Tales of Suspense* offered an Iron Man T-shirt, a Spider-Man poster, and the Marvel Comics Group Offi-cial Swingin' Stationery. In the September 1966 *Fantastic Four* fans could find an offer for the poster, stationery, a Fantastic Four T-shirt, and sweat-shirts featuring either the Thing or the Hulk (in two sizes, "monstrous youth" and "gargantuan adult"). As time went by, more posters, clothing, and other Marvel products were offered to fans eager to proclaim their loyalty.

Membership in Marvel's official fan clubs was another way of announc-ing this loyalty. Beginning in 1965, fans could join the Merry Marvel March-ing Society (MMMS). In 1967 membership included a pin, a recording of the official song, eight stickers, "a nutty new notepad," "a magniloquent Marvel mini-book," a Marvel pencil, a certificate, and a membership card, all for only one dollar (*Thor* #146 [November 1967]: 23). By the 1970s the MMMS had apparently outlived its usefulness, and Marvel began a second fan-club, FOOM (Friends of Old Marvel). Although FOOM was billed as the "ultimate fan club," it offered fans fewer products and less fellowship. An early advertisement for the club explained that for $2.50, members would get a poster, a fistful of stickers, a membership card, and year's subscription to *FOOM Magazine* that would include the "Spider-Man Code" so fans could read the "secret" messages occasionally included in "Bullpen Bulletins" (*Avengers* #119 [January 1974]: 28). The magazine was essentially an expanded form of the bulletins, with inside information plus articles and other items of interest to Marvel fans. One issue also included a poster by Steranko, at the bottom of which was inscribed FOOM's creed: "Stand tall! Thou hath reached the peak and plucked the proudest prize! Hang loose! Thou shalt flee from fear no longer, nor suffer pangs of doubt! Face front! The past doth lie behind thee. The beckoning future now is thine! 'Tis true! 'Tis true! O, how proudly we proclaim: thou hast joined Marveldom assembled! Thy name hath been inscribed, now and evermore, in the blessed book of FOOM! Come take thy place, believer, within the hallowed ranks. The eyes of FOOM are upon thee. They behold thee with fondness and favor. The heart of FOOM embraces thee. The hands of FOOM clasp thine. For FOOM hath summoned thee, and claimed thee for its own! Thou hath chosen a creed, a code, a way of life. And by thy choice, and by thy faith, the legends ne'er shall perish! Excelsior!" (*FOOM* #20 [winter 1978]).

Whether fans took this rhetoric seriously is hard to tell. They were certainly used to Marvel not taking itself entirely seriously. All of its fan features, from the "Bullpen Bulletins" to the ads for the fan clubs, include their share of humor, or at least a mocking tone aimed at the company, its employees, and its readers. Marvel even managed to poke fun at its own never-ending hucksterism. A 1965 MMMS page told fans about a new gimmick in which members' names and addresses would be printed in each Marvel comic, twenty-five at a time. But, the ad explained, members would not be told in which title their names would appear, so "half the fun will be trying to find" them. And, the ad admitted, "if this keeps you buying all our titles regularly, that won't break our avaricious little hearts either!" (*Journey into Mystery* #117 [June 1965]: 23).

Outsiders' reactions to Marvel's hype were mixed. Some members of the mainstream media subscribed to Lee's image of himself and his company. Writing for the *New York Times Magazine*, Sol Braun valorized both Marvel Comics and especially Lee, arguing that he "very likely saved comic books from an untimely death" almost single-handedly (47). In *Rolling Stone*, Robin Green offered an insider's view of Marvel Comics that depicted the Bullpen as a group of men trapped in adolescence. The walls, she wrote, were covered with comic book images, often of naked women in pornographic poses, and the writers and artists were paid to freely exercise their fantasies about men in skintight costumes battling evil. Green was also aware that Marvel's image differed substantially from reality. After explaining the official version of the happy-go-lucky Bullpen, she pointed out that "management doesn't tell the artists what the sales figures are because 'they're afraid you'll ask for a raise or something.'" The article ends by focusing on Lee and how he had remade himself and his company in the now-familiar image. Born Stanley Leiber, he is old and balding. But Stan Lee is eternally young and hip and has a full head of hair. The old self is so buried that Stan "doesn't even recognize him in the mirror" (30, 34). Green's Lee was in many ways the ultimate con artist, the ultimate salesman.

For the first ten to fifteen years of Marvel's existence, Lee and his company were selling more than just comic books. They were was selling a participatory world for readers, a way of life for its true believers. According to Darcy Sullivan's article, "Marvel Comics and the Kiddie Hustle" (1992), Marvel was "a gestalt experience, a universe whose interconnectedness implied the inclusion of the knowledgeable reader" (35). This relationship ended, he argues, in the early 1970s, the period during which Marvel and its "House of Ideas" (Lee's nickname for the company's creative staff) achieved dominance of the comic book industry and began emphasizing making money over creating quality entertainment. Still, Marvel's residual energy lasted throughout that decade, giving the Marvel zombies the illusion of dynamic innocence and fun that had characterized the company's early years. Instead of cementing this relationship with its fans, however, Marvel began to experiment—without much forethought or expertise—on ways to expand its audience.

In 1969 Marvel began publishing two romance comics, *Our Love Story* and *My Love,* both clearly aimed at a female audience that traditionally had not been part of the Marvel community. Although these publications included work by prominent Bullpen members (including Steranko, John Buscema, Gene Colan, John Romita, and Lee himself), neither title reached its fortieth issue. Perhaps Marvel and its marketing department just did not know how to sell romance comics to its devoted fans; perhaps they did not know how to sell Marvel comics to nonzombies.[2] Around the same time, perhaps realizing that the romance comics were not working, Marvel began publishing comics starring female superheroes. The Black Widow (a former Russian spy and martial artist) costarred in eight issues of *Amazing Adventures* beginning in 1970, while both the Cat (a woman imbued with feline abilities) and Shanna the She-Devil (a female jungle queen) debuted in 1972 and were canceled before their sixth issues. A few years later, Marvel apparently decided that female heroes would have a better chance if they were based on male heroes along the lines of DC's Supergirl. Ms. Marvel and Spiderwoman were introduced in 1977, while the Savage She-Hulk made her first appearance in 1980. Beyond being based on older, male heroes, all three of their comics were filled with established supporting characters that made the stories difficult for non-Marvelites to follow, and none of these titles achieved long-term success.

The company also tried out other genres in continuing attempts to expand its audience. Monster comics were important for time, with characters such as Brother Voodoo, the Golem, Man-Wolf, Werewolf, and Ghost Rider, starring (usually briefly) in their own series. Horror comics were also important, as were sword-and-sorcery titles. Marvel also began reprinting many of its own rather unremarkable post–Comics Code science fiction and mystery comics from the 1950s and early 1960s in an effort to capture that market.[3] The company even allowed some of its less famous comics to edge toward a new audience: real adults. Writer/artist Jim Starlin filled Marvel's science fiction titles *Captain Marvel* and *Warlock* with complex, universe-spanning epics and cosmic, philosophical contemplation. Marv Wolfman's and Colan's *Tomb of Dracula* told complex supernatural stories with a large supporting cast, while Steve Gerber's *Howard the Duck* was filled with satire and cultural criticism. The other most prominent examples of this trend toward an adult audience were Don McGregor's *Jungle Action,* starring Black Panther, an African hero engaged in battle with the Ku Klux Klan, and the new *Amazing Adventures,* starring Killraven, a sword-wielding rebel fighting a Martian invasion force. Stories and visuals (especially the P. Craig Russell art in *Amazing Adventures*) were complex and challenging to mainstream comic readers.

Fan letters responding to both these series almost always praised their creators for providing comics that older readers could truly enjoy.

Also in the early 1970s, Marvel began a separate line of black-and-white, magazine-sized comics that were aimed at an even older audience that did not necessarily read comic books. The bigger format allowed the publications to be sold with magazines, like *Mad,* and consequently bypass the Comics Code). Other than these cosmetic changes and the potential for increased violence and occasional nudity, the new magazines were very much like the old comics. Some of these publications, though, offered the company a chance to try out new genres (for example, martial arts comics in *Deadly Hands of Kung-Fu*) or to portray old characters in more realistic ways (the Ka-Zar appearances in *Savage Tales* and the various barbarians in *Savage Sword of Conan*). Other newcomers simply seemed to be attempts to cash in on the success of Warren Publishing's *Creepy,* a magazine-sized comic inspired by the EC horror stories of the 1950s.

In 1980 after much hype in "Bullpen Bulletins" in the company's regular comics, Marvel introduced *Epic Illustrated,* a magazine of graphic science fiction and fantasy. Just as *Creepy* influenced Marvel's horror magazines, *Epic Illustrated* clearly imitated the highly successful magazine *Heavy Metal.* Although derivative, the new magazine was clearly another attempt to attract an older audience. Near the end of the magazine's thirty-six-issue run in 1986, Marvel began to publish traditionally sized comic books for adults, its "Epic Comics" line. Despite critical acclaim for such comics as J. M. DeMatteis and Jon J. Muth's *Moonshadow* (a fable about the teenaged son of a hippie and a disembodied extradimensional intelligence) and Rick Veitch's *The One* (the story of superheroes made into doomsday weapons by the nuclear powers), Marvel ended the decade without any truly adult material and without having successfully tapped into this audience of non- or ex-Marvelites.

By the 1980s Marvel needed this enlarged audience, despite the company's continued dominance of the comic book industry throughout the decade. Marvel was simply no longer as innovative as it had once been, even within the narrow definition of the superhero genre. Sullivan argues that "what seems clear is that the House of Ideas no longer knows how to create characters kids want to read about. It can rake in the dough on a presold character, its own or someone else's, but it's just not up to the tough job of selling a truly new comic book." In the 1980s Marvel's biggest successes were characters created in the 1970s (such as the Punisher and the X-Men) and product crossovers (such as *G.I. Joe,* based on the Hasbro action figures) (Sullivan, "Marvel Comics" 36) Even its biggest success in the 1990s, Kurt Busiek's and Alex Ross's *Marvels,* was basically a rewriting of classic stories from Marvel's history.

Perhaps success spoiled Marvel Comics. As the company grew and began publishing more comics, the overall quality of the line dropped as second-rate artists were assigned to the new titles. When Ditko and Kirby left the company in the early 1970s, this problem became even worse as much of the creativity behind Marvel's initial success was gone. And as Lee became less involved in the company's day-to-day workings, the comics seemed to lose some of their enthusiasm and energy. Lee's new position as a kind of Hollywood schmoozer trying to get the Marvel heroes into the other media epitomized the company's decline. Television programs and films were produced, but most were embarrassing if not downright silly, despite Lee's promotional ability. (Or perhaps the Marvel style simply did not translate well to other media, resulting in the awful film version of *Howard the Duck,* the direct-to-video *Captain America,* and the rather unexciting television version of Spider-Man.)

As Marvel's universe — and its monthly output of comics — expanded, its audience became less exclusive, and the company no longer had to try quite as hard to maintain its relationship with its fans. As the company's output increased from the nine titles published before 1968,[4] perhaps the Marvel zombies simply were no longer able (or willing) to identify with the vastness of the company's output. Although the company's sense of humor still exists, its broader, less devoted audience has made Marvel less willing to take risks and make fun of itself. Perhaps the "grim and gritty" trend of the mid-1980s took the innocence out of the company and shifted emphasis away from Spider-Man and the Fantastic Four and toward darker and more violent characters such as Wolverine, a mutant with razor-sharp claws and a bad attitude, and Ghost Rider, a motorcycle-riding demon from Hell. This shift meant that young readers were less likely to discover heroes and then grow up with them. Whatever the cause, Marvel Comics's special relationship with its audience in the 1960s and 1970s was not the same thereafter.

Furthermore, although Marvel tried to convince its readers that the boundary between them and the creators was permeable, the reality of the situation was that Marvel was as much of a business as any other publisher. The fans of Marvel Comics were not editors, as Lee suggested. They were readers and consumers and hence were no different from those people buying and reading any other brand of comics. And despite its rhetoric, Marvel was not terribly different from other publishers when it came to fans. In fact, by the mid-1980s, the company and its staff seemed to have become cynical about its readers. In 1984, then editor-in-chief Jim Shooter put together a long cross-over series called *Marvel Superheroes Secret Wars* that involved most of the company's major characters. Because of the way the series was marketed, it was popular with the Marvel zombies, but some fans were concerned that the characters did not act the same in that series as they did in their home publications. In a memo under his signature, Shooter urged his editors, "If you guys would talk up the wonderful job I'm doing, we could ~~trick the little fucks~~ make it clearer to the charming readers that, despite my stylistic differences from the other writers, we're all writing the same characters" ("Newswatch" 14). After the *Comics Journal* published the memo a year later, Marvel staffers argued that it and especially the "little fucks" comment were examples of in-house humor. Even if that contention is true, the memo still implies that Marvel's editorial staff in 1984 was not as friendly to its readers as the company's rhetoric suggested. Many older fans undoubtedly realized it, but other fans remained true believers in the Marvel rhetoric of close fan involvement with their comic books. Even if based on an illusion, the closeness many fans felt to Marvel's creative staff and characters was unique and important.

In 1974, when Marvel was still attempting some innovation, its willingness to take chances led to an effort to attract readers of underground comics (known as *comix*) through a publication called *Comix Book*. Edited by Denis Kitchen (founder of Kitchen Sink Press), this magazine-sized comic was even less successful than Marvel's other attempts to expand its audience, lasting only five issues (with Marvel publishing only the first three). *Comix Book* did, however, provide one of the few outlets for creators after the end of underground comix's golden age. This period lasted only from 1968 to 1974, but those years were important for the comic book medium and its audience. According to Joseph Witek, "The underground comix were the first significant group of comic books in America aimed at an entirely adult audience, and the comix proved to a whole generation of readers who had been raised on the vapid Code-approved comics that the sequential art medium is a powerful narrative form capable of enormous range and flexibility" (52).

The underground comix's creators were artists embittered by the con-formist, middle-class values of America in the early 1960s. (Hence the novel spelling of *comix*, as these creators sought to differentiate themselves from traditional comics.) As Robert Crumb explains in Ron Mann's 1988 docu-mentary, *Comic Book Confidential*, "In the '60s, the mainstream media was so atrophied and locked into a certain way of doing things that you were pretty much locked out if you had any idea of doing things your own way." Crumb had read funny-animal comics growing up in the late 1940s and early 1950s, but by the 1960s he was ignoring mainstream comics and working in the commercial art field producing greeting cards (and not enjoying it much). Other creators, such as Gilbert Shelton and Jack Jackson, worked on univer-sity humor magazines. Some, such as Frank Stack, obtained traditional fine-arts educations. A few, including Rick Griffin and Victor Moscoso, lived in San Francisco and produced psychedelic posters for rock concerts. But after the inspiration provided by Crumb and his *Zap Comix*, first published in 1967, other artists quickly banded together to form a comic book–producing community. *Comic Book Confidential* includes a film clip of Crumb, Shelton, Spain Rodriguez, and other underground creators frolicking during one of the many jam sessions that would result in "multi-person comic strips in which each artist draws something, taking off from what the previous artist has done" (Estren 222). Eventually, these sessions evolved into publishing cooperatives.

Since the underground creators had grown up roughly at the same time, many of their influences were also similar, creating a strange sort of conti-nuity with comics of the past. In addition to influencing Crumb, funny-an-imal comics clearly played a role in the artistic development of Jay Lynch, whose "Nard 'n' Pat" strips (about an average guy and his talking cat) could easily fit into a 1940s Disney comic if it were not for the frequent sexual sit-uations illustrated. Later, Crumb and others were influenced by Kurtzman's *Mad* (Groth 56). EC comics were a more general inspiration for many under-ground creators. Witek argues that comix such as *Skull* and *Slow Death Comix* had "philosophical connections" with EC's horror and science fiction comics of the 1950s, taking "much of their tone and graphic format" from these pre–Comics Code stories (56, 54). Many underground creators also attacked the Code, some by breaking all the rules, others by parodying the Code seal found in the upper-right-hand corner of mainstream comics published after

1954. Some underground creators, particularly Shelton, also criticized the most popular contemporary comics — those published by Marvel. Shelton mocked Marvel in various "Wonder Wart-Hog" stories and "Smiling Sergeant Death and His Merciless Mayhem Patrol," a parody of *Sgt. Fury and His Howling Commandos* (Estren 191–93). At an even more basic level, though, almost all underground creators attacked the idea that comics were only for children.

Of course, most Americans still agreed with the notion of comics as kiddie fare, but the adult audience for these comix was not the mainstream but rather the emerging 1960s counterculture. The Print Mint, a San Francisco company that published psychedelic posters, was among the first publishers of underground comix, and many ties connected the Haight-Ashbury district's rock culture and the underground comix community. Comix such as *Zap, Insect Fear, Bijou Funnies, Snarf, Slow Death,* and many more reflected the concerns of both political protesters and hippie cultural radicals. According to Todd Gitlin in *The Sixties: Years of Hope, Days of Rage* (1987), underground comix were part of the dynamic that divided radical youth from the rest of America: "In the iconography of the underground press, *they* were uptight, uniformed, helmeted goons; *we* were loose, free, loving freaks. *They* harrumphed about law and order; *we* desecrated their temples. *They* threw tear gas canisters; *we* threw them back. *They* swung their clubs; *we* threw rocks and trashed windows. *They* brought up their battalions of National Guardsmen; *we* sang, 'We Shall Not Be Moved.' *They* put us on trial; *we* denounced 'Amerika,' with its Teutonic look, or 'Amerikkka' " (288).

Underground comix were clearly aimed at this *we,* creating a cohesive, if limited, audience: members of the counterculture who could take comics seriously. Jackson explained, "Comix were for aficionados and dopers and whatnot from the beginning. We were just entertaining our friends, so to speak" (Harvey 204). Drugs and the culture surrounding them are almost ubiquitous in the comix. According to Mark James Estren in his *History of Underground Comics* (1974), "The use of drugs is, in fact, an assumption lying behind many of the stories in the underground comics" (206). Stories about drugs, especially marijuana, worked to reinforce the community between the creators and their audience by emphasizing their shared experiences (Estren 211).

Many stories focused on the drug culture itself: buying marijuana or LSD, avoiding the police, rolling a joint, marijuana-induced hunger pangs, and more. Shelton's *Fabulous Furry Freak Brothers* is a perfect example. His characters' adventures are almost always about marijuana; their jokes poke fun at the drug culture and mock the police and "straights." Other underground creators focus more on the effects of drugs, either trying to illustrate a hallucinogen-inspired trip or using the chemicals as inspiration for nonnarrative, abstract comics. Taking hallucinogens radically changed how many underground creators viewed the world. In a 1988 interview, Crumb explained that LSD "so totally alters how you see reality and your perspective on your own personal identity that what everything means is changed. All the old meanings become absurd, so it heightens your sense of the absurdity, or mine, anyway, of all the things you're taught or programmed to believe is important or significant about reality, so that it made it easier to poke fun at everything" (Groth 69). Many underground comix's readers were taking similar drugs and having their realities altered, creating a kind of synergy between creator and audience that would not exist for most straight readers.

The underground comix were also about violating and even destroying the taboos — especially sex — that the establishment had created for society as a whole and for comic books more specifically. Crumb, S. Clay Wilson, and many others had no qualms about including depictions of all manner of sexual acts in their stories, and depicting sex acts seemed to be the point of some comix. Sex (often combined with violence) was just another element to shock readers of Wilson's stories of bikers, demons, pirates, and lesbians. Although Crumb certainly was not above doing sex stories for their own sake, his explicit comics often had an element of satire behind them. A New York City court declared obscene the issue containing his famous "Joe Blow" (*Zap Comix* #4 [June 1969]) because of its graphic scenes of incest and oral sex, but the story itself is really a satire of mainstream notions of family togetherness, as the Blow family learns that the best way for it to stick together is not by eating dinner, playing board games, or doing chores but rather by having sex. Creators also did not hesitate to depict a variety of bodily functions (urination and defecation, among others) that were sure to offend the sensibilities of most Americans — but not the underground comix's audience of open-minded countercultural types.

The more overtly political content of the underground comix would also have certainly offended the majority of Americans. Rodriguez's "Trashman," one of the most class-conscious of the comix, told the story of "a sort of anarchist superhero who thinks nothing of gunning down a few braying members of the bourgeoisie" (Sabin, *Adult Comics* 40). Greg Irons and Tom

Veitch's *Legion of Charlies* challenged the morality of the Vietnam War by illustrating the parallels between Charles Manson and Lieutenant William Calley, the American soldier who led the My Lai massacre. *Slow Death Funnies* concerned ecology, while many of Crumb's comics from this period (as well as Shelton's "Freak Brothers" stories) have obvious political messages. According to Estren, most underground creators sought to illustrate the injustices in the American system so that "even a reader who is unwilling to take radical action himself will have his consciousness sufficiently altered by these comics so that, when others do take radical action to change society, the reader will support that action — or at the *very* least will not oppose it" (163).

Like the counterculture itself, the underground comix movement was not devoid of sexism, though. In fact, as Sabin writes, "When it came to sexual politics, there was often a surprising ignorance and insensitivity" among men in both the counterculture and underground comix (*Adult Comics* 224). Too often, this insensitivity turned into misogynistic fantasies, which prompted female creators including Trina Robbins, Shary Flenniken, Melinda Gebbie, Aline Kominsky, and Lee Mars to establish their own titles and publishing groups. *It Ain't Me Babe, Wimmens Comix,* and *Tits and Clits* were among those inspired by the women's movement and focused on feminist concerns, often through autobiography. Other times, their creators attacked the sexism of both underground and mainstream comics. In Robbins's 1970 *It Ain't Me Babe,* female characters including Supergirl, Olive Oyl, Betty and Veronica, and Little Lulu revolt against their male counterparts and form a feminist collective.

Underground comix's countercultural content helped to create a sense of unity among their readers. In an essay entitled "Icons of Alternate Culture: The Themes and Functions of Underground Comix," Clinton R. Sanders argues that "the most important function of the comix is the cohesion of a group of people who feel alienated from the dominant culture and who are seeking social support for their anger and disgust. In that they reflect shared values and sharpen shared perceptions, the comix sustain the alienated group and play an important role in the affiliation process by which new members are socialized and become a part of the counter-cultural community" (849). This process created a strong sense that the hip readers of underground comix were in direct opposition to the straight Americans who thought comics were for kids and found comix repulsive and dangerous. Witek argues that this sharp sense of boundaries unfortunately reduced underground comix "to preaching to the converted" and often resulted in a sense of "sophomoric in-group smugness" (52–53).

This relatively small audience also meant sales of comix were limited by countercultural affiliation. Sabin reports that during the 1968–74 period the six major publishers were selling one hundred thousand comix per month (*Adult Comics* 41). According to Harvey Pekar, as of May 1969, Crumb had sold eighty thousand copies of the first four issues of *Zap* (679) Most of these comix were sold in head shops alongside drug paraphernalia and other elements of the hippie subculture. When these shops began to close or be more careful about their merchandise in 1973 because of changes in obscenity laws, the golden age of underground comix waned. At the same time, the counterculture itself was beginning to shrink as hippies and political protesters shifted into more established social roles. Still, a few underground comics—for example, *Comix Book* and *Arcade,* an anthology edited by Bill Griffith and Art Spiegelman—survived into the late 1970s, but by then the heyday was over. The golden age of underground comix may have been brief, but their effects were long lasting, as they helped to establish the potential of comics to be an important form for adults as well as children.

In many ways, comic books have waged this struggle since their beginnings in the 1930s. When soldiers in the 1940s read comics, publishers began to develop new genres of stories—such as crime and romance—in an attempt to appeal more to adult readers. This emerging audience was squashed in the mid-1950s, as the Comics Code essentially mandated that all American comics would be acceptable reading for children, but the adults who would become the first wave of comics fans kept interest in the format alive. When Marvel differentiated itself from DC in the 1960s, one way it did so was by suggesting that Marvel's readers were smarter, older, and more mature than the readers of *Superman* and *Detective Comics.* A truly adult audience for comic books did not emerge until the advent of the underground comix later in the decade, however. Their fans and creators would help develop the alternative comics of the 1980s and 1990s, thereby keeping this struggle for intelligent, adult comics alive through the end of the twentieth century.

From Speculators to Snobs

The Spectrum of Contemporary Comic Book Readers

New comics usually arrive at Daydreams and other Midwestern comic book shops on Wednesday afternoons. As a result, Wednesdays and Thursdays are the busiest days for Daydreams. When the shop was in its previous location, in Iowa City's Hall Mall, eager readers often lined up outside the door waiting for their new comics as the shop had to limit the number of people inside. The new, larger store and its bigger staff often serve more than two hundred people on one of these busy days, including many regular patrons and the 160 pull-list customers. Weekends are also busy at Daydreams as the shop attracts people visiting Iowa City for football games, concerts, or other cultural activities.

Of course, some visitors just browse — to see how much the comics they read as a kid are worth, to reminisce about old issues of DC's *World's Finest Comics* or EC's *Tales from the Crypt*, or to flip through the latest issue of *Gen-13* or *Optic Nerve.* But most shoppers become paying customers. These customers vary widely, from ten-year-old boys yelling as they search for the most violent, bloody comic they can find to middle-aged men in business suits looking to fill holes in their Robert Crumb collections. Comic book readers may not be the most demographically diverse group of people — as mentioned earlier, most readers are young and male — but the variety in this popular culture audience is important, helping to make comic book culture an important site for the study of audiences and the cultures they create around themselves and their favored texts.

Daydreams employees are certainly aware of the differences among their patrons. Sheila Glennon, an employee for a year and a half, quickly categorized many customers:

> There are the truly snobby people — they'll be anybody.... And they will pick up very obscure things, titles that we don't get more than, say, five copies

of. And they use big words, and they are always involved in some project, and they're usually involved in graduate-degree programs of some sort. We've got sort of an elite, and you can usually tell them by the way that they dress. And then you've got the weekend people, who are just browsers. They used to read when they were kids and what have you. They wind up spending quite a bit of money, but I think it's more nostalgia than anything else. You have the odd woman who comes in — not as many as I'd like to see. That's my pet peeve. They do show up and they buy Vertigo titles mostly. You have the big base, which is the people who either have pull lists with ten titles or more or are buying that many off the racks themselves, and they're buying superhero comics mostly. It's nice to see them starting to round it out with a few independent titles . . . that aren't what they've been reading the whole time. They tend to be guys anywhere from their late teens to their — we've got people who are probably into their forties or fifties. They tend to pick up things by title grouping. They're the people who pick up all the X-Men titles and all Spider-Man titles. They are habit people. They are the people who will tell you, "I hate the way my title is going, I hate the way this book is going," and they'll still keep reading it. There are guys who have been saying that the whole time I've been working here about one title. They're still on there, they're still getting it, bag and board it, every month, putting it away. And then there are the people who I really hate, and they're the collectors and the investors, and they're coming in and picking up things with gold covers and foil stamping and signed and numbered and — garbage. It's not going to be worth anything. They're sort of inflating it. What disturbs me most is to see kids getting into that whole thing. They're not really reading things because they enjoy them, and in some cases they're not really reading at all. They're just bringing them home, putting them in a box, and checking up on the price in *Wizard* every month.

This chapter will examine all of these contemporary comic book readers and more. Some of them fit the traditional idea of fans, while others can be described by the more derisive term *fanboys,* a word that is as controversial among comics readers as *Trekkie* is for regular viewers of *Star Trek.* Still other readers would never associate themselves with the mainstream of American comic books, preferring to identify themselves as fans of alternative comics. Many of these people find their status as part of Generation X regularly reinforced in these independently published comics. There is even diversity among mainstream readers based on fans' very different kinds of relationships with their comics. Nonetheless, many similarities exist in comic book fans' lives. Their reading backgrounds are certainly comparable, but the diverse communities of comic book readers are truly united by their devotion to the medium of comics itself, a medium mocked by some and ignored by others.

Although, as Bill Schelly argues, the golden age of comics fandom ended in the early 1970s, most readers of mainstream comics can still be considered fans. Not all, however, are fans in the sense that the organizers of comic book fandom—for example, Jerry Bails, Roy Thomas, and Don and Maggie Thompson—were fans. These fans were involved in the production of their own (professional and amateur) comics, in the development of outlets for commentaries on comic books and their creators, and in the organization of others like themselves into a movement that formalized their hobby into a specific culture. In the 1990s there are still fanzines, organized discussions about comic books (in the fanzines and on the Internet), and comic book conventions where fans can find fellowship and meet professional writers and artists. But there are also other regular readers who do not or cannot get involved with any of these activities yet remain devoted to and identify with comic books.

Involved and uninvolved groups of fans are present in other forms of popular culture, too, even if scholars focus their academic energies on the more dynamic among them. In his book *Textual Poachers: Television Fans and Participatory Culture,* Henry Jenkins seems to suggest that all media fans, all fans of *Star Trek* and other television series, are actively involved in writing fan fiction, producing videos, or participating in "filksings" (fan sing-alongs with lyrics about favorite texts and fan lore) at media conventions. However, many *Star Trek* fans, for example, are satisfied with regularly watching the television series, occasionally reading novelizations, and generally discussing the show and its universe with others. These fans may not be involved in fandom, but they remain fans. In "The Cultural Economy of Fandom," John Fiske argues that fans are "active producers and users" of their chosen cultural texts (33). This production can involve simply creating meanings ("semiotic productivity"), the sharing of fan meanings and affiliation ("enunciative productivity"), or the creation of new texts based on the originals ("textual productivity") (37–39). This division of fans works well for those individuals devoted to comic books. Some are satisfied with creating their own interpretations of what they read, while others need to talk about comics with others or wear T-shirts featuring characters or work by favorite artists. Another group is actively involved in the creation of new texts — either comic books themselves or fanzines focusing on comic books — and actively participates in comic book fandom.

Still, there are similarities among these groups. In most cases, being a comic book fan is central to fans' identity. For some, identifying with the medium as a whole is most important. Others find themselves identifying more with a particular title, character, creator, or even period of comic book history. These fans' particular identification might determine particular collecting strategies. A fan of Alan Moore, the writer behind *Watchmen, From Hell,* and other highly acclaimed comics, might search out the particular issues of any title with which he was involved. This fan might even create a web page devoted to Moore, travel to conventions to meet him, or become involved in a fanzine to interview the writer. Many fans come to sincerely care about their favorite creators whom they have met and conversed with at conventions. As a result, some fans become friends with their favorite creators. Others are simply protective of artists or writers and their work. A group of Jack Kirby's fans, for example, ran a campaign during the 1980s to get Marvel to return to him the original artwork that he produced for the company in the 1960s.

Some fans wear T-shirts announcing their identity as comic book readers, but others prefer to keep their interest a secret, at least at the beginning of a relationship. Catherine, a graduate student at the University of Iowa, explained,

There are lots of secret signals that I have to wait for to discover if it's an okay thing [to talk about being a comic book/science fiction fan]. It's an interesting situation. Just to give you an example of how I wait for secret signals, Tami [a fellow fan] and I were working one day with study partners, interpreting poetry — Japanese poetry — the other night. The study partner had suggested she would like a little change of pace. Suddenly, Tami is volunteering much fan stuff to this friend. And I'm sitting there thinking, "Hm. I'm not reading the secret signals that this is okay from this person, so I will be very subdued." For example, if they can usually give me some sort of counter, like "I read issue X of whatever," or "Golly, I watch public television late, and I've seen this show," then it's okay for me to talk about it a little bit. But I won't bring it up first. And the reason I don't bring it up first is that I'm very concerned about how I look as a professional, as a teacher, as an academic, and I don't want to be classified as a geek.

For some, then, being a comic book fan is source of pain, perhaps because it has become an important part of many fans' identity and they know how American society tends to look down on the medium and its readers. The author of a regular comic book review column in the *River Cities' Reader,* a Quad Cities alternative newspaper, began his first column, "My name is Eric, and I'm a comics reader. If that sounds like a confession, it's because comics readers feel they have to explain whenever they identify themselves" (Larew 9). The stereotypes of being a fan — and especially a fan of a thoroughly devalued medium such as comic books — may make one hesitant to admit one's interest or cause the admission to be accompanied by a longer explanation, but social pressures usually do not stop fans from seeing themselves as such.

Also important to the concept of being a comic book fan is play and pleasure. Fans certainly get a sense of enjoyment from reading or rereading comic books. Many fans find that reading a stack of old Thomas-written *Avengers* or Kirby's postapocalyptic *Kamandi*s can be the perfect way to spend a rainy Sunday afternoon. Even if the stories themselves are not great, the memories associated with those comics and the time when they were originally read make reading a fun activity. Pleasure also comes from the use of imagination, which comic books are quick to inspire. Talk in comic shops quickly turns to what ifs: What if Spider-Man joined the Fantastic Four? What if the rocket that brought Superman to Earth landed in Nazi Germany or the Soviet Union instead of Kansas? For fans, this kind of play — examining possibilities, comparing characters, immersing themselves in fictional universes — is an important part of comic books' appeal, much in the same way that baseball fans discuss trades and rosters during the off-season or that soap opera viewers imagine themselves in the place of favorite characters or try to figure out what will happen next. For some fans, this kind of imaginative play turns into fan-fiction, amateur comics, or role-playing-game scenarios. Other fans enjoy playing with characters by doing sketches, creating their own T-shirts or posters, or even constructing their own action figures or models. *Wizard* has recently featured a regular column, "Homemade Heroes," devoted to photographs of action figures made by fans.

Perhaps the most important element of being a fan, though, is the perception of having a vested interest in comic books. Many fans take events in their favorite titles — and in the industry as a whole — very seriously. If they perceive characters as being misused or misrepresented, fans often become angry and will not hesitate to share these feelings with creators. Many fans become so frustrated that they stop reading the comics despite devotion to a particular character or group. Silver-age DC characters such as the Flash and Green Lantern are common focuses for these frustrated fans, explaining the success of a limited series such as 1998's *JLA: Year One* that features these characters, but comic shops are often filled with talk about how the *Avengers* or *Fantastic Four* have not been "right" for a hundred issues or more. When the "real" hero returns, or when a new creator recaptures the character's original sense of adventure and fun, fans enthusiastically return. This attitude defines some fans' relationship with the comic book industry as a whole: frustration with current trends, with the lack of good stories, with the killing or reformatting of certain characters, or with the high price of comic books causes fans to quit (or, more often, nearly quit) reading the publications. Nevertheless, these readers still identify themselves as comic book fans, and it is not uncommon to find letters in the *Comic Buyers' Guide* that explain just this position.

The bottom line is that many comic book fans feel a sense of ownership and hence become very angry when they see professionals and publishers destroying "their" hobby or ruining "their" favorite characters. For some fans, this intensity evolves into a sense of obligation to defend the medium/industry/hobby against those threatening it or attempting to promote it among nonreaders. Fans might feel obligated to attend a comics-inspired film (even if they know it is not supposed to be good) or watch a comics-inspired television series. Fans in academia might expose their students to comic books ranging from *Conan* to *Maus*. The medium's harshest internal critics often become its most vocal defenders against outsiders.

Sometimes, though, this intensity backfires, thereby helping to create fanboys, comic book readers who take what they read much too seriously. The concept of fanboys very closely corresponds to the typical depiction of fans in popular culture as well as to the Trekkie stereotype that Jenkins works to debunk in *Textual Poachers:* "Trekkies," he explains, "are brainless consumers who will buy anything associated with the program or its cast, ... devote their lives to the cultivation of worthless knowledge, . . . place inappropriate importance on devalued cultural material, . . . are social misfits who have become so obsessed with the show that it forecloses other types of social experience, . . . are feminized and/or desexualized through their intimate engagement with mass culture, . . . are infantile, emotionally and intellectually immature, [and] are unable to separate fantasy from reality" (10). These outsider characterizations apply equally well to popular conceptions of comic book fans, the fanboy stereotype. And just as Jenkins explains that the Trekkie description may apply to some fans of *Star Trek,* the same is true of its application to fans of comic books. There are, in fact, fanboys — twelve- to eighteen-year-old pubescent males who search the aisles of comic book shops for hot new titles or heroines or villainesses clad in revealing leather bikinis. Other fans simply have trouble separating the adventures of Superman or Spawn from reality. In truth, however, fanboys make up only a small percentage of comic book readers. In fact, the term *fanboy* is used almost exclusively among comic book fans to refer to practices with which they disagree, titles they do not like, or people with whom they simply do not want to be associated.

One place this stereotype has been used is the novel *What They Did to Princess Paragon* (1994), written by former fan (and *Comics Journal* contributor) Robert Rodi. His novel is the story of a mainstream comic book company (much like DC Comics) that decides that its fifty-year-old characters needed updating. After Moonman (essentially Batman) is made "grim and gritty" by a British writer (kind of a cross between Moore and Frank Miller) and Acme-Man (Superman) is updated and simplified, Brian Parrish, a gay comics writer, offers to try his hand at Princess Paragon (a Wonder Woman analog). Parrish's decision to make Paragon into a lesbian and radical feminist, though, is not greeted with joy by fanboys, including Jerome Karnacher. After Karnacher decides to kidnap Parrish from the Chicago Comicon, the novel quickly devolves into little more than a bad Hollywood caper movie.

Rodi's portrayal of Karnacher and other mainstream comic book fans fits the fanboy stereotype perfectly. Jerome is overweight, slovenly, lazy, and obsessive (he keeps the drapes shut in his bedroom to protect his mint-condition posters from fading). He lives with his mother and lacks interpersonal skills, and his sexual activity is limited to daily masturbation. The comic book shop is Jerome's refuge, at least until he begins to see the changes in Moonman, Acme-Man, and Princess Paragon (of whose publications he has nearly every issue). Even the convention, where at first Jerome "saw himself reflected again and again," turned on him, attacking his insecurities and torturing him with the real world. Unlike him and people selling superhero comics, those selling comics about the real world were "clear-eyed young men and women who came from that world, who did not have the look of the hidden, the hopeless, and the hunted" (116). Rodi's message is clear: fans of mainstream comics are insecure fanboy types for whom obsessive reading of superhero stories has made the real world a frightening and intimidating place. Alternative fans—readers who enjoy (but do not obsess over) comics such as *Love and Rockets* and *Eightball* (titles that Rodi does not fictionalize in the novel, unlike those of mainstream comics)—are normal, well-adjusted, healthy young people.

Of course, Rodi's novel is not the only place where the fanboy stereotype can be found. It is also common in alternative comics. One of the first uses of the term appears on the cover of Jay Kennedy's *Official Underground and Newave Comix Price Guide*, published in 1982. There, Bill Griffith, creator of the bitingly satiric adventures of Zippy the Pinhead, illustrates four members of "Fanboys of America, Inc." engaged in a typical fan conversation, except that they are talking about undergrounds instead of mainstream comics (see fig. 6). Griffith continued his attack on fanboys in "Pinman and the Chastiser" (*Zippy Quarterly* #12 [December 1995]: 1–11). In that story, Zippy and Griffy (Griffith's autobiographical stand-in) wander into a local comic book store, where they are shocked by superhero comics and their readers. After being attacked by Testosterono, a huge superpowered character, the pair are transformed into superheroes themselves: Pinman and the Chastiser. The story ends when they manage to remove all superhero content from comic book fans, creating new fanboys arguing about the work of Crumb and other alternative creators.

Fanboys also appear in the fourth issue of *Minimum Wage*, Bob Fingerman's narrative about comics artist Rob Hoffman, his lover, and his friends ("Conventional Behavior," *Minimum Wage* #4 [1996]). Rob attends a comic book convention as a professional trying to sell his independently published comic. The fans at the convention are almost all fanboys: overweight, lacking in sexual experience, petty, obsessive, and completely inflexible regarding their reading matter. Evan Dorkin's stories about "The Eltingville Comic-Book, Science-Fiction, Fantasy, Horror, and Role-Playing Club" in *Instant Piano* and *Dork* create a portrait of fanboys as insecure, juvenile,

Fig. 6 Bill Griffith mocks both mainstream fanboys and readers who take underground comix too seriously. This cover may also mark the first use of the term *fanboy* (*Official Underground and Newave Comix Price Guide* [1982], by Jay Kennedy, published by Boatner Norton Press; cover © Bill Griffith.)

greedy, sexually frustrated teenagers totally divorced from the real world as experienced by the rest of America (see fig. 7). One of these stories, "Bring Me the Head of Boba Fett!" won a 1996 Eisner Award for best short story, suggesting that professionals have a certain degree of respect for Dorkin's vision of comics fans.

These are all alternative comics, and most fanboys do not read these publications. For their creators, however, this fact is almost irrelevant. These artists and writers are not trying to change anyone's mind about which comics are best to read (although they do have ideas on that subject, too). Instead, these creators are commenting on the industry itself and trying to distance

Fig. 7 Josh and Bill battle over comics, *Star Wars,* sci–fi, and other fanboy trivia for the rights to a much-sought–after Boba Fett figure ("Bring Me the Head of Boba Fett!" *Instant Piano* #3 [February 1995]: 10; © 1998 Evan Dorkin).

themselves from what they see as the worst aspects of comic book culture—
fanboys, whether in stereotypes, reality, or overgeneralizations. When alternative creators use that image, mocking the stereotype and thereby distancing themselves from it, they are telling their readers, "Yes, you read comic
books, but you are not like these losers. You can laugh at the people who
read *Wolverine* and who obsessively collect every comic with an appearance
by Lobo. You are different from them and better than they are." This attitude helps to create one of the most important boundaries between readers
of mainstream and alternative comics.

At the same time, not every comic book reader of any type takes this
term completely seriously. In recent years, many people have come to use
the term *fanboy* with self-depreciating irony, particularly when mainstream
comics readers are admitting an unfashionable way of interacting with their
favorite titles. In a letter to *Legion of Super-Heroes*, Marc Wilkofsky of Pomona,
New York, wrote, "I've gotta wax fanboyish again and do what I used to
love to see letter writers do way back when—list a few pages or scenes that
were my faves in the issue." He also admitted that Ultra Boy was his favorite
Legionnaire, adding, "Man, I'm getting *really* fanboyish" (*Legion of Super-
Heroes* #82 [July 1996]: 30). Michael Slark of Burnaby, British Columbia, suggested that part of his enjoyment of the new *Justice Society of America* came
"from my fanboy-type, knee-jerk, excited reaction to anything JSA" (*Justice
Society of America* #8 [March 1993]: 32). Even fans of alternative titles have
been getting in on the act. In *Hate*, Craig Paeth of North Olmstead, Ohio,
referred to himself as a "drooling fanboy." In the same letters column, Laura
Mitchell of Somerville, Massachusetts, wrote, "One of the my favorite things
about *Hate* is reading the letters section, because that's where the fanboys
really shine!" (*Hate* #23 [June 1996]: 26–27). These letters show mature
comic book readers reflecting on their fun with their favorite titles. These
fans may obsess over minor details, get angry about the treatment of a particular character, or simply take the stories a bit too seriously. For them, being a fanboy or acting fanboyish involves a certain degree of irrationality,
especially in regard to choosing favorite characters or comics based not on
aesthetic criteria but rather on some gut-level determination of "coolness."

Other members of comics culture who admit to being fanboys or having
fanboy tendencies focus on their own childhoods. *Comics Journal* critic Ray
Mescallado argues that *Astro City* is "an unabashedly fanboy series," especially
good for helping readers "tap that Inner Fanboy"—like an inner child—

hiding inside intelligent, adult comic book fans (review 38). J. Torres's and Tim Levins's *Copybook Tales* has two simultaneous narratives, one of a beginning alternative comic book writer struggling to make ends meet and the other of the writer as a child enjoying comics such as *X-Men* and *New Teen Titans*. The first issue of the series was entitled "Portrait of the Artist as a Fanboy." Other creators also have owned up to their fanboy tendencies. In his cartoon diary originally published in the humor anthology *Snarf*, Joe Matt refers to himself as a "terminal fanboy" while trying to explain an episode of writer's block. (*Peepshow* 48) (see fig. 8). In his fanzine, alternative creator Scott Saavedra refers to himself as "a goofoid fanboy" (*Comic Book*

Fig. 8 Even such creators of alternative comics as Joe Matt admit that, deep down, they are fanboys (*Peepshow: The Cartoon Diary of Joe Matt* [1991]: 48; © Joe Matt).

Heaven #1 [May 1995]: 2). In his send-up of mainstream fisticuffs, Scott McCloud admits to having read superhero comic books as a kid, adding, "It's true! I'm a fanboy! Put on the cuffs! There's no denying it now" (*Destroy!* 33).

Some comic book fans certainly have been able to take the term *fanboy* and make it almost a badge of pride. "Around here, we all realize that we're fanboys deep down — some of us not that deep — and there's nothing wrong with it," explains Don Hughes, a Daydreams employee. For Hughes and others, acting fanboyish or tapping their inner fanboy is something that can be turned on and off, so the term lacks any negative connotations. For example, Daydreams employees enjoyed talking about *Kingdom Come* (#1–4 [1996]), a DC "Elseworlds" story that imagined a future in which heroes such as Superman and Wonder Woman had to come out of retirement to save the world from new, more violent superpowered beings that lacked any sense of responsibility toward humanity. The series was fun to talk about because of the cameo appearances by various DC characters and, more often, their descendants. Finding old favorites and their children gave Hughes and others a chance to be fanboys again for a little while: "We were back there talking [about *Kingdom Come*] like, 'I can't believe that was Billy [Batson, the original Captain Marvel's alter ego],' referring to these guys by their first names like they're our pals," Hughes explained. "It's just a 'throw reality to the side' kind of thing."

Of course, not all fans of mainstream comics can laugh at the fanboy image, let alone use the term to refer to themselves. Rick Olney, executive director of the Organized Readers of Comics Associated (ORCA), a club of comic book readers and collectors based in Utica, New York, expressed his view of the term *fanboy:* "The tag name of 'fanboy' is demeaning. It is a forgone conclusion that 'fanboys' are a specific type of comic book reader. In fact, the references are more likely to indicate that 'fanboys' don't actually read their comics. It's thought that these type of readers are pimple-faced adolescents with no interests in anything but a certain title or industry professional. 'Fanboys' are more likely to buy a book and put it away awaiting the day when those issues will have turned to gold. I *am not* the Executive Director of a 'fanboy' club. The close to 400 members of ORCA are male and female between the ages of 8 to 56 years of age. Their combined reading interests span the entire spectrum of known comic book product currently on the market. I think that the time is right for people prone to using the word 'fanboy' as a descriptive to grow up and realize that it is demeaning" (personal correspondence). Olney is certainly right; the term *fanboy* is demeaning when it is applied broadly to all comic book readers or even only to all readers of mainstream comics. But it is possible that some readers fit the stereotype, and it is also possible for comics fans to read or enjoy a particular story—whether *Kingdom Come, Astro City,* or even *Sandman* or *Hate*—as fanboys would. Mescallado is on the right track when he talks about "tapping the inner fanboy"; a good part of the enjoyment that adult readers of mainstream comics derive from their hobby comes from associations created when they were children, when they were concerned about an argument between Mr. Fantastic and the Thing or about the exact effects of red Kryptonite on Superman. Recapturing those feelings, that excitement—and sharing them—is part of what binds mainstream comic book readers into a particular kind of reading community. And as a result, being a fanboy, remembering a fanboy past, and talking with friends about fanboyish topics are important elements of comic book culture.

Olney and others critical of the term *fanboy* seem to object primarily to certain kinds of comic book collectors. While most comic book fans of all sorts save and sometimes protect what they purchase at the local specialty shop, there are different reasons for collecting. "The whole idea of collecting comics has two distinct, separate entities within it. You collect either for yourself or you collect with the idea that someday I'm gonna make a lot of money off this," explained Adam Mix, a fan and Daydreams employee. In fact, many members of comics culture would not even consider speculators who treat comic books as investments to be real fans or even readers.

Because of a desire to keep their comics in mint condition, many speculators do not read their books, and others buy two copies, one for reading and one as an investment. Other speculators are not interested in comic books as storytelling devices and began buying them simply as money-making commodities. Fans also criticize this practice for a couple of important reasons. First, speculators tend to drive up the price of back issues on hot titles— for example, *Sandman* or *Uncanny X-Men.* "They are the oil-sheiks of fandom," commented Frank V. Priore. "In fact, they don't even really collect comics; they accumulate them. They say to themselves, 'Hmm, if this book is worth $100, I'll bet I can get some sucker to pay $200 for it tomorrow'"

(263). In the late 1980s, many speculators began their own comic book shops or started dealing at comic book conventions. This boom ended in 1994, though, and nearly all of these speculators have left for greener pastures.

Second, fans are angry because speculators generally seem to know little about comics or about the medium's history. A participant in a comics bulletin board on the Internet argued, "Where pure speculators go wrong is that they don't know the difference between Neil Gaiman or Jack Kirby and Joe Schmoe. They tend to hit the first issues of ANY HYPED UP TITLE, and expect to sell it for oodles of money later." This statement is not true of all speculators, however. High-level investors may buy very rare comics for later resale, but the motivation behind the purchases is rarely as simple as greed. Many speculators view their purchases as artworks in the same way that others view Pablo Picasso's paintings. Lower-level speculators, conversely, are often teenage boys who become so caught up in the checklists, price guides, and constant information about what will become hot that they begin buying multiple copies, variant covers, or whatever gimmick publishers can use to declare a comic an instant collector's item. Other collectors may occasionally speculate by buying the work of an unknown artist they think will become popular or a comic with an appearance of a character they believe (or have heard) will become important to a longer story line. Despite this, most fans are like Hughes. "I never went out and specifically said, 'That [comic] will make me money. I don't care what it's about.'"

Fans such as Hughes who are primarily interested in the stories nonetheless often have substantial collections of comic books that are important regardless of monetary value or lack thereof. Hughes explained, "I've got somewhere close to forty long boxes in my basement, with 200 to 250 [issues] in each one. It's been so long since I played with my list, [but] I think at last count I was just around sixteen thousand, and there's been probably three or four boxes since then. As far as collecting for value goes, I could probably get more for most of my comics by pulling out the staples and selling them by the pound." Although most readers who get their books through pull lists have the publications bagged and boarded, many are simply not terribly concerned about it. According to Mix, "[W]ell over half of [my comics] — and even my older books — aren't in plastic containers. They're not cardboard backed." The purpose of the bags and boards is to protect the comics from the elements — heat, moisture, light, and so forth — and a variety of companies sell a number of different grades of materials for different levels of protection. The *Overstreet Comic Book Price Guide* and other similar indexes are very specific about temperature and humidity levels. Nevertheless, following these guidelines to the letter is simply not a very popular practice except among high-level speculators.

Fans collect comics for a variety of reasons. "I'm kind of looking at [my collection] as something to not necessarily pass down monetarily to my kids," Hughes explained, "but when they're growing up, I can say, 'Hey, read this. Have some fun. Go downstairs into the library and dig through and pull out some comics and have a good time.' " Others collect for nostalgia, buying up old copies of *Sgt. Fury and His Howling Commandos* or *Little Lulu* that they read as children. Priore, writing in *Fandom Directory*, suggests that collecting is a mania, an explainable mystery: "What mystical force propels [collectors] headlong into the frenzy of a comic convention dealer's room in full-swing, when they know that the chances of leaving it with both their wits and their wallet intact is, at best, minimal?" (262).

People collect comic books for many of the same reasons that people collect anything. In their essay "No Two Alike: Play and Aesthetics in Collecting," Brenda Danet and Tamar Katriel argue that collecting "is a sheltered way of confronting chaos and the ephemerality of human existence," that it gives those involved a chance to "create an agenda for the production of, and reduction of, manageable tension" (271, 264). To reduce this self-imposed tension, collectors must be able to achieve a sense of closure, perhaps by completing a set or aspiring to perfect objects. The initial motivation for collecting, though, lies in the ideas of play and aesthetics. This sense of play can be found in the competition between collectors for artifacts, in the paradox between rationality (found in the assessment and classification of the objects collected) and passion (falling in love with objects), and in the elements of fantasy that allow collectors to return to their childhoods through the collections (Danet and Katriel 256). The aesthetics arise primarily in the reframing of the original object — usually something mundane or something considered ephemera — as a work of art. Part of the beauty of this art comes from repetition, in having a group of objects that are the same but also different. This repetition then creates a unique kind of logic for the collection and allows the individual items to "rhyme" (Danet and Katriel 262), to link themselves together in a complex matrix of sounds, images, and ideas. It is not hard to see how this theory applies to collectors of comic books as well as to those involved in stamps, coins, baseball cards, beer cans, or nearly anything.

Some comic book readers prefer even more sameness than the average collector and hence focus their interest on a single genre or title. Two mainstream series have especially devoted readerships, Marvel's X-Men titles and DC's *Legion of Super-Heroes*. Having followed their favorites from *Adventure Comics* (the superhero anthology series where the group of futuristic, interplanetary teenaged heroes first appeared in 1958) to the group's two 1990s series, *Legion of Super-Heroes* and *Legionnaires,* devotees of the Legion are especially loyal. By the 1960s, DC editors had recognized the special relationship between the Legion and its fans. Readers constantly suggested new members and villains, demanded romances between characters (there has always been a strong female component to Legion fandom), and generally wanted more background information about the characters. Readers eventually received the right to vote in annual elections for the team's leaders. In 1966 one reader, a thirteen-year-old named Jim Shooter, was named writer and went on to produce many of the Legion's most beloved adventures (Jacobs and Jones 85). In one of the fanzines devoted to the group, Paul Decker tried to explain its appeal: "I think that one of the reasons so many of us really loved the Legion is that it was *our* feature. . . . I really felt a part of that Legion, when I knew my vote had been counted, when [editor] E. Nelson Bridwell printed my letters and then my costume designs. I really felt that someday I was going to be another teen-aged Jim Shooter genius. I wrote story idea after story idea and created new Legionnaire after new Legionnaire and sent them in to some poor editor who had to sort through the mess. It was something more to do than just use up my spare time" (*Legion Outpost* #9 [1975]: 28). Despite sales that have rarely been stellar, the Legion's devoted fans have kept their favorites in print for nearly forty years.

A more recent source of fan devotion is Marvel's X-Men. Although not a big seller when it was first introduced in the early 1960s, *Uncanny X-Men* always attracted a very loyal readership. When the series was canceled in 1970, fans were angry and began clamoring for the return of the teenage mutants wherever any of them appeared as guest stars. After the X-Men returned to their own comic in 1975, enthusiasm for the group grew slowly until John Byrne, a favorite of comics fans, took over the art for the book in 1978. At that point, the book took off and quickly became the centerpiece of

Marvel's domination of the mainstream comics market in the 1980s and 1990s. For the comic's core readership, though, *Uncanny X-Men* was always more than just a hot title. They identified with their publication in ways that fans of other superhero comics did not. Carolyn Amos wrote:

> I—and my friends—encounter ourselves so beautifully in this book.... Night-crawler [a demonic-looking mutant with the ability to teleport himself across short distances] is the most special of all the X-Men characters, new or old, to me. I alluded to being physically deformed earlier. I may not be pointy-eared and blue or able to go "bamf," but because my hands and feet are mis-shaped and I wear an artificial limb I can no more pass for "normal" than Kurt [Nightcrawler's real name]. So it is that his and my life experience and outlook most interlock; and he becomes both a mirror and a self-portrait of sorts, as well as a role-model. Like Kurt, and sometimes with or through him, I discover that it is truly better to be a whole "me" than "normal," that humor helps defuse anger and to dissolve self-pity, that one's self is infinitely preferable to any "image" and so much more (*Uncanny X-Men* #149 [September 1981]: 31).

The devotion of fans such as Amos, who saw personal messages in the group's adventures, made *Uncanny X-Men* an important comic with a unique core readership.

Although *Legion of Super-Heroes* and *X-Men* attract a large part of the comics audience, other comics, albeit very different ones, also have devoted readers. Fans of these alternative comics make up a distinctive (if relatively small) part of the whole comics audience through their rejection of most of the industry's mainstream products. The labels *mainstream* and *alternative* are controversial, and it is best to view them as ends of a spectrum rather than as discrete categories. As a comic book moves to the more alternative end of the spectrum (in terms of diverging more from the corporate prod-uct published by the mainstream companies), its audience often becomes more distinctive and, hence, smaller. While most mainstream readers are male (most estimates put the number between 90 and 95 percent), alterna-tive comics' audience is substantially female, with the actual numbers vary-ing according to title. Furthermore, alternative fans often read and collect their comics differently from their mainstream counterparts. Despite these generalizations, there is a great deal of variety among alternative fans, who range from devotees of the widely distributed Vertigo titles to snobs inter-ested in the most obscure comics available.

Among alternative readers, those dedicated to the comics published by the Vertigo imprint of DC Comics are the closest to the mainstream. The imprint was started in January 1993 out of a handful of titles, focusing on offbeat superhero-type concepts, that the company was already aiming toward a more mature audience. Most of the Vertigo titles were written by British writers or women, and nearly all involved horror, the supernatural, or psychological science fiction. With the new imprint (and its own editor), DC took *Sandman, Swamp Thing, Hellblazer, Doom Patrol, Animal Man,* and *Shade the Changing Man* out of the company's superhero universe. DC also began marketing these products more aggressively to an audience not accustomed to buying comic books. High production values, nontraditional comics art, and challenging story lines made these publications attractive both for readers who had grown bored of Batman and for those more accustomed to reading their fiction in traditional books. Since its beginnings, Vertigo has successfully created a line of comic books that had an alternative attitude despite being supported by mainstream marketing.

This new Vertigo audience included college-age young adults, women, readers of Anne Rice novels, and those interested in the occult. In 1995 the company even sold a set of high-priced tarot cards with art by prominent Vertigo creator Dave McKean (best known for his *Sandman* covers) and featuring many of the imprint's characters. Goths, a youth culture tribe of "pale-faced, black-swathed, hair-sprayed night dwellers who valued imagery both religious and sacrilegious, consumptive poets, and all things spooky" seemed particularly drawn to Vertigo titles (Daly and Wice 94). The imprint soon began to connote a specific image very different from that of DC's other comics. The company advertised Vertigo's publications as comics for people "on the edge" who collected experiences (rather than comics). A 1994 subscription ad urged readers to "stand apart from the crowd" by subscribing to a Vertigo title (*Sandman Mystery Theatre* #21 [December 1994]: 31).

Some longtime comics fans, many of whom read some Vertigo titles, became angry at the company's use of a sense of elitism to sell comics. Some readers resent the Johnny-come-latelys who have usurped the hobby simply because it is suddenly cool in a certain crowd. Others fans are angry about what they perceive as a generally anticomics attitude among Vertigo fans. Explained Michael Ayers, "There are a lot of literary folks coming into the industry because of Neil Gaiman [writer of *Sandman*] and a couple of other people, making a big deal of 'This is . . . good literature done in comic books, . . . and it's not like any of the other comic books. This is a good one; the rest of them are still bad.'. . . I know some people who have the attitude of 'I just read Vertigo because they're the only good comics.'" Others are more critical of the creators and editors at Vertigo for apparently catering to this crowd at the expense of the readers who had been following characters such as the Swamp Thing since the beginning of the series many years before the imprint began.

Sandman was Vertigo's most important title prior to the comic's conclusion in 1996. The series began in 1989 with little fanfare, but it quickly developed a highly committed readership. Older comics fans were attracted by the use of obscure DC characters, including some from the company's horror comics of the 1970s, while readers from the alternative end of the spectrum were more interested in Gaiman's use of ancient myths, European folktales, and world history. Just as these readers came together to help form the comic's devoted audience, so did the different elements — from comics, literature, and myth — that Gaiman introduced into *Sandman* work together to form a new kind of contemporary mythology that acknowledged powers and forces beyond those of humankind but demanded no worship of them. Along with the overall quality of Gaiman's writing, these elements excited readers, creating one of the most loyal followings in all of comics and resulting in fan letters gushing with praise.

The complexity of the *Sandman*'s story lines were important to defining and limiting the comic's audience. Gaiman gave the series a very tight continuity, with story arcs of between five and ten issues becoming what amounted to unified graphic novels. These novels, though, built on each other, so that the plot of the final long sequence, "The Kindly Ones" (*Sandman* #57–69 [February 1994–July 1995]), hinged on events from some of the earliest issues of the series. The short sequel, "The Wake" (*Sandman* #70–73 [September–December 1995]) included guest appearances from many of the characters who had played important roles in earlier stories. The final issue, "The Tempest" (*Sandman* #75 [March 1996]) demanded that readers not only have knowledge of previous *Sandman* events but also have a certain amount of understanding of Gaiman himself. That story, an adaptation of the play of the same name, was a thinly veiled autobiography, with Gaiman as William Shakespeare, that worked to explain to readers why he had decided to end the series. Like many *Sandman* stories, "The Tempest" also demanded that readers have some knowledge of history and literature, in this case, knowledge of Shakespeare.

The fact that these graphic novels and short stories were quickly collected in trade paperbacks also helps to reveal *Sandman*'s audience. Most of these paperbacks sold for around twenty dollars, adding to the idea that the comic's audience was primarily adult. For people who did not read other comics (and *Sandman* was the only series read by many people, especially spouses and significant others of broader comics fans), the trade paperbacks certainly looked more dignified than comic books. The quality bindings and paper — along with McKean's surrealistic covers — suggested that these publications were books and hence were meant to be shelved with other works of fiction found in more traditional text forms. This format is also more durable than standard comics, thereby encouraging loaning, sharing, and multiple reading, all of which were common among *Sandman* fans. That this audience was quite literate was demonstrated by the fact that introductions to the trade paperbacks were written by prominent, well-respected writers, including Harlan Ellison, Gene Wolfe, Samuel Delany, Clive Barker, and Steve Erickson. The introduction to the collected version of the spin-off *Death: The High Cost of Living* was written by musician Tori Amos.[1]

Sandman's strong female characters have attracted many women, like Amos, to the series. Although Dream of the Endless is the nominal central character, many of the stories' important actors are young adult women. In *Sandman: The Doll's House*, for example, the hero is Rose Walker, a young woman looking for her long-lost brother. Rose also plays a part in "The Kindly Ones," but the main story focuses on the wrath of Lyta Hall, a woman who believes that Dream stole her child, and the Furies, female spirits of vengeance who must punish Dream for taking the life of his son. The most popular female character in the *Sandman* mythos, though, is Death (see fig. 9). The older sister of Dream, Death is the fundamental force of the universe, but she is not grim, and her job is not depressing. It merely *is*. Of all the Endless, Death is clearly the most well adjusted, most able to look at the world and her job with a serene sense of duty and even a sense of humor. Her popularity has spawned two miniseries, 1993's *Death: The High Cost of Living* and 1996's *Death: The Time of Your Life*. Visually, Death is a very appealing character for both men and women. She is smart, sincere, and sensitive, and, importantly, she does not look like an exaggerated Playboy Playmate.

Fig. 9 Neil Gaiman's Death (right) appeals to many Vertigo readers, both male and female (*Death: The High Cost of Living* [1994]: 18; by Neil Gaiman, Chris Bachalo, and Mark Buckingham, © DC Comics).

She is someone with whom women can identify or imagine as a friend or even strange sort of role model. Many young men also might see her as a potential friend but hope to take the relationship further. She is "the way-cool hipster babe alternately inaccessible and great to hang out with, who can dazzle with a smile or send you off with a withering put-down, who knows Sylvia Plath and Patti Smith, and can mosh all night while you ache for a slower (horizontal) dance" (Mescallado, "Day" 50). Some male readers certainly would not be attracted to this type of woman, but *Sandman* and the Death miniseries are neither aimed at nor read by an all-inclusive audience.

Many of Vertigo's readers also read independent comics published either by smaller companies or by individual creators. Such titles as *Strangers in Paradise, Stray Bullets, Bone,* and *Madman* may not be aesthetically or culturally challenging, but they do provide a clear alternative for readers raised on mainstream superhero or genre comics. These former mainstreamers may still read an occasional issue of one of Marvel or DC's well-written superhero comics, but most such readers have found that their tastes have changed and that the larger companies generally cannot keep up. For these independent readers, superhero stories hold no real stigma as long as they are intelligently written, clearly drawn (or painted), and more complex than the comics of their childhoods. As a result, Mike Allred's *Madman,* Kurt Busiek's *Astro City,* and other comics that recapture the earlier era's innocence but add an intelligence and maturity that was relatively rare have achieved a good deal of popularity among older fans.

Other independent comics are also filled with genre stories. David Lapham's *Stray Bullets,* first published in 1995, is a crime comic in the tradition of Quentin Tarantino's *Pulp Fiction* (which, not surprisingly, is a favorite among comics fans). Each issue has its own self-contained story, often about the almost random effects of violence and crime, but the series also forms a larger whole that links all the characters into a single narrative that takes place over the span of many years. Terry Moore's *Strangers in Paradise* is, at different times, a soap opera, a sitcom, and a romantic comedy. The strong female characters, Katchoo and Francine, help to attract a strong female audience. Jeff Smith's *Bone* and Zander Cannon's *Replacement God* are classic fantasy works in the tradition of J. R. R. Tolkien's *The Hobbit.*

Bone has been particularly important in encouraging the production of "all ages" comics that feature clean, well-told, exciting, inoffensive stories with a gentle sense of humor. Independent publishers such as Caliber Press have even begun special imprints for comics that both adults and children can enjoy. Marvel and DC also have created series devoted to younger readers. Adults respect *Batman and Robin Adventures* (based on and drawn in the style of the animated series) and its brethren for telling intelligent stories with a simple elegance. Independent readers often especially like these comics because they help to re-create the (perceived) innocence of the comics of the 1960s and 1970s that these readers would have encountered as children. Furthermore, these adults are also looking for comics that they will not be embarrassed to give to their children. Visually, many of these independent comics also create a sense of nostalgia. Compared to the often cluttered, highly exaggerated, usually sexist style of art in most comic books published by Marvel and especially Image Comics, many independent comics have a sense of visual simplicity. The women in *Strangers in Paradise* are attractive, but they are drawn in a realistic way that does not offend readers' intelligence or sensibilities. *Bone* features clean, curved lines, simple and clear layouts, and solid storytelling, and its art style certainly reminds readers of Walt Disney cartoons and that company's comics drawn by Carl Barks, a favorite artist of many independent and longtime mainstream fans.

The direct ancestor of these black-and-white independent comics is *Cerebus*, which since its inception in 1977 has been written, drawn, and published by Canadian Dave Sim. *Cerebus* is filled with crisp, detailed art that certainly constitutes part of the series' appeal. Devoted readers are attracted to many other elements of the series as well. *Cerebus* began as a parody of Marvel's *Conan the Barbarian* and other sword-and-sorcery comics but quickly evolved into a long narrative about the life of an aardvark warrior. These adventures take place in a three-dimensional world where city-states have their own political and religious systems, where ideological forces battle each other for control of those small nations, and where the characters have lives that grow and change like those of real people. The stories are complex, often focusing on the machinations of political and religious power that often surround Cerebus. Other stories are more satirical, attacking both current affairs and comic books.

Sim is also part of the series' appeal. Early on, he announced to his readers that *Cerebus* was really a single, long story — the title character's life history, in many ways — and that it would not be completed until the last issue. That issue would be number three hundred, a point that was many years in the future. But Sim made a commitment to reach this point without using guest writers or artists to reduce his workload. Many devoted fans admired this commitment and admired the fact that Sim made the story accessible to new readers. After he completes a *Cerebus* novel, Sim and his publishing company reprint it in a relatively inexpensive paperback. Fans have come to call these works phone books because of their size and the relatively low quality of paper used to ensure low prices. All of the books are perpetually in print, so access to them is easy. Many readers are also attracted to the long letters pages that often take up nearly half of the comic book. There, readers engage each other and sometimes Sim in conversations about events in the comics as well as broader topics such as the comics industry or North American sexual politics.

Some comic book fans debate whether these independent comics that generally do not challenge their readers are truly alternative. Observers of 1990s culture have also debated extensively whether the term has any meaning at all. Steven Daly and Nathaniel Wice explain that in the 1980s *alternative* "became a handy description for the [college rock] milieu, but it was soon reduced by overuse to just a cooler way of saying 'cool.'... Even spread this thin, alternative — with its roots in white, middle-class rock — couldn't describe American youth culture in all its fragmented glory: what about Snoop Doggy Dogg or Nike or Mortal Kombat or *Melrose Place?*" (xiv). The use of the term to describe music has become especially problematic when "alternative" bands such as REM and Pearl Jam now perennially appear on the top of the Billboard charts.

In comic books, though, the difference between the mainstream and the alternative is often (but not always) very clear, especially concerning the very different audiences for the two branches of contemporary comics. The content of the comics is certainly important in determining alternativity, but so is the publisher (with the exception of the Vertigo titles, almost all are published by small companies or individuals), the creator (most creators have positioned themselves in one camp or the other), the presence or kind of advertising (most alternative publications feature only ads for other comics and zines done in the same spirit, but some have begun featuring ads for compact discs from indie rock bands), and the sales figures.

Most alternative comics contain a certain degree of criticism, particularly of the aesthetics of their mainstream counterparts. Alternative art styles differ greatly from that of mainstream publications: clearly cartoony, grittily realistic, dramatically expressionistic, purposefully ugly, interestingly Picassoesque, exaggeratedly simple (see fig. 10). This art works as a kind of de facto criticism of the clichéd styles found in mainstream superhero comics. Stories about average, everyday people in alternative comics such as *Hate, Minimum Wage, Naughty Bits,* and *American Splendor* also emphasize the silliness of mainstream comic book stories about overly muscled men and

Fig. 10 Alternative comics are filled with diverse art styles, from the sketchy to the cartoony to the primitive (top: *Naughty Bits* #18 [January 1996]: 13; © Roberta Gregory [www.robertagregory.com]; middle: *Yahoo* #5 [December 1991]: 22; © Joe Sacco; bottom: *New Hat* [August 1995]: 21; © Tom Hart).

women in impossibly skintight costumes saving the universe from other similarly garbed individuals.

Other alternative comics directly criticize mainstream comics and culture. Some alternative publications are like the old underground comix that worked to assault middle-class society on every level imaginable. Early issues of Chester Brown's series *Yummy Fur* were perfect examples of this phenomenon, with stories about penile transplants, clowns spontaneously fracturing their limbs, Ronald Reagan's head transplanted onto a penis, alternate universes where toilets had never been invented, and a man who cannot stop defecating (collected in *Ed the Happy Clown* [1992]). In many issues, though, Brown juxtaposed this seeming chaos with a retelling of the Gospel, albeit one with images of open sores, festering wounds, and typically private bodily functions. Many of Dan Clowes's stories in *Eightball* are also very disturbing. His graphic novel, *Like a Velvet Glove Cast in Iron* begins with a man seeing his wife in a strange sadomasochistic pornographic film and ends with the amputation of his arms and legs and his romantic involvement with a woman with a similar disfigurement. "On Sports" contains images of male and female genitalia in the place of common sports equipment (*Eightball* #14 [1994]: 10–14). Clowes's comics are generally drawn in an odd retro style reminiscent of an early 1960s cocktail lounge patronized by lonely salesmen who carry playing cards or cigarette lighters with cheesecake photos of scantily clad women. In many ways, Clowes seems to be trying to offend as many people as he can, from puritanical right-wingers to liberals troubled by sexist images.

More direct political criticism is also a part of many alternative comics. Joe Sacco's *Yahoo* contains a series of stories under the title "How I Loved the War" that scathingly attacks the U.S. role in the Persian Gulf War and the media's complicity in the American people's general lack of anger about the whole affair (*Yahoo* #5 [December 1991]) A series of issues of Roberta Gregory's *Naughty Bits* features the Bitchy Bitch's younger self and her search for an illegal abortion (*Naughty Bits* #6–8 [August 1992–February 1993]). As an adult, Midge comes out squarely against prolife forces. In comics such as *New Hat* and *Hutch Owen's Working Hard,* Tom Hart advocates a philosophy of aggressive anticonsumerism and constructive anarchism, attacking the values of the middle class not only through his allegorical stories but also through his primitive, minimalist art.

One reason for this variety of criticism is that nearly all alternative creators are devoted to a personal vision that helps to define both what and how stories are told. This vision — a desire to create high-quality stories without interference from publishers or corporate lawyers telling creators what they can and cannot do — keeps many alternative creators from sacrificing their integrity for the sake of improved sales. It also helps to create specialized audiences that are somehow in tune with the creator's vision and sense of humor and beauty. Not every reader — and not even every alternative comics reader — can laugh at Gregory's "Crazy Bitches" (*Naughty Bits* #1 [March 1991]: 1–4), in which a gang of women rape and bite the penis off a man guilty only of sexism and reading comics by Crumb. Many alternative readers simply cannot get past Sim's misogyny and general egotism to enjoy the political and human stories in *Cerebus*.[2] Not every reader can identify with autobiographical stories, tolerate existential despair and weird cynicism, or manage to remember complex character relationships — all of which exist in alternative comics. Many alternative fans read only a handful of titles that somehow mesh with their personal tastes and identities.

Some alternative comics are directly aimed at specific demographic groups. *Naughty Bits*, starring Midge, the "Bitchy Bitch," is clearly aimed at women. The main character is an everywoman. This comes through especially strongly in the stories collected in the *A Bitch Is Born* trade paperback. There, readers discover what made a young Midge — an average girl growing up in the 1960s — into an angry, bitchy woman: sexual abuse, overbearing parents, social expectations about her appearance, laws that made abortion illegal, and a religion that made both sex and contraception sinful. In other words, the elements of Bitchy Bitch's origin are common to most woman of her generation. Other stories depict Midge's frustration in the sexual arena and in the workplace. Sarah Dyer's *Action Girl Comics* is aimed at a female audience of all ages. This anthology series seeks to provide an outlet for young female cartoonists and to offer stories relevant to a wide variety of female experiences but remain "boy friendly" (Dyer, inside cover).

Action Girl is also one of the many comics seemingly aimed at Generation X. Like the term *alternative*, the label *Generation X* has been the source of a great deal of controversy, misuse, and misunderstanding. Too often, it has become a quick, simplistic, superficial marketing generalization, but there is also a reality to the idea of a generational culture uniting contemporary young adults. As defined by Douglas Coupland in his 1991 novel of the same name, Generation X is a group of people born between 1958 and 1970 who have decided to uncomplicate lives characterized by bad jobs, fears of apocalypse, and boomer-inspired pop culture. His *X* is a variable, allowing for specific, individual voices within the larger generational culture. Demographers Neil Howe and Bill Strauss, in their *13th Gen: Abort, Retry, Ignore, Fail?* (1993), expand the generational grouping to include nearly all Americans born between 1961 and 1980, but these authors also recognize intragroup diversity based on race, ethnicity, sexual orientation, and even age. Although Coupland's term has come to have more cultural currency, Howe's and Strauss's more complicated characterization is more accurate.

The Generation X label is a viable descriptor because of the cultural and political background in which contemporary young people grew up. This historically unique environment has helped to shape Xers' child- and adult-hoods and is often demonstrated through their culture and attitudes. Many of these attitudes appear in texts favored by members of Generation X: movies such as *Slacker, Singles,* and *Menace II Society;* novels such as *Generation X* and Jeff Gomez's *Our Noise;* music by Public Enemy, Nirvana, Green Day, and others; and comic books. In fact, the comics industry is one of the primary sites where the generational culture is expressed and explained (see fig. 11). These Gen X comics include *Love and Rockets,* where Jaime Hernandez's stories focus on Maggie and Hopey, two Chicana friends involved in the punk subculture of Los Angeles; Jeff LeVine's *No Hope,* with stories about getting old and struggling through McJobs; Adrian Tomine's *Optic Nerve,* with more stories about McJobs and Xer angst; and even Shannon Wheeler's *Too Much Coffee Man,* about a superhero whose abilities come from the contemporary coffeehouse milieu. Many of the stories in Clowes's *Eightball* fit the Gen X idea, especially the "Ghost World" series (collected in *Ghost World* [1998]), starring Enid and Becky, two alienated young women living "in a limbo between childhood and adulthood, between the past and the future" (Raeburn 5). The ultimate Generation X fable, though, is *Hate,* created by Peter Bagge.

First published in 1990, *Hate* is the story of twentysomething Buddy Bradley, a cynic with few marketable skills and little desire to become part of the middle-class working world. The series began in Seattle, where Buddy struggled through a variety of dead-end jobs (including briefly managing a grunge band). With the sixteenth issue, he and his sort-of girlfriend Lisa moved back to New Jersey to live with his parents. There, he opened up a pop-culture nostalgia shop with a partner and had to deal with his now adult siblings, their bratty children, and his father's death. Buddy's lack of

Fig. 11 Generation X sensibilities are common in alternative comic books (top: *Hate* #8 [spring 1992]: 2; © Peter Bagge; bottom: *Too Much Coffee Man* #1 [July 1993]: 27; © Shannon Wheeler [www.tmcm.com]).

direction and enthusiasm can be found in many other generational texts. Richard Linklater, in his film *Slacker,* focuses on characters who have, in their words, "withdrawn in disgust" from society and are trying to lead truly free lives on their own terms in individualistic, anarchistic worlds of and about themselves and their friends. Almost all of the characters in Gomez's *Our Noise* wander aimlessly through relationships, jobs, and the American landscape.

Hate differs from these and many other Gen X texts because of the amount of reader interaction with the stories and their creator. Bagge opens the first issue (*Hate* #1 [spring 1990]) with Buddy greeting readers at the door, as if old friends were making a surprise visit. After offering a tour of his new apartment, there is a conversation, with Buddy speaking directly to the readers and sometimes responding to comments. The story's construction makes readers Buddy's friends, someone like him who can understand his life and experiences. And Buddy is the readers' friend, too: he commiserates with the loss of a job, a breakup with a significant other, or parental frustrations. Bagge also encourages his readers to literally become part of the comic. In one issue, he initiated a "Win a Date with Stinky" contest (*Hate* #3 [fall 1990]: 23) in which winners could appear in the comic as cartoon characters paired up with Buddy's disreputable and frequently disgusting roommate. Even those who entered but did not win had photos or drawings of themselves printed (*Hate* #5 [summer 1991]: 21–24, back cover). In the next issue, Bagge started the "Buddy Bradley Look-Alike Contest" and subsequently published the winner's photo (*Hate* #6 [fall 1991]: inside back cover; #10 [fall 1992]: cover, 22).

Fans also interact with Bagge and each other in the comic's letters pages, praising the stories and art, criticizing Bagge for selling out as the series became more popular, commenting on events, and trying to get him to listen to tapes of their bands. More than anything else, though, readers constantly tell Bagge how much they are like Buddy and his friends. Richard van Busack of San Francisco wrote, "I was really surprised to find out that Buddy and I had gone out with the same girl" (*Hate* #3 [fall 1990]: 23). Erick Kuerstein of Bridgewater, New Jersey, explained, "My similarity to Buddy is so disturbing that my hands were shaking as I turned the pages" (*Hate* #9 [summer 1992]: 24). Lauren Tillinghast of Chicago asked, "What does it say about us that we actually know people like Lisa?" (*Hate* #11 (winter 1992–93]: 23). Janna Kriens of Oakland, California, opined, "*Hate* #7 came a little too fucking close to this chick for comfort. Bagge, have you been following me around? Lisa's place looks like mine. . . . Am I that much of a fucking cliche? I beg you Bagge please stop and think before you draw again or at least make it seem desirable instead of merely pathetic. But I forgive you, we are a generation that is much too easily pegged" (*Hate* #12 [spring 1993]: 23). Like Kriens, many other readers see *Hate* as a generational text. Alonso Duralde of Dallas, Texas, argued that Bagge "and Douglas Coupland (author of *Generation X*, a must read) are about the only people who really understand the aesthetics and ennui of the post-boomer generation" (*Hate* #9 [summer 1992]: 24). This kind of identification and interaction makes comic books important tools for the study of Generation X and makes the Xers an important audience for alternative comics.

Some readers have developed very specialized tastes, prompting other fans — even readers of alternative comics — to consider them snobs. The prime source of this snobbery, according to some, is the *Comics Journal* and especially its editor, Gary Groth. Among mainstream and many independent fans, the *Journal* is well known for its negativism, never-ending elitism, and constant willingness to attack mainstream comics, even those generally well considered by readers. Many fans are put off by the magazine's attitude of superiority and simply stop reading it. To a certain extent, this accusation of snobbery is accurate. Although the magazine lacks a unified editorial policy that determines what comics and graphic novels get positive or negative reviews, it does tend to publish reviews that its readership will find useful — that is, the magazine reviews comics that might interest alternative readers. Still, reviews of important mainstream comics (such as Busiek and Alex Ross's *Marvels*) do appear and are on occasion positive. All reviews reflect individual reviewers' tastes rather than editorial policy. Although many of the creators interviewed work somewhere on the alternative end of the comics spectrum, mainstream writers and artists (especially those active since the 1940s or 1950s) receive some exposure. The *Comics Journal* has even devoted a column, Mescallado's "Fanboi Politik," to superhero comics as read through the twin lenses of ironic nostalgia and academic literary theory.

Still, reading the *Comics Journal* can sometimes feel like perusing a club newsletter or fanzine where writers use the publication as a vehicle for their rantings and ravings. At least once a year, Groth seems to write an editorial blasting mainstream comics for their general awfulness, their lack of literary values, or for the publishers' increasing reliance on licensed characters from other media. Many of these editorials also include dire predictions about the effect of mainstream publications on alternative comics and their creators, prophesies that have never quite come true but have also never quite been proven false. A 1992 issue dedicated to mainstream comics gave Groth multiple opportunities to make his traditional complaints, first in an editorial entitled "Comics: The New Culture of Illiteracy" and later in interviews with *Spawn* creator Todd McFarlane and writer Alan Moore (*Comics Journal* #152 [August 1992]: 3–6, 45–70, 89–100).

The *Journal's* saving graces have been its occasional sense of humor about its own elitism and a willingness to take criticism. Kent Curry of Bridgeton, Massachusetts, wrote about his attendance at a *Comics Journal*–sponsored panel at the 1996 San Diego Comic Book Convention: "I finally left in disgust as you continued to epitomize the worst kind of snobs—the high school clique, shallow but all-knowing, better than everyone else, yet never open for others to join. It never seemed to occur to any of you that there were newcomers in the audience seeking substance, intelligent conversation, and differing viewpoints in and about this vibrant field; [it must be] easier to play to the Fantagraphics fanboys who understood all of the in-comments" (*Comics Journal* #189 [August 1996]: 9). Of course, printing the letter without any response does little to solve the problem but at least shows that the editors are aware of it. Generally, though, the *Comics Journal's* elitism can be seen as reflecting high standards regarding comic books. The *Journal's* writers seem to expect more from the medium than do many other comics readers, and these expectations come from being truly devoted fans. In an essay entitled "Triumph and Despair in the Temple of Elitism," Heidi MacDonald argued that she became a *Journal* critic because of her love of comics (183). Just as fans of a sports team might offer its strongest criticism (to other fans), so too might comics fans be unwilling to accept a lack of quality from the medium that they love.

Some alternative snobs are primarily interested in the most obscure comics they can find, usually self-published minicomics. Usually produced by individuals at local copy shops, minicomics are customarily small (an 8½-by-11 or -14 inch piece of paper divided into halves or quarters), short, and idiosyncratic. As a result, they are hard to find. A few urban and extremely alternative comic shops stock them (usually only those by local artists), but most fans of minicomics purchase them directly from their creators, either at comic book conventions or through the mail. (Many alternative comics include a list of recommended minis, and many creators keep their back issues in print for newcomers.) Because these comics are produced by amateurs, many are not of high quality, but fans value their authors' enthusiasm, energy, and especially the fact that they clearly have not sold out.

Many creators of minicomics go on to work in regulation-sized comics, but doing so almost always produces anxiety for their fans, many of whom worry that the creator will give up his ideals for money. Adrian Tomine poked fun at these concerns in the last issue of his mini *Optic Nerve*, depicting his alter ego explaining to the audience that the comic will subsequently be published by Drawn and Quarterly, a Canadian company with a very alternative reputation. Throughout his little speech, the audience members call him a sellout, a "bourgeois scum," an "ass-kisser," and a has-been, suggesting that "all he cares about is money" (*Optic Nerve* v1 #7 [summer 1994]: back inside cover). Tomine knew that his real audience would respond in the same way. Bagge was also called a sellout after Fantagraphics began publishing *Hate* in color and running advertisements (in this case, for various indie rock labels). These fans seem to worry that their favorite alternative comics will somehow become mainstream, or at least a little bit less obscure, thereby robbing the fans of some of their alternative credibility. Many of these snobs find obscurity—in comics, fiction, or music—important in determining something's alternativity and hence its worthiness of patronage.

Other alternative snobs look more to the limited high culture of comics. Art Spiegelman's graphic novel, *Maus,* is at the top of this list because of its broad acceptance outside comic fandom. Its original source, Spiegelman's anthology *RAW,* also helps explain *Maus*'s status. *RAW*'s audience is limited in part by its design, perhaps following trends in contemporary art, and its list of regular contributors, including Charles Burns, Mark Beyer, Sue Coe, Ben Katchor, and Drew Friedman, few of whom appear in more traditional comic books. *RAW*'s acceptance in the world of contemporary art may alienate many comic book fans, even readers of alternative publications. In addition to including the work of contemporary cartoonists, *RAW* also published deceased masters of comics art like Winsor McCay, creator of *Little Nemo in Slumberland* and other strips from the turn of the century. Many alternative snobs are as devoted to the work of McCay, George Herriman, and others as they are to any contemporary cartoonist. *RAW,* like another high-comics-culture anthology, *Drawn and Quarterly,* includes the work of many European artists. Many alternative snobs believe that the best comics come from Europe, where comic book creators are respected and rewarded by society at large.

The limited ranks of scholars studying comic books often include these alternative snobs. Increasing numbers of graduate students in English, American studies, communication studies, women's studies, and other disciplines are becoming interested in comic books' academic potential. Although now defunct, a small journal called *Inks* was devoted to the academic studies of the comic art medium, and scholarly articles appear occasionally in the *Journal of Popular Culture,* among other places. There is also an annual comics art conference held in conjunction with either the San Diego or Chicago comic book conventions. Panels on comic books and strips are among the best organized at the annual meetings of the Popular Culture Association and its regional organizations. Other academic discussions of comic books appear in Internet newsgroups and occasionally in the *Comics Journal* and *Indy,* another magazine focusing on independent comics.

Although some comics scholars are snobs, most seem to be the direct opposite: comics omnivores, reading everything from *RAW* to *Amazing Spider-Man,* from *Kamandi* to the work of European masters. Many scholars write about some aspect of mainstream comics from the perspective of popular culture, focusing on the evolution of superheroes, the careers of prominent artists, or the historical/cultural meanings of the EC horror comics of the 1950s. Hence, many academics write about comics that they read as children. Others examine comics from a more literary perspective and focus on alternative comics or graphic novels—the comics they are more likely to be currently reading for personal as well as professional reasons. Many academics are simply so interested in the whole gamut of the comics medium that they are familiar with everything. In Internet newsgroups devoted to alternative comics, it is not uncommon for posts from a single academic to include an explanation of poststructuralist theory as applied to *Watchmen,* a description of the joys of *Master of Kung-Fu,* and a review of the latest issue of *Eightball.*

Many comics scholars share a sense of ambivalence about how their colleagues (especially those making financial aid or tenure decisions) view their academic specialty. In "X-Bodies: The Torment of the Mutant Superhero," Scott Bukatman admits that the autobiographical subject "entrenched" in the essay "isn't me, the adolescent dreaming of bodily strength and cosmic consciousness, but me, the adult academic who feels compelled to write about superhero comic books.... Beyond the not-so-shocking shock value of comics, ... I *do* like the things. In early drafts of this essay I 'sutured' the complex pleasures I derive from comics to the reductive discourses of the academy; the very approach I abhor the most. Academia presented me with

an imperfect double of my self—*Bizarro Scott*—and now it was clobberin'
time. I had to rediscover my fondness for the medium, and for the genre of
the superhero fantasy, without surrendering my intellectualism. I needed to
recapture my own fragmented experience—my trauma, my anxiety, my hurt,
my humor, my play, my intelligence, my body, my grace, my clumsiness, my
fantasy, and my creativity. This would be my greatest battle" (96, 98). Many
comics scholars wage this battle: coming to terms with their comics' past
and future in light of academic pressures to produce something unique but
marketable, something original but also part of a larger intellectual tradition.
In many ways, these fears help to unify academics studying comics into a
real community. At academic conferences, this community can become real,
whether in a discussion of the possibilities of teaching a course on comic
books or a search for comic shops.

The diversity within the comic book audience goes beyond divisions between mainstream and alternative. Many female readers feel marginalized
by an industry they see as generally sexist. In response to this feeling, in
1993 a group of female fans formed Friends of Lulu, an organization devoted
to involving more girls and women in comic books as both readers and creators. Gay and lesbian readers have felt that their experience has also been
marginalized by the industry, prompting the production of titles such as
Gay Comix, Dykes to Watch Out For, and *Hothead Paisan, Homicidal Lesbian Terrorist* that might better speak to this audience. African American
comic fans have long endured stereotypical depictions of their race. In the
early 1990s, a number of creators started their own lines of comics aimed at
African American and multicultural audiences. This diversity certainly needs
to be examined more closely, as do comics audiences that focus their reading on Japanese *manga,* anthropomorphic stories, and pornographic titles.

Despite these varying interests and the mainstream-alternative differences, many of the basic experiences of comic book fans are similar. Many
fans fondly remember their first comic book or the first comic that they
purchased for themselves. Many remember their first trip to a comic book
store and their sense of awe at the vast selection of comics, which pushed
them into becoming more involved in comics culture. Some discover fandom
at this point; many others begin to dream of becoming professional comic
book writers or artists.

The life of a typical comics fan begins with the first comic book. Some
who began as young children may only remember a genre or a character.

Others have very specific memories. Explains Olney, "The first comic book that I ever read was *Fantastic Four* #1. I was in grade school and a friend of mine brought a copy to class. He let me borrow it. . . . I took it home and as I think about it, the Thing was kind of scary. I remember thinking that he was ugly. . . . After reading *FF* #1, it was only a few months before I had my mom buying everything that Marvel was publishing" (personal correspondence). Another fan, Chris Coleman of Bolivar, Tennessee, remembers, "The first comic I ever read was also the first one I ever bought: *Marvel Tales* #61 from summer of 1975. It was a reprint of *Amazing Spider-Man* #80, featuring a battle royale between Spider-Man and the Chameleon. I can't recall ever even noticing comic books before then, but there it was on the spinner rack in the local drugstore and it just looked like the coolest thing on earth; I had to have it. I still have this book. The pages are yellowed and chipped, the cover is worn out and stapled back on, but I don't think I could ever bear to throw this issue away" (personal correspondence).

These early comics were read or purchased for a variety of reasons, often depending on the fan's age at the time. Parents often purchased the books to keep children occupied during long car trips or while waiting at an airport or train station. Other children got comics when they were home sick from school. Some parents would purchase comic books for educational reasons, consciously or unconsciously using the publications to encourage reading, especially for children who had difficulty with text-only books. "Originally what attracted me to comics was that when I was a kid I was a very slow reader," Hughes said. "I liked to read books, but it took me a minute or more to get through a page of a paperback. And if I wouldn't lose interest, I'd lose my place and have to go back and re-read. Especially in reading groups, I'd feel kind of stupid. It's not that I wasn't retaining it or had some kind of reading problem, I was just a slow reader. And with comics I could go and I could read through the balloons and the captions and if it seemed like it was taking a while you had the picture to bring you back into it. I guess at my pace it gave me a better feel of what was going on." Other readers, especially fans who learned about alternative comics sometime in college, discovered the publications through friends or spouses. Others became interested in more "mature" comics when the industry received some press coverage in the mid- and late 1980s: "I wasn't a habitual reader of comics until I was in college and I ran across an article in *Time* magazine that described *Sandman* and *Hellblazer,* neither of which I read any more, but at the time they sounded really intriguing and they weren't my idea of what comic books were," Glennon explains.

Many childhood readers made comics and their characters an important part of play. Dennis Kiniger of Whitesboro, New York, admitted that "some of my childhood play involved comics, comic book characters, and characters in popular genre TV shows of the time (ex. *Six Million Dollar Man*). Being of an artistic nature in my youth, I enjoyed cartooning and copying artwork from comic books. I played with action figures. I had a whole drawer in my dresser *full* of Mego superheroes, *Planet of the Apes* figures, *Star Trek* figures, and many others" (personal correspondence).[3] Other fans would act out superhero stories with their friends, sometimes even adapting the comics into audio plays that they would tape-record. During the 1980s both Marvel and DC created role-playing games that allowed fans to act out the parts of their favorite characters in Dungeons and Dragons–style adventures. A number of independent companies also developed role-playing games in which players could create their own heroes and villains. In the mid-1990s, both Marvel and DC licensed collectible card games.

As young readers began to become more enthralled with comics, they became collectors, and many had specific strategies for getting the comics they thought they needed. Fans who began reading comics in the 1960s and 1970s often faced a true challenge. Luck was sometimes the most important element in building a collection: "I really got serious about collecting comics at age 11," recollects Rick Chandler, a journalist from Redwood City, California. "A friend of my father's — a guy in his mid-twenties — drove up to the house one day, and I noticed that his car was literally filled with comics. That's where he kept his collection, piled in the back seat. He noticed my interest and told me to dive in and take what I wanted. What a treasure trove! I filled out my collection of *Spider-Man, Daredevil,* and other Marvel titles — comics which I still own. Can you imagine any collector these days keeping his comics in the back seat of his car? But that was the attitude back then" (personal correspondence). Other young collectors acquired comics in less-than-reputable ways. Olney explains, "While most of my comics were obtained legally, I had my dark side at times back then. There was a period of time when I would steal new comics from a local drug store. I'm not proud of this, mind you. I never got caught and it bothers me sometimes. I had one former friend that stole books from me. I would loan him comics and he'd never give them back. I'd go to his Mom and tell her. She'd scoop his books up by the armful and tell me to take them home. I'd do it, never letting him know that his Mom had given most of his collection to me" (personal correspondence). Most collectors, however, found the best way to get old comics was at flea markets and garage sales, where people who assumed that comic books had no value would sell them for a dime or a quarter.

New comics were usually purchased at drugstores or newsstands. Many fans somehow came to learn when the comics arrived at these stores. Explains Chandler, "The big day for myself and two or three of my friends was Friday. That's when the magazine truck would arrive at a local liquor store/market in our small community and deliver the new comics. I would take the two or three dollars I had saved all week and load up on my favorite titles.... Single issues were 12 cents each, '80-page' annuals cost 25 cents. This was in 1966–68. We were there before the school bus arrived, loaded up on comics and took them home, then got back (hopefully) in time to catch the bus" (personal correspondence). Other collectors developed a route that would take them from grocery stores to convenience stores to drugstores looking for that month's comics.

Having to search for comics this way was so difficult that, for many fans, going to a comic book shop for the first time was a moment of epiphany (see fig. 12). Brad Winter of Great Bend, Kansas, writes, "I went to my first comic book shop at...13 or 14. The experience blew me away. I finally saw all these comics that fanzines had been raving about for a long time, and I got a chance to try them" (personal correspondence). Mix also remembers his first comic book shop: "My parents took me to a town that was a couple of towns over...and I remember walking in, and it's like—I still consider it the greatest day of my entire life because I had access to books I didn't even know existed....It was a day in December. I can remember it was snowing." Being in comic book shops gave many fans the sense that they were surrounded by every comic ever published, mentioned in "Bullpen Bulletins," or discussed by friends—in short, by every comic fans ever dreamed about owning. Some fans had such a strong experience that even years later they still dream about comic book shops, finding that one missing issue or the issue that disappeared and is now only a dim memory. For some fans, exposure to a comic book shops accelerated their desire to collect and resulted in the creation of elaborate "want lists" to make shopping and searching more orderly and efficient.

Fig. 12 Jamie and his younger brother, Alex, enter their first comic book store in *Copybook Tales,* a series about an aspiring comic book writer and his childhood as a fanboy (*Copybook Tales* #1 [July 1996]: 16; © J. Torres and Tim Levins).

Avid collectors often had very strong loyalties to particular comics and publishers. Bryon Stump of Iowa City explained his loyalty to DC: "I would never pick up a Marvel comic, and the main reason is, as a little kid, I knew that if I went to the store and bought a comic I would probably never see the next issue. A DC comic, there's a beginning, there's a middle, there's an end. It's complete. Marvel, you pick it up and it's like, 'What are they doing? They're starting someplace, something's up, the Vision's arm has melted off. How did this happen? Blah, blah, blah. And how does it end? Who is it? Who's in the shadows?' I'll never know. So I pick up a DC because it's all there. A Marvel's going to start in the middle, end in the middle. It'll just be a piece, and I'll never find the next piece, so I never picked up Marvels. Ever." The loyalties of other fans changed with time and their own needs as a reader. J. David Clarke wrote to an alternative comics newsgroup on the Internet, "I started reading comics by picking up whatever looked interesting on the rack, and that was usually *Fantastic Four, Flash,* or one of the Superman Family books (I thought Krypto [the Superdog] was the COOLEST). Eventually, I decided DC books sucked.... [I] still remember clearly leafing through an issue of *Batman* and thinking it was the most moronic thing I had ever read. So I became a Marvel zombie and read only Marvel Universe superhero books.... Then in the mid-eighties I hipped to this 'black & white' thing and that led me further and further into alternative & mature readers titles. Today, I read a lot of supers still, mostly DC because Marvel's quality is terrible and they are pissing me off by screwing around with their little corporate war games. (Trying to destroy my hobby, dammit!) But I also read a wide variety of other stuff, from *Tyrant* to *Eightball* to *Bone.*"

As fans became avid collectors with specific likes and dislikes, they began to think about comics with much more complexity. Many fans became aware of creators for the first time and as a result began to think seriously about professionally producing comics. "It took me until my junior year of high school to realize that people actually do this for a living, or what passes as one," Ayers explains. "I really started thinking about [trying to do comics professionally] my junior year and got much more serious my senior year." In late 1995 Ayers and a handful of other Iowa City comics fans and prospective creators formed Crop Circle Comics, which is producing its own comic books in an effort to help the group's members gain experience for future professional work. Although Ayers and his partners are more serious than most fans about becoming professionals, many readers do have fantasies about taking over their favorite title and making the necessary changes to make it into a great book again.

As they began taking comics more seriously, many fans researched the medium's history, sometimes as part of an effort to read every possible comic. Stan Lee's *Origins of Marvel Comics* and *Son of Origins of Marvel Comics* (1975), Jules Feiffer's *The Great Comic Book Heroes,* and DC's books that reprinted selected adventures of Superman, Batman, and Captain Marvel from the 1930s to the 1970s were important because they gave fans a chance to read earlier stories. Also important were Marvel and DC's reprints published in the 1970s. For a time, Marvel seemed to be reprinting all of its major series from the 1960s, while DC Comics reprinted stories from the 1940s in hundred-page giant-sized editions of many of its comics and oversized (approximately 10 by 13½ inches) "Treasury Editions" devoted to landmarks such as the first issue of *Action Comics.* All of these works helped to give comics fans information about the history of the medium and particular characters.

Comics readers also began to discover fandom as they became more involved in collecting and the culture in general. Some people began to attend comic book conventions, while others began to subscribe or contribute to fanzines. Many became regular correspondents to a variety of different titles, including both comics and fanzines, and sometimes writing directly to other fans. The discovery of fandom kept many people involved with comics into adulthood. Dan Tyree, a fan and columnist for the *Comic Buyer's Guide,* admits, "I probably wouldn't be buying comics if not for fandom" (personal correspondence). Fandom was particularly important in giving older fans a sense of community and belonging. Michal Jacot of East Tawas, Michigan, explains, "Fandom has become more important to me in the last few years than ever before. I think many older collectors, at first, feel a sense of separation from others because of their involvement in a hobby that's supposedly for younger people. After attending conventions and getting involved in the fan circuit, we learn that there are many others out there like us, and that it is nothing to be ashamed of" (personal correspondence).

Some comic book readers did not find fandom and stopped reading the publications. Many readers simply became bored with comics, or at least with the comics to which they had access. As some fans grew older, they found superhero stories clichéd or dull. While in high school, many fans developed other interests — music, football, realistic literature, or girlfriends or boyfriends. Many readers certainly succumbed to social pressures and began to feel that comic books were really for children. Collections that had developed over many years were sold at this point, and former fans realized that the comics' value was fairly low.

It is common to encounter people who used to read and collect comic books as well as fans with long gaps in their reading histories. Some older fans have returned to comics through their children; the discovery of comic book shops brought others back. Coleman explains, "I was out to see a movie with a friend and on the way home he asked if I'd mind stopping by the comic store so he could pick up his 'weekly fix.' I honestly had no idea that such a thing as 'comic store' existed. It was like being that eight-year-old kid again, discovering the coolest thing in the world" (personal correspondence). At the new comic shops, many former fans discovered more mature comics for the first time. Returning fans often mention *Batman: The Dark Knight Returns* and *Watchmen* as important inducements, as well as alternative comics including *Cerebus* and *Love and Rockets*. For others, the return to comics involved nostalgia. When Ed Thomas saw a new issue of *Superboy,* starring the Legion of Super-Heroes, he decided to collect comics again because of the associations that comic books had for him: "It was like seeing an old friend you hadn't seen for years" (Massara 61). Often, even confirmed fans of alternative comics would feel nostalgia for their earlier favorites. Mark Nevins explains to an Internet newsgroup, "I don't know how, otherwise, to explain the delight I still take in '60s and '70s Marvel comics. . . . I generally *loathe* modern-day superhero stuff—hell, I can't even read it. . . . But when I think of The Jackal and Man Mountain Marko and Foggy Nelson and the Nomad and all that '70s Marvel stuff, I just get real happy. (And I'm not even talking about stuff I *love,* like Killraven, early *Luke Cage,* and, of course . . . *The Master of Kung-Fu!* :-)."

Some fans realize their dreams of becoming industry professionals, working in comic book shops or starting their own stores. After long years of work and sacrifice, some readers become professional writers and artists. For this reason, David Yurkovich could announce that "anyone *in* comics is a fan" (*Threshold* #1 [October 1996]: 31). Often, it is hard to tell the difference between the fans and professionals. And just as comic book fans are very protective of the medium and care about particular characters, genres, and audiences, so too are comics creators. Well-known creators such as Sim and Byrne fill their letters pages with commentary not just on their own comic books but also on the industry as a whole. Alternative creators Fingerman (of *Minimum Wage*) and Jessica Abel (whose *Artbabe* is filled with her own Gen X–ish short stories) actively participate in a comics newsgroup on the Internet, commenting broadly on trends within the industry and the content of recent releases. Other creators give interviews about the changes in the industry. In an interview published in the special twentieth anniversary issue of the *Comics Journal,* Busiek speaks at length not only about his acclaimed comics *Marvels* and *Astro City* but also about the problems facing the mainstream comic book industry. He comments on the dwindling children's audience, the problems of cost and format, and the economics of newsstand distribution networks (*Comics Journal* #188 [July 1996]: 85–94). Busiek clearly cares about what is going on in comics, much in the same way a devoted fan would. Like many comic book professionals, Busiek is a fan.

This proximity between consumers and producers makes the relationship between comic books and their readers unique in American popular culture. *Star Trek* fans may write fiction based on their favorite characters and edit tapes together to create new narratives, but very few, if any, get the opportunity to help create texts recognized as official by the fan culture. A tiny percentage of sports fans may grow up to be athletes or executives, but it is very unusual when a spectator can have any impact on the outcome of a game. Every city and college town has its share of rock bands, but very few are heard extensively outside their hometowns. Most Americans are more than happy to leave the production of music and movies to the stars. But comic book fans regularly become professionals, and professionals continue to identify as fans. As a result, these fannish writers and artists fill their stories with content that is about comic books. And this content, this self-referential cycle, helps to limit many comics' audiences to people who already know about the publications. How this process works is the subject of chapter 4.

4

Comics Literacy

Creating Culture through Content

Sometime late in the fall of 1993, a comic book fan makes his weekly trek to Daydreams Comics and Cards. Carefully looking through the racks of new issues, the fan spies issue 679 of *Radioactive Man* and carefully removes a single copy from the display. A few minutes later, he decides to spend the $2.25 to purchase it. Perhaps he has read the previous four issues of the limited series. Maybe he has read reviews of the series in *Wizard,* a mass-market comic book fanzine, or on the Internet. Or perhaps he is interested in getting the *Simpsons* trading card promised on the comic's cover. Or maybe the cover itself—and the resemblance of Radioactive Man to Homer Simpson—attracted this fan. The comic is, after all, produced by the company founded by *Simpsons'* creator Matt Groening and advertised as "Bart Simpson's Favorite Comic Book!" The fan might have even glanced through the issue and seen something that made him laugh, such as the opening page that both made fun of and paid tribute to the opening page of one of his favorite comics, *Watchmen* (see fig. 13).

Reading this issue of *Radioactive Man,* the fan finds a self-reflexive comic book that relies on his knowledge of the industry's history and practices and of the superhero genre's conventions for its humor. *Radioactive Man* is not alone. Tens of thousands of comic books have demanded this kind of devoted, educated, "comics literate" reader. Some of these publications violate the basic rules of comics, while others twist the conventions of the superhero genre or allude to the industry's history. Parodies of other comics are very common, as are issues that rely on readers' knowledge of previous stories within the comic's universe or narrative sequence. Some of these comics even comment on fans and their culture. All these different categories of recursive comics require a knowledgeable audience for their impact and for sales. Comics literacy, then, contributes to the construction of

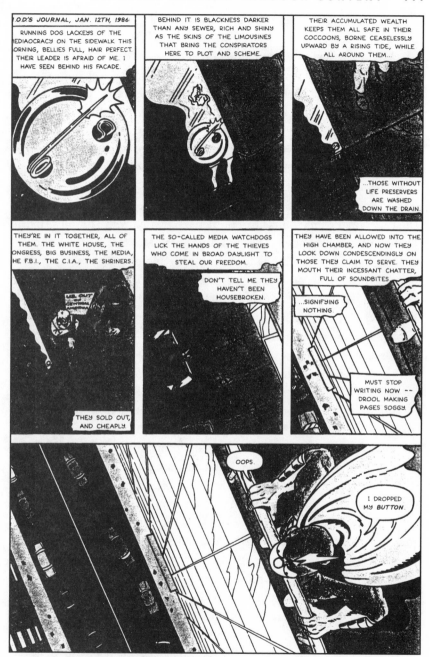

Fig. 13 This opening page from *Radioactive Man* mimics the cinematic visual style and grim narration of the first page of *Watchmen* (*Radioactive Man* 679 [#5] [1994]: 1; by Steve Vance, Tim Bavington, and Bill Morrison, © Bongo Entertainment).

comic book culture by limiting the audience and giving it a body of common knowledge.

Self-reflexive texts are also among the favorites of devoted consumers of other forms of popular culture. Devoted fans of *Doctor Who,* for example, have very different tastes in the long-running British science fiction series than do average, nonfan viewers. Both enjoy well-written episodes that provide new insights into the series's characters and situations, but, according to John Tulloch's essays in *Science Fiction Audiences: Watching* Doctor Who *and* Star Trek (1995), "many fans particularly enjoy episodes which call up that knowledge and so address them directly *as* fans" ("We're Only a Speck" 147). The same is true of all popular media fans, including those of comics. What separates comic books from other U.S. media with fan followings is the much smaller number of nonfan consumers. Most mainstream publishers seem to have ceased trying to expand their audience to nonfans, instead focusing their energies on tapping their current readership even deeper than in the past. As a result, companies such as Marvel and DC do not need to worry about alienating a more casual comic book reading audience because, in many ways, no such audience exists. Consequently, vast numbers of comics address readers as fans.

This chapter seeks to describe and analyze the different categories of these fan-oriented comics. The primary question here is "Why?" Why do fans enjoy comics steeped in comics literacy? Why do creators continue to do stories that demand highly knowledgeable readers? The relatively small number of devoted comic book readers certainly constitutes part of the reason. For years, publishers have struggled with attracting new readers to this group. Feature films such as *Batman Forever* certainly bring people to comic book shops, as did the well-publicized (if short-term) death of Superman in November 1992, but many of these people are former readers looking for a quick nostalgia fix, and the effect passed quickly. Animated series such as Fox's *X-Men* and the *Tick* have also garnered interest, but the industry's difficulty in attracting (and keeping) a new audience of children suggests that these series are not as effective as the companies might hope.

Most Americans are unaware of and thoroughly uninterested in comic books, and many publishers have consequently resigned themselves to selling comics solely to their devoted readership, believing it a waste of advertising money to try to sell comics to outsiders. In contrast, television producers need to be aware of both their devoted fans and their casual viewers.

There are many more casual viewers watching any given episode of *X-Files* than there are X-Philes who tape every episode, participate in on-line discussions of the show, buy Scully and Mulder T-shirts, and attend *X-Files* conventions. Hence, episodes that rely on the show's continuity are relatively rare, although they are among those most talked about by fans.

Comics' publishers' tendency to aim comics at a core audience continues for a number of reasons, most involving the pleasure of both consumers and producers. Many professionals, most of whom were once fans themselves, are quick to create the sorts of fannish stories — aimed directly at devoted readers — that the creators would have liked to read. Many also clearly enjoy writing for a knowledgeable audience. And, suggesting that comic book readers are among a select group can help sell comics. This kind of salesmanship was part of the reason for the success of EC Comics, and it certainly contributed to the growth of Marvel Comics during the 1960s and 1970s.

Many of these comics-literate stories directly mirror fan thinking, especially when stories violate continuity. The letters pages of Marvel's *What If,* a title devoted to alternate versions of critical events in the Marvel universe, were constantly filled with ideas from readers, some of which actually became story lines. Creator and historian Jim Valentino suggested that DC's imaginary (or noncontinuity) stories appearing in various Superman titles from the late 1950s through the mid-1980s were an effort to placate fans who wanted to see Lois Lane and Superman marry (48). Thinking about super-characters is a natural result of reading comics about them, so it is not surprising that many comic book fans imagined meetings between their favorite heroes. When crossovers began to appear, fans were overjoyed. Now they had "real" evidence to use in their arguments about who was stronger, faster, or more powerful. When Marvel and DC began to join together to team up their characters (for example, *Superman vs. the Amazing Spider-Man* [1976]), another fan dream came true. Now, they have become commonplace.

The crossovers and increased reliance on continuity helped to make the fantasy world that much more real, or at least more like the one in which fans lived. To be sure, part of the pleasure of continuity-based comics is having this developed fantasy world at one's fingertips. It is a world that is manageable, that comic book fans can almost literally hold in their hands. Making sure that world has a past and future, gods and goddesses, and definite rules makes it more three dimensional without taking away any of its manageability. Many fans feel comfortable in this world, where they are the experts. This sense of expertise is no small thing for people who may feel powerless, at the mercy of parents, teachers, and classmates. As the labyrinth of this comics world grew, it became increasingly difficult to navigate, requiring explorers to become ever more expert in their mastery of the minute details of the superhero universes. In the process, Marvel's and DC's worlds became too intimidating for most newcomers to enter.

Like sports fans, comics fans enjoy being experts, even when there is no one with whom to share their knowledge. When both types of fans are fortunate enough to be among the like-minded, an element of competition also certainly exists. Baseball fans challenge each other to name lineups or batting averages; comic book fans challenge each other to identify the first appearance of Sabretooth or to list all of Luba's children in *Love and Rockets*. This kind of knowledge is one of the primary identifiers for being a fan of any genre, as Tulloch suggests: "standard knowledge of minute details... is prodigious, and is a major marker of being accepted as a 'real' fan" ("Time Lord" 134). Comic book fans' expertise is also important for other reasons. Many such fans feel as if they are under attack from the ordinary world, which sees their hobby as at best slightly goofy and at worst potentially dangerous and which sees comic books as a form of worthless popular culture better suited to children. A kind of siege mentality can develop among comic book fans, and the information that they use to challenge each other works as a kind of secret handshake, allowing a new person with the requisite expertise into a group where fannish experiences are openly shared. The information can also serve to intellectualize the hobby. After all, a fan might argue, people who do not read comics cannot understand the significance of the jokes and allusions in *Radioactive Man* and therefore are unqualified to label it stupid.

All of these practices and the comic books analyzed in the rest of this chapter add up to a culture that is created both about and through these comics. Richard Reynolds suggests that only some hypothetical ideal reader can envisage the metatext surrounding comic books (43). To an extent, he is correct. No one can have read every comic book or even every comic book published by a single company, but devoted comic book fans have more detailed knowledge of their texts of choice — even of stories they have never read — than most people in the outside world can imagine. Still, all of that knowledge is held at the cultural level. As a result, the ideal reader at which these stories steeped in comics literacy are aimed is not an individual: it is comic book culture itself.

The most fundamental element of comics literacy is the visual grammar of comics. That comics constitutes a unique language in and of itself is the central argument of Scott McCloud's *Understanding Comics: The Invisible Art* (1993). Although McCloud alludes to comics being a "natural" form of communication in his history of the medium, he argues that people have to learn how to read comic books and develop a certain amount of comics literacy. This process includes understanding how the basic language works as well as knowing certain bodies of information without which comic books could be virtually indecipherable. Although McCloud's book is not meant as a tool for readers and critics to analyze comics as much as it is meant to be a tool for creators, giving them more ways to create meaning than they might have had previously, *Understanding Comics* still works to provide the basic vocabulary for talking about the language of comics. Without expertise in this language, an expertise that many fans have internalized, comic books can prove to be difficult reading for the uninitiated. McCloud argues that every aspect of a comics page, from the panel layout to the use of color, from the interaction of words and pictures to the artist's tendency toward (or away from) the abstract, is important in creating meaning.

A spread from McCloud's comic book, *Zot!*, is illustrative (see fig. 14). One of the first things that comic book readers must understand is the meaning behind the arrangement of panels on a page. For McCloud, this arrangement is essentially the machinery of narrative. In the sample from *Zot!* he divides the scene to achieve maximum emotional impact by emphasizing Jenny's desperation to find the missing Zot, her extradimensional crime-fighting boyfriend. Movement from panel to panel is smooth, simple, and quick, perfectly fitting a scene that the clock indicates takes perhaps three minutes.

Of course, comics pages are not always so orderly. In fact, in the first two decades of the twentieth century, before the movement from panel to panel became part of the comics language, Winsor McCay and other artists commonly numbered individual panels so that readers would know in what order to read them. Later comic book artists included arrows to show the progression of panels on a page. Now, both techniques are rare except in cases where an artist is consciously breaking the rules of panel progression (the traditional left-to-right reading direction). One example of this approach

Fig. 14 Scott McCloud's *Zot!* began as a fun, wholesome superhero comic. At the end of its thirty-six–issue run, McCloud switched gears and transformed it into a realistic series about the adolescent problems of the title character's girlfriend and her friends. Here, Jenny urges her brother, Butch, to help her find the missing Zot, gone into the city to fight crime (*Zot!* #36 [July 1991]: 8–9; © and ™ 1998 Scott McCloud).

appears in Chris Ware's *Acme Novelty Library,* where the formal rules of comic book language are broken to reinforce "an airless, choking space of despair and heartless pragmatism" that his characters experience (Gilbert 47). In both of the first two issues, Ware has pages that are almost completely non-linear (see fig. 15). Panels are not laid out left to right, top to bottom. Instead, the story can almost begin anywhere, and from one panel the reader might be able to read to two or three others. In some ways, Ware's work is like a visual hypertext, a web where every panel fits into a matrix instead of a simple sequence. However, these matrices have no easy entry point and certainly no easy way out. These strips are like unending cycles of despair and pain that emphasize the minute details of our worlds that constantly remind us of the mistakes we have made.

Understanding the transitions between panels is also an important part of developing comics literacy. McCloud devotes an entire chapter of *Understanding Comics* to how the closure between panels happens in the readers' and the creator's mind. He argues, "If visual iconography is the vocabulary of comics, closure is its grammar. And since our definition of comics hinges on the arrangement of elements, then, in a very real sense, comics **is** closure" (67). What happens in closure is that readers use their imaginations to transform two separate but adjacent images into a single idea. During an average comic book, this act of imagination could take place hundreds of times, constructing "a continuous, unified reality" (67). In a comic produced by quality storytellers, closure results in a sense of seamless, fluid motion, of the narrative flowing from panel to panel, from page to page. Of course, closure is achieved only if the reader understands how the different kinds of panel transitions work, something that most experienced comic book readers have internalized.

McCloud suggests that his six different kinds of panel-to-panel transition demand different levels of involvement from the reader. The first, moment-to-moment transition, focuses on a single subject at two subsequent moments. Little closure is needed here because the interpretive space between the two panels is small. Action-to-action transition involves a single subject in a brief sequence of movement or change: a baseball player hitting a ball. This transition is demonstrated in the first three panels on the right page of the *Zot!* sample, as an imaginary camera focuses on Butch as he considers Jenny's situation, asks her a question, and gets a response. Action-to-action transitions can also be found in panels 8 through 11 on that

Fig. 15 In these nonlinear pages from Chris Ware's *Acme Novelty Library*, arrows direct the reader because the panel arrangement differs greatly from that of more traditionally laid out comics. This reading experience is almost cyclical (*Acme Novelty Library* #1 [winter 1993]: 12; © C. Ware).

page, as Jenny sits down, lowers her head, begins to cry, and raises her head again as Butch begins to reassure her.

Subject-to-subject transition focuses on a single scene or idea but moves its focus from place to place during the sequence of panels. This technique appears during the exchange between Jenny and Butch in the bottom tier of panels on the left page, as the focus closes in to show her anguished face. Scene-to-scene transitions demand a certain amount of deductive reasoning, as the reader fills in the gaps of time and space between the panels. These transitions usually are used to separate specific sequences and can be found throughout the comic as McCloud divides the story into separate scenes. Aspect-to-aspect transitions involve a montage of elements reflecting a single place, idea, or mood. McCloud briefly uses this technique in the first three panels on the left side as the clock, the cereal, and Jenny indicate that Zot missed his deadline and that she is clearly worried about him. Finally, non sequitur transitions involve no logical relationship between panels, but McCloud argues that even they can create "meaning or resonance" (*Understanding* 70–73).

Without these interpretive tools at hand, readers will have difficulty figuring out certain comics where the narrative jumps unexpectedly between time and place or between reality and fantasy. In Alan Moore and Dave Gibbons's *Watchmen,* flashbacks are unannounced and jarring, with only a line of dialogue or a repeated shape to give readers a sense of continuity. But as the novel progresses, readers discover that everything fits together and makes sense. Readers' initial perspective made it look random, but by learning more and identifying more with the virtually omniscient Dr. Manhattan, readers can see universal patterns at work. In Gilbert Hernandez's *Poison River,* part of the long-running *Love and Rockets* series, flashbacks are also unannounced, but few signals tell readers how information fits together. No godlike entity reminds readers that events make sense. Instead, readers are easily confused, lost in the intricate details of the lives of Luba, her ancestors, and her lovers. Confusion is an important element in Paul Karasik and David Mazzuchelli's adaptation of *Paul Auster's City of Glass* (1994). As writer Daniel Quinn interviews Peter Stillman, readers see a series of seemingly unrelated images, fitting McCloud's non sequitur transition. But experienced comic book readers might come to see patterns and realize that the rapidly changing images are part of Stillman's insanity, part of his lack of ego. The transitions in all three of these graphic novels demand a great deal of imagination and involvement from readers, skills honed by patient, experienced comic book readers. Although people learn how to read these works during the process of reading, they can be a true challenge to people who are comics illiterate, especially in comparison to the relative simplicity of something like Art Spiegelman's *Maus*.

Panel arrangement is also important, defining of the flow of time in a narrative. An individual panel can depict a single, frozen moment in time or a series of moments involving motion and dialogue. McCloud suggests that panels "have no fixed or absolute meaning" except for acting as "a sort of general indicator that time or space is being divided" (*Understanding* 98–99). Time — both the amount depicted and the amount readers should spend on a particular sequence — can be controlled by the content, number, and shape of the panels. In the example from McCloud's *Zot!*, the consistently shaped panels signal the reader that time flows at a regular rate. Each tier of panels takes up the same space and thus takes up the same amount of time for readers. The larger panels — numbers 4, 5, and 6 on the left side and numbers 7 and 12 on the right — involve more time than the narrower panels. The relatively small size of these panels, especially those on the right, provide important information about the relationship between Jenny and Butch. Although he is clearly hung over in the first panel, he does not take long (one panel) to take into account his sister's near panic regarding the missing Zot. And it only takes a few moments (panels 8 through 11) for Butch to realize that she needs his reassurance. A longer panel, or additional panels, would have signaled that more time elapsed between her pleading and his offer of help. McCloud could have also elected to show a despairing Jenny in a panel without borders that bleeds off the edge of the page. This effect would have been very different, giving the image a sense of timelessness, especially if it lacked captions or dialogue (*Understanding* 101–3).

Experienced readers also come to understand comics language's basic vocabulary — words, pictures, and other icons — and how these elements interact. It can be difficult to learn these other icons, shorthand images that have come to work as symbols for common actions, emotions, or states of consciousness. In *Understanding Comics* McCloud demonstrates the basic visual images for smoke, odor, love, and grogginess, among others. In *Zot!* he uses slightly scrawled lettering to show Butch's hangover. All of these images, McCloud suggests, have become symbols, "the basis of language" (128). Artists gradually develop new ways to represent the invisible, and as others imitate these images, they too become part of this language. In Japan, though, where comics can be very different visually from those originating in America and Europe, these conventions are different. Just as written or oral languages evolve differently, so do the languages of comics (*Understanding* 131). As a result, readers may at first find it difficult to decipher even the visual elements of a comic book from another culture.

According to McCloud, art style too can have meaning. Emotional meaning is produced by an artist's use of different lines. Gentle curves might communicate innocence, while sharp, jagged lines might create feelings of anxiety, and dark, heavy lines might be best suited to the grim worlds of crime and horror (*Understanding* 126). McCloud's clean lines in *Zot!* encourage readers' youthful optimism. Combined with the often serious story line from which this sample comes — Jenny and her friends' motivations for wanting to escape their adolescent lives — this sense of optimism both kept the series from falling into despair and emphasized the true sadness of their situation.

In many ways, comic book readers do not need *Understanding Comics* because they have already internalized the language that McCloud explains. They do not need to learn how to understand comics because they already do. Some experienced comic book readers interviewed called McCloud's book boring for just this reason: it failed to tell them anything they did not already know. Although some praised the book as a comic, these readers were not impressed by the lessons it taught. Young, hopeful creators, though, tend to appreciate the book more, as do beginning or novice comic book readers, many of whom have suggested that without *Understanding Comics*, *Watchmen* and *Stuck Rubber Baby*, for example, would have been too confusing, not because of content (although it is a concern with *Watchmen*) but rather because of the medium.

Comic books demand a unique set of reading practices that many Americans lack. The ability to read comics differs from the ability to read text-only forms. Ronald Schmitt, in his essay "Deconstructive Comics," suggests that comic books are subversive "in their effects on traditional, hierarchical modes of reading and on the entire notion of literacy" (153). Schmitt sees comic book reading as a kind of postmodern activity "in which pictorial and word texts continually exchange emphasis, effectively eradicating the primacy of either" (157). Physically, the act of reading a comic book is unlike reading a traditional book. The eye cannot simply go from left to right in the same linear way it can when reading words only. Lawrence Abbott suggests that, with comics, "eye movement in a panel is determined by both the left-to-right, top-to-bottom conventions of reading and by the freer patterns associated with the contemplation of pictures" (159). Looking at the fifth panel on the left page of the *Zot!* example, the eye first briefly focuses on the whole image, the kitchen, and then on the two figures in it, Jenny and Butch. Next, the eye flashes back to read the written text, following the order of dialogue. First there is Jenny's exclamation, "Butch!" followed by his question about his mother's whereabouts and Jenny's response. Readers glance once more at the scene and then move on to the next panel. Abbott suggests that there are "only three significant moments of picture contemplation" in a panel with two main images—once for the secondary image and twice for the primary or central image (161)—but most readers will look at the panel as a whole both before and after reading the dialogue. Abbott's study focuses on a single panel, but when reading a whole comics page, most people will begin by quickly scanning the entire page and then going to the uppermost left panel.

Some commentators have worried that this different kind of reading would make young people less able to read traditional books. In *Seduction of the Innocent* (1954), Fredric Wertham claimed not only that comic books harmed children through their content but also that the physical reading of comic books would cause problems: "habitual picture readers are severely handicapped in the task of becoming readers of books later, for the habit of picture reading interferes with the acquisition of well-developed reading habits" (140). Wertham and other critics suggested that comic book readers do not learn to read left to right as English text is written and that a lack of practice of this physical skill would make later text-based reading more difficult for these children. Today, concerns about comics causing reading disabilities have been replaced by worry over the effects of television and video games. Some contemporary teachers and parents now use comic books to teach reading and to encourage reluctant children to read.

Still, reading comic books is a different skill than other kinds of reading. Regular readers of comics practice their literacy every time they pick up a comic. Since this literacy is not held by all potential readers, telling a story in comics form automatically limits its potential audience to comic book readers, something of which members of this culture are keenly aware. This literacy thus functions as one of the primary boundaries between comic book readers and nonreaders. But comics literacy is more than just knowing the transitions that McCloud explains or understanding the symbols that serve as a quick shorthand for ideas or emotions. Literacy also includes specific knowledge about a huge body of texts with stories, information, characters, and even genres. The language of comics helps to unify comic book culture, just as any common language helps to unify any group of people. In some ways, then, the language of comics—and the information that contributes to comics literacy—can work as an entry test that novices must pass. This situation may harm the industry by automatically limiting the pool of potential consumers, but such tests are effective for the culture itself, weeding out casual fans and pretenders.

The first part of this test is knowledge of the rules of comics narrative, among them the notion that characters and creators exist in different worlds. This concept carries with it an idea that is central to nearly all fictional forms: the characters within a story do not know that they are fictional constructs that exist only in the context of the story. Of course, this rule has been broken in fiction, theater, and film—and in comics. As in other forms of storytelling, breaking the "fourth wall" in comics allows creators to comment on the form itself and its restrictions. This technique also demands comics-literate readers who are experts on the form and are interested in what the creators have to say about it. In the two most important examples of these kinds of stories, breaking the rules is central to creators' goals.

In Marvel's *Sensational She-Hulk,* writer-artist John Byrne broke these basic rules for the sake of comedy. Many of the jokes in the series revolved around the fact that She-Hulk—a green, superstrong, statuesque woman—was one of the few characters who was aware of being in a comic book. This ability allowed her to directly address both the audience and Byrne himself (see fig. 16). Because she knows she is in a comic book, She-Hulk takes advantage of the shortcuts and conventions of comics, including those governing time and movement. Frequently, the green superheroine uses the gutters (spaces between panels) to try on a number of different outfits at an incredible speed or to travel from place to place instantaneously. (For examples of both practices, see *Sensational She-Hulk* #4 [August 1989].) She also passes through panel borders, the walls that would have otherwise limited She-Hulk's world to that within the traditional comic book stories. In one issue, she leads a group of people out of a world of realistic cartoons by ripping through the comics page and emerging onto a double-page ad selling back issues of Marvel Comics (*Sensational She-Hulk* #5 [September 1989]).

Fig. 16 One of the more comics–aware superheroes, She–Hulk complains to her writer/
artist about his choice of villains (*Sensational She–Hulk* #2 [June 1989]: 13; by John Byrne,
© Marvel Comics).

In an issue published after Byrne's return from a nearly two-year hiatus from
the series, she wakes up from a particularly weird dream and glances down
from the splash page to the indicia (the space giving information about the
publisher, copyrights, and subscriptions) and is surprised to learn that more
than twenty issues have passed (*Sensational She-Hulk* #31 [September 1991]).

It would be easy to call these moments of self-referentiality postmodern critiques of the limitations placed on comic book creators by the medium and industry in which they are involved, but doing so would be wrong. Apparently influenced more by the television program *Moonlighting* than by contemporary literature, Byrne's violations of the basic rules of comics are jokes done in the Marvel tradition of hip self-depreciation. In the late 1960s, it was not uncommon to find writers, artists, editors, and especially Stan Lee poking fun at the company's own products specifically and the comics medium more generally. Just as Byrne tried to emulate the energy and style of the classic early Marvel stories in comics such as *Fantastic Four,* he tries to echo this genial mocking tone in *She-Hulk.* And to a great degree, Byrne succeeded, at least among longtime comic book readers. Trying to successfully tell the jokes from the series to non–comic book readers would be virtually impossible, perhaps by design.

The other series that relied on violations of formal comics rules, DC's *Animal Man* as written by Grant Morrison from 1988 to 1990, contained more postmodern awareness and was certainly more ambitious and complex than Marvel's offering. Morrison's Animal Man, with the power to mimic nearby animals, was a reluctant hero and only vaguely super, an animal activist more interested in convincing his family of the importance of vegetarianism than in fighting criminals. His stories, especially in issues 19–26, led to the title character questioning his "reality" and wondering if everything was arbitrary, as if it were thought up by a single creator for the purposes of entertainment. Like much contemporary postmodern fiction, these issues also encourage readers to question the reality of their universe.

Animal Man begins to learn the truth—that he is just a comic book character—when he and a physicist experiment with some peyote. After hallucinations allow him to reexperience his origin, our hero finds himself in a blank, white space where he encounters another Animal Man. Longtime readers quickly recognize this Animal Man as the original 1965 version of the character, who was replaced by the new, more sensitive version. Anguished, the original claims that he is Animal Man but that he is somehow no longer real. He was destroyed, he claims, when *They* decided to change continuity. "They twist us and torture us. They kill us in our billions. For what? For entertainment," he cries. "Our lives are not our own" (*Animal Man* #19 [January 1990]: 9). Slowly, the original fades away, but he grants the new Animal Man the ability to see who *They* are. He turns and sees the readers. After the revelation that he is only a comic book character whose life is manipulated by someone else, Animal Man returns home to another shock, the ultimate manipulation: his family has been murdered.

After avenging their murders, Animal Man tries to go back in time to try to prevent their deaths, but he is ultimately unsuccessful. He eventually realizes that he must go to the top, to the force or being that has created his universe. After a long journey, he finds a house—his house, albeit a neglected version thereof. Animal Man enters and slumps down against the wall. There, he opens an envelope and pulls out a script for a comic book story—for this story. "*Animal Man* #25, 'Monkey Puzzles,'" the first page says. "I read my own words, my own thoughts, and I realize they're not mine after all. They were **never** mine," he thinks to himself, taking another important step in the slow realization of his true existential status. Just as the script says, Animal Man goes into the kitchen and cuts out a paper key. Leaving his house, he enters a fenced-in neighborhood. Drawn to one particular house, he goes to the door. After a few moments, a man opens it—a man named Grant Morrison (*Animal Man* #25 [July 1990]).

The long story line ends in the next issue with a dialogue between Animal Man and his writer. Animal Man finally realizes the truth, that he is in fact a comic book character and that Morrison controls everything that happens to him (see fig. 17). The comic then turns into Morrison's commentary on his occupation. He apologizes for turning *Animal Man* into a preachy, animal-rights comic. He thanks his editor, artists, and fans for their support. He agonizes over the fact that violence stills excites readers, that death and torture would make the comic more "realistic," more "adult." He complains about superheroes and their inherent silliness. But Animal Man does not care. He merely wants to regain his family and to escape Morrison's "pseudo-existential narratives." Of course, Morrison cannot bring Animal Man's family back. "It wouldn't be realistic. Pointless violence and death is 'realistic' now. Comic books are 'realistic' now," he explains. But he can—and does—give Animal Man the hope that the new writer will improve Animal Man's situation. Eventually, Morrison disappears. Shortly thereafter, Animal Man finds himself sitting on a comfortable couch in a middle-class American living room—his living room. The doorbell rings, and Animal Man's family appears (*Animal Man* #26 [August 1990]).

For comic book fans unfamiliar with contemporary metafiction, Morrison's *Animal Man* was truly innovative, asking previously uncontemplated

Fig. 17 Animal Man is finally convinced that he is a comic book character when he meets "Grant Morrison" and gets a chance to look at a few recent issues of *Animal Man* (*Animal Man* #26 [August 1990]: 6; by Grant Morrison, Chas Truog, and Mark Farmer, © DC Comics).

questions about the medium, putting characters into radically new situations. The comic also took advantage of readers' knowledge about the comics medium — especially its conventions of realism — to tell a very distinctive story. To be sure, readers with a broader understanding of contemporary literature might have seen *Animal Man* as a relatively simple exercise in postmodernism of the sort that had occurred decades earlier in traditional literature. Linda Hutcheon, for example, argues that the postmodern novel "begins by creating and centering a world . . . and then contesting it" (108) — clearly what happens in the first twenty-six issues of *Animal Man*. Perhaps Morrison was merely trying to mimic what he had been reading in his favorite novels.

Or perhaps he was trying to "explicitly [lay] bare the conventions of realism," a tactic that Patricia Waugh argues is central to metafiction (53). *Animal Man* may not be grounded in the kind of realism to which Waugh is accustomed, but the comic is certainly grounded in the peculiar realism of superhero comics, where reality is created out of continuity and specific formal rules. In part, Morrison seems to be responding to some of the other peculiarities of mainstream comic book realism, including those that declare that violence, not compassion, is "realistic." The realism that he creates in issue 26 is, finally, a more authentic version where Animal Man is a fictional character in his world as well as our own. Of course, it is also possible to read the final issue of Morrison's run on *Animal Man* as a kind of autobiography. Critic Josh Lukin suggests that the final issue is an exercise in Morrison's guilt over writing comic books about superheroes, which he feels on some level is ultimately trivial (85). Whatever the motivation, Morrison's *Animal Man*, Byrne's *She-Hulk*, and other publications that break formal comics rules are aimed squarely at the comics literate, who suspend their disbelief long enough for people in tights to become realistic and are so involved in the comics medium that breaking its rules becomes a heroic act.

Another set of rules that govern comic books, continuity — the intertextuality that links stories in the minds of both creators and readers — also helps to define and limit the audience. By establishing a coherent universe with definite physical laws and an established chronology, continuity adds depth and a kind of realism to comic books, especially mainstream superhero publications. Because of the emphasis on action and adventure, very little characterization usually can occur in a single issue or story. But over the course of years and scores of issues, those little bits of characterization and information can add up to something complex: a character readers come to care about, worlds that become part of readers' lives. As a result, part of fans' pleasure comes from the mastery of continuity knowledge.

The intricacies of continuity may please longtime readers but can also limit a comic book's (or even a company's) audience. Writing about 1970s fan favorite *Tomb of Dracula,* Will Jacobs and Gerard Jones argue that writer Marv Wolfman "wrote too much for Dracula's loyal body of fans; after a couple of years, it became virtually impossible for a new reader to pick up a single issue and understand who all those characters were and what they were trying to accomplish" (201). In the 1990s, this kind of problem can be found in comics of all types, from mainstream titles such as *X-Men* to alternative comics such as *Love and Rockets.* Devoted fans, however, do not see a problem. All of these continuity-heavy comics have very loyal, highly knowledgeable followings. In some cases, fans even like new readers' difficulty in understanding the series and joining that particular reading community.

In the comics of the 1940s, continuity was not important. With a few exceptions, stories did not continue from issue to issue. By the 1950s and 1960s, though, the repetition of stories starring characters such as Superman and Batman had created a limited continuity centered on characters and basic plots. Readers knew, for example, that Lois Lane would never marry Superman (or Clark Kent) and that Bruce Wayne would never fire Alfred. Superman was vulnerable only to Kryptonite, and Batman had no superpowers beyond his tremendous intellect and athleticism. And readers knew these things would not change. In his essay "The Myth of Superman," semiotician Umberto Eco called these story elements "irreversible premises" whose power was that they maintained a sense of timelessness. "In the same comic book, or in the edition of the following week, a new story begins," Eco writes. "If it took Superman up again at the point where he left off, he would have taken a step toward death. On the other hand, to begin a story without showing that another had preceded it would manage, momentarily, to remove Superman from the law that leads from life to death through time" (114). As a result, DC heroes seemed to be immortal and unchanging.

The stories in Marvel Comics, regularly continuing from issue to issue, lacked this sense of timelessness and hence depended on a more modern concept of continuity that would theoretically demand a certain amount of change from issue to issue. In Marvel's publications, characters had an often historically specific past, as heroes and villains remembered their previous encounters. The editors at Marvel prided themselves on keeping their universe very orderly. To do so, the Marvel comics of the 1960s through the 1980s in particular were filled with footnotes directing readers to earlier appearances and other situations. For example, *Avengers* #119, a typical Marvel comic from January 1974, includes references to fourteen other issues of six different titles. Fans who wrote letters to the editors pointing out continuity problems received "No-Prizes" if they developed cogent explanations for mistakes. Still, some basic, "irreversible" premises made Marvel Comics relatively timeless. Secret identities remained the same, alliances were consistent, and Peter Parker's Aunt May, although seemingly always on her deathbed, remained an important presence in his life.

By the mid-1990s, though, as continuity became tighter at Marvel, many of these premises disappeared. Aunt May died, and the person known as Peter Parker for twenty years was revealed to have been a clone of the original. DC too has allowed its characters to change: Dick Grayson abandoned his identity as Robin to become Nightwing, and Superman's cousin, Supergirl, died and was replaced by a shape-shifting alien. Continuity has become more important, and stories that in the past were sometimes loosely connected have become tightly linked together. Typically, the cover of a superhero comic will now include not just the issue number but also a number showing where the issue fits into the ongoing story line (for example, *Batman* #497 [July 1993] is also the eleventh issue in the long story line "Knightfall"). This increased serial continuity has made it almost impossible for potential readers to pick up random copies of superhero comics such as *X-Factor* or *Legion of Superheroes* and expect to understand them. Because of this problem, publishers have advertised certain issues as being good starting points for new readers. In recent years, Marvel has begun including background information with all its comics, telling new readers about both characters and continuity.

The growth of the direct market for comic books is at least partially responsible for this increased reliance on continuity. In the past, publishers could never be sure that fans shopping at newsstands and drugstores would be able to find the next issue of a continued story. Now, however, with most comics sold at specialty shops serviced by direct distributors, readers can easily collect serials. In some ways, continuity has become the planned obsolescence of comics in the 1980s and 1990s. In the 1940s, comics would become obsolete as they were read repeatedly and eventually simply disintegrated. Readers would then simply go to the corner newsstand or drugstore and buy a new comic. In recent years, though, readers have protected and preserved their comics so that they are no longer ephemera. But to insure that new issues are purchased, publishers have emphasized the importance of readers buying every issue. With each new issue, continuity is theoretically revised, making previous stories important as history but obsolete as contemporary guides to a superhero universe. Devoted readers do not want to miss a piece of the continuity puzzle. Stories have become more complex, but publishers have found monetary concerns at least as important as aesthetic ones in the emphasis on continuity.

Continuity becomes even more complex because of the presence of multiple titles devoted to the same characters. During 1997 there were as many as twenty different titles devoted to the X-Men's various permutations and individual members. This trend is one of the newest in comic book publishing: superhero franchises in which a single character or group and their spin-offs star in a number of titles united by very tight continuity. In addition to the X-Men, there are also important franchises surrounding Superman, Batman, and Spider-Man. The franchises work well for the publishers because they almost demand that readers purchase the whole group of titles on a monthly basis. For example, to completely follow the "Death of Superman" story line from 1992, readers had to purchase issues of *Superman: The Man of Steel, Justice League America, Superman, Adventures of Superman,* and *Action Comics,* along with a handful of stray publications.

Continuity is also important in more realistic series where complexity comes in the form of character interaction instead of fantasy settings. In *Love and Rockets,* an alternative series published from 1982 to 1996, Jaime and Gilbert Hernandez created distinctive worlds with very large casts of characters. Both narratives revolve around communities and the interactions that take place within them. As in real life, those interactions can become quite complex and always demand a great deal of attention and knowledge from readers. Gilbert Hernandez's graphic novel *Poison River,* for example, depicts the childhood and adolescence of Luba, the central character of his Palomar stories. Although the events of *Poison River* take place early in Hernandez's long narrative, the novel appeared in its finished form in 1994, twelve years after the series premiered. The novel is filled with brief glimpses of characters that readers had seen earlier — and often considerably older — in the *Love and Rockets* series. Readers who get the most out of *Poison River* have read all of the previous Palomar stories.

Although continuity serves the needs of the comic book publishers, it also adds to the reading experience. Continuity, comments Richard Reynolds, "forms the most crucial aspect of enjoyment for the committed fans" (38). After reading more than 135 issues of *Uncanny X-Men* over the course of almost twenty years, it is not surprising that fans had strong reactions to the 1982 death of the Phoenix, a character who began her existence as Marvel Girl in 1963. It is not surprising when readers, thanks to their knowledge of continuity, come to feel they know the Flash, Hawkman, or Captain America after reading their adventures for years. It is not surprising to see longtime fans of such characters get angry when radical changes are made or when the comic books starring these characters are canceled.

Continuity is, of course, violated, often on purpose. Stories that obviously break continuity by putting familiar characters into new situations or by putting different heroes into familiar settings give fans a chance to recognize their expertise by seeing how different the divergent story is. Eco suggests that such violations are "necessary to find continually new narrative stimuli and to satisfy the 'romantic' demands of the public" (115). These violations also help to unshackle writers whose creativity is limited by the irreversible premises and the strict rules of modern continuity.

The first form of continuity violation was the imaginary story, an innovation that began in Superman comics in the late 1950s and early 1960s. Valentino defines the imaginary story as "any story which alters or in any way repudiates any pre-existing continuity, ergo creating a completely self-contained continuity in the process" (48). The first imaginary story (*Superman* #132 [October 1959]) discussed what would have happened if Krypton had not exploded. As with most of these imaginary stories, little changed. Kal-El (who we would have known as Clark Kent) befriends a superhero named Futuro, is inspired to become a space pilot, and eventually gets superpowers, after which he decides to call himself Superman and fight for truth, justice, and the Kryptonian way. In the 1990s, DC stopped doing imaginary stories, instead publishing "Elseworlds" tales in which "heroes are taken from their usual settings and put into strange times and places," according to the standard explanation included with all of these comics. *Justice League of America: The Nail* (1998), for example, depicts a world where a flat tire prevented the Kents from discovering the infant Superman. Marvel's official continuity violations come in the pages of *What If*. Consistent with its devotion to continuity, the stories in *What If* are closely based on past events, almost always on some turning point in the history of the Marvel universe. For example, the first issue of *What If* (February 1977) used the first issue of *Amazing Spider-Man* as its starting point, speculating on what would have happened if the Fantastic Four had taken up the hero's offer to become a fifth member of that team.

Although publishers have attempted to bring new readers up to speed regarding a company's or a title's continuity, the increasing reliance on this kind of complexity has traditionally limited the comics' audience. *X-Men, Love and Rockets,* and many other comic books demand knowledgeable, highly comics-literate audiences. In many ways, fans seem to particularly enjoy these kinds of series, perhaps because they automatically work to separate fans from nonreaders. Fans also enjoy being able to use their knowledge from previous issues. Information based on continuity becomes the source of discussion, jokes, and arguments, making it the raw material for the interactive glue that holds comic book culture together.

"Superheroes and comic books were made for each other," suggests scholar Robert Harvey (35), so it is not surprising that another element of comics literacy is knowledge of this genre of stories. Superhero adventure gave the format action-filled, formulaic stories that took advantage of comics' serial nature and bright illustrations; the format gave the genre (virtually born in comic books) a place where characters' adventures could be "imbued with a sufficient illusion of reality to make the stories convincing" (35). Because of this close relationship, superhero stories have been the most common comic book genre. Hence, comics-literate fans need to have a strong knowledge of the conventions of these stories and characters.

These conventions have been established, explained, expanded, revised, criticized, and strengthened in the hundreds of thousands of superhero comics published since 1938. To be sure, though, some important texts explained many of the genre's basic elements and encouraged its evolution. The first key text is the initial Superman story (*Action Comics* #1 [June 1938]). The second important text is the 1962 introduction of Marvel's Spider-Man (*Amazing Fantasy* #15 [August 1962]). The final work central to the superhero mythos is Moore and Gibbons's *Watchmen.* Building on the genre conventions established decades earlier, this revisionist graphic novel demands that its readers know about both the original, primitive elements of the genre and the more mature, classic superheroes of the 1960s. This primitive to classical to revisionist development is traditional for any genre.

Jerry Siegel and Joe Shuster's story introducing Superman is usually considered the beginning of the superhero genre (see fig. 18). Richard Reynolds argues that "much that would become central to the superhero genre is established in these 13 pages." He points to the seven parts of a "working definition of the superhero genre," all introduced in this first story: separation from parents, heroes with the powers of gods, devotion to justice overwhelming a devotion to law, the extraordinary hero in an ordinary world, the mundane alter ego who was very different from the hero, the element of patriotism and national loyalty, and mythical stories that use science and magic "to create a sense of wonder" (12–16).

Another important convention introduced in this story is the brightly colored costumes that superheroes seemed to be required to wear. The costume had to protect the hero's secret identity (a convention itself) and somehow demonstrate or recapitulate the hero's name or powers. In some cases, such as that of Batman, the costume was also supposed to strike fear into the hearts of criminals. The story also sets up the basic superhero love triangle — the hero, a female admirer, and the hero's secret identity. In this first story, Lois Lane gives Clark Kent a chance, allowing him to take her to a dance. Once she meets Superman, even though she is clearly frightened by him, she has a reason to be even colder than usual to Clark: she now has a man who is clearly superior all her other suitors.

By 1962 these and a handful of other conventions had been clearly established as important parts of the superhero genre. A small number of new titles published by a company that would soon be known as Marvel Comics would challenge some of these foundations, producing new conventions in the process. The character who most clearly represents Marvel's innovations was Spider-Man. His initial appearance introduces Peter Parker, beloved nephew at home, nerdy pariah at school. Unlike the DC heroes, Parker is clearly the "real" person and the superhero, Spider-Man, clearly the act. Unlike Batman, originally motivated by anger over his parents' murder, or Superman, apparently motivated by his acute sense of morality, Spider-Man is motivated by guilt, and this motivation often was not enough to keep Parker devoted to fighting crime. As the series continued, readers discover Parker to be a deeply flawed human being: frequently selfish, self-absorbed, fearful, and generally neurotic. In short, readers found someone psychologically more like themselves. The Marvel universe was filled with such characters with problems. While the members of the Justice League were friendly

Fig. 18 The first Superman story helped to establish the superhero genre, but it also contained some unexpected plot elements that failed to catch on. Top: The power of Superman frightens Lois Lane during their first meeting; bottom: Superman exercises his social consciousness by attacking a wife–beater (*Action Comics* #1 [June 1938]: 10, 5; by Jerry Siegel and Joe Shuster, © DC Comics).

and professional, the Fantastic Four frequently bickered, like the family they were, and occasionally broke up for short periods of time. At one point, Captain America became so troubled, so worried about his home and his place in it, that he gave up his patriotic costume to become Nomad, the Man without a Country (*Captain America* #176–83 [August 1974–March 1975]). Tony Stark, Iron Man's rich industrialist alter ego, struggled with alcoholism (*Iron Man* #128 [November 1979]). These and other real-life problems made the superheroes into something closer to actual people and made Marvel fans feel that they were reading something more than a simple, childish comic book. Of course, these conventions — which for a time certainly seemed revolutionary to readers — became clichés. Fans now groan when they read another story about the Thing quitting the Fantastic Four or Peter Parker deciding that he can no longer be Spider-Man, partially because the same story has appeared twenty times previously but also because readers know that in a handful of issues everything will be back to normal.

By the mid-1980s, the conventions of the genre were so well established that creators began to write revisionist superhero stories, the most important being DC's *Watchmen*. First published as individual issues beginning in the summer of 1986, *Watchmen* is a dense novel that, among other things, attempts to go beyond Marvel's angst-filled hero to describe characters with true psychological complexity. None of these heroes is simple; all have dark sides, personality problems, or complex fears that make them the people they are. The psychology of the vigilante Rorschach is particularly rich. His life had made him into a raving paranoid who saw conspiracies and portents of disaster all around him, and he believed in absolutes: "There is good and there is evil, and evil must be punished," he writes in his journal in the first chapter of the novel. "Even in the face of armageddon I shall not compromise in this" (Moore and Gibbons chap. 1, 24). The almost antisexual Rorschach also has an important identity problem: he believes that his mask, a constantly changing pattern of black ink on a white hood, is his real face.

Rorschach's psychology is abnormal to say the least, but it is only a step beyond that of most classic superheroes. These characters, such as Superman and Batman in the early 1960s, saw clues everywhere, in every piece of information. They were endlessly dedicated to fighting "evil," an absolute concept that they would have never questioned or made more complex. They were also so chaste as to be dysfunctional and so dedicated to their superhero identity that they might have been diagnosed with multiple personality disorders. Moore's work, as with most revisionist forms, makes readers ask difficult questions about the genre's conventions and the stories that come out of them. Other revisionist stories would also look deeply into superhero (and supervillain) psychology. *Batman: The Killing Joke* (1988), by Moore and Brian Bolland, and *Batman: Arkham Asylum* (1989), by Morrison and Dave McKean, analyzed the strange abnormal psychology of Batman and his most famous nemesis, the Joker. Rick Veitch's *Brat Pack* (#1–5 [August 1990–May 1991]) focused on a variety of superhero archetypes and their neuroses, especially those regarding their costumes.

One of the questions raised in *Watchmen* is in the background of every superhero story. What does it mean to do "good"? What are the heroes' responsibilities to their fellow humans? Are heroes responsible for individuals, the nation, or humanity as a species? In *Watchmen,* different characters answer these questions in very different ways. The vigilante Rorschach feels responsible to some higher, abstract notion of good. Ozymandias, the adventurer whose elaborate plan to frighten the world powers into cooperation and peace is the plot that drives the novel, believes it is his duty to improve the world, and if that means sacrificing three million lives for the sake of the other untold billions on the planet, then so be it. The omnipotent Dr. Manhattan, having spent most of his superpowered existence sleepwalking from capturing criminals to winning the war in Vietnam, is not exactly sure of his responsibility. At the end of the novel, he leaves our galaxy, deciding that he has no particular responsibility to do good here on earth. Moore criticizes Manhattan's withdrawal from human affairs as well as Ozymandias's direct involvement and Rorschach's absolutes. Moore's answer is some kind of middle ground in which average people come to the aid of their neighbors not out of devotion to a philosophical ideal or to fulfill some sort of psychological need but rather out of human concern and empathy.

Watchmen also reworked many of the basic superhero archetypes central to the genre. Where Superman at times was able to do virtually anything, Moore's Dr. Manhattan is almost literally God. At the end of the novel, he announces that he is going to another galaxy to create his own human race (Moore and Gibbons chap. 12, 27). Where characters such as Batman were driven to frighten and threaten the criminal element of Gotham City, Rorschach does not hesitate to kill and maim when he deems it necessary. To be sure, both these characters (and, in fact, all of the Watchmen) are exaggerations of their earlier counterparts, but the exaggerations rest on a foundation of the comics-literate reader's knowledge of the conventions of the superhero genre. Without that knowledge, reading *Watchmen* is still a complex, engaging experience, but it loses one of its many layers of meaning.

For the comics literate, these layers of meaning can also be found in comic book parodies, one of the medium's most common forms. Defined by critic Margaret Rose as "the comic refunctioning of preformed linguistic or artistic material" (52), parody relies on a knowledgeable readership for its impact, making it an important element in the limiting of the audience through comics literacy. In comics, parody has been put to three sometimes overlapping purposes: criticism, homage, and marketing strategy.

The beginning of parody in comic books can be traced back to the 1950s and EC's *Mad*. As edited by Harvey Kurtzman, *Mad* became successful when it began mocking other companies' comic books and strips. The feature that epitomized the attitudes of the people working on *Mad* was the Kurtzman and Wally Wood parody "Superduperman!" (*Mad* #4 [April–May 1953]: 1–8). The story pokes fun at the basics of the Superman mythos, especially the Lois Lane–Clark Kent relationship; here, Superduperman and his alter ego, Clark Bent, are both pathetic losers who will never have a chance with the aloof Lois Pain. Other *Mad* targets included Wonder Woman, Archie, Plastic Man, Batman, and Mickey Mouse (Reidelbach 18–41). *Mad*-style criticism of other comics became more common in the late 1960s with underground parodies of mainstream characters and forms. Gilbert Shelton is perhaps the most important practitioner, especially with his character Wonder Wart-Hog. Like Superman, the Hog of Steel is chaste on the surface, but in this case, the superhero is really a lecher, sexually violent, and impotent (Estren 123–24).

Parody that functions as criticism continued into the 1980s and 1990s. Don Simpson's *Megaton Man*, a grotesquely muscled but unbelievably stupid Superman type, debuted in 1984 (see fig. 19). On the most basic visual level, his exaggerated physique functioned as a critique of the depiction of other superheroes. The parody went deeper, though, because of the close resemblance of a handful of his supporting characters to their referents. At the start (*Megaton Man* #1–2 [November 1984–February 1985]), Megaton Man meets the Megatropolis Quartet—a dead-on parody of the Fantastic Four with Liquid Man, Yarn Man, See-Through Girl, and the Human Meltdown standing in for the original team. Wall-Man—a parody of Spider-Man—subsequently enters the narrative (*Megaton Man* #4 [June 1985]).

Fig. 19 The muscle–bound Megaton Man tries to seduce the See–Through Girl, a member of the Megatropolis Quartet. *Megaton Man* was one of the best parody comics of the 1980s (*Megaton Man* #4 [June 1985]; © Don Simpson 1985. Megaton Man is a trademark of Don Simpson, all rights reserved).

These characters were clearly meant as commentary on their Marvel counterparts. The Megatropolis Quartet stories, for example, pointed to the obvious age difference between Mr. Fantastic and his wife, Invisible Girl, and emphasized her decidedly second-class status on the team. When Wall-Man is introduced, a reporter quickly explains why that character (and Spider-Man) has lost his appeal: "Face it, Wall-Man, you're not a teenage underdog anymore! You're a yuppie — a winner — you've gotten your act together! Who wants to read about **that**?" (*Megaton Man* #4 [June 1985]: 8). This kind of criticism certainly went beyond what Marvel's hip, self-depreciating sense of humor would allow, prompting a lawsuit from the company ("Marvel Comics").

A similar kind of criticism of Marvel Comics could be found in Moore's 1993 miniseries *1963*. Over the course of the six issues, Moore and his collaborators worked to re-create the tone and hokeyness of the early Marvel universe, criticizing the comics at the same time. The element of criticism was perhaps strongest in the fake editorial pages where the writer mocked Lee's rhetoric and predilection for alliteration. In the fifth issue, "Stan's Soapbox" becomes "Al's Amphitheater!!! (in which our arguably amiable anti-Christ agitates aimlessly about almost anything and also arrogantly airs an astonishing affinity for actual avarice" (*1963* #5 [August 1993]: 10). The text is a thinly veiled attack on Lee and his portrayal of himself as the creator of the Marvel universe. In *Parody: Ancient, Modern, and Postmodern* (1993), Rose argues that parodies can be "both critical of and sympathetic to their 'targets'" (47), as *1963* demonstrates. The attack on Lee is truly scathing, but most of the series is actually a loving reproduction of the comics that he and artists Jack Kirby and Steve Ditko produced in the early 1960s. Moore and his collaborators managed to almost perfectly capture the innocent strangeness of the early Marvel characters and their adventures, so much so that the series is more of an homage than a criticism. In many ways, *1963* seems most critical of the fact that Marvel's current output is almost entirely unlike the stories told in the company's early years.

A more clear homage can be found in Bongo Comics's *Radioactive Man*. The characters featured in the six-issue miniseries from 1994 (and a special edition that was published in 1995) clearly echo ones central to the superhero genre. Radioactive Man himself is a hero with superstrength and the power of flight, powers created through an unfortunate mishap that left him with a lightning bolt stuck in his head. He is clearly reminiscent of

Superman and virtually every other bland superhero that followed him: Radioactive Man is powerful but good-natured, politically naive but devoted to justice. In his secret identity, reporter Claude Keen, he is a bumbling idiot. Unlike Superman, however, Radioactive Man is also a fool. His sidekick, Fallout Boy, is as devoted to his mentor as the classic teen sidekicks from the 1940s. The hero's love interest, Gloria Grand, is a reporter like Lois Lane but is much more politically astute and much more aware of her potential boyfriend's shortcomings than her counterpart.

All of these touches would be funny to longtime comic book fans, but the authors of the parody added another important element. The limited series works as a recapitulation of the history of superhero comic books, with each issue focusing on a single era. For example, the story in the issue numbered 679 (but in reality only the fifth issue published) makes fun of *Watchmen, Batman: The Dark Knight Returns,* and crossover series. For devoted comic book readers, this kind of humor is effective, in part because it is filled with details, trivia, and dialogue that take fans back in time. Comics such as *Radioactive Man* are also effective because they appeal to readers' specialized knowledge used only in reading other comic books.

Parodies, of course, are produced to sell comics: fans enjoy laughing at themselves and at the sillier aspects of their reading. In the 1960s especially, Marvel took this phenomenon a step further, integrating parodies into its entire marketing strategy. As with EC Comics, Marvel used a self-deprecating sense of humor to show that it really did not take its comics too seriously. Even the title of its first parody series, *Not Brand Ecch,* reflected this style of humor. For many years in Marvel letters columns and editorials, DC Comics was never mentioned by name but was instead known as Brand Ecch. By calling the comic *Not Brand Ecch,* the editors at Marvel (at this time, primarily Lee) were telling readers that although it might be stupid, at least it was still a Marvel Comic and was therefore better than anything its rival published. Including characters such as the Fantastical Four, Sgt. Furious and the Hostile Commandos, and the Sunk-Mariner, the first issue was published in August 1967. According to responses printed in letters columns, Marvel fans loved *Not Brand Ecch,* especially its demands on readers' comics literacy. Norman Elfer of New Orleans wrote, "The entire purpose of our beloved *Not Brand Ecch* is satire, and it cannot be appreciated for its richness unless the reader is aware of the rest of comicdom. You do not try to fake it out for the ignorant with a plot they can grasp without knowing more. We, your readers, thank you for not insulting our intelligence" (*Not Brand Ecch* #5 [December 1967]: 31).

Parodies returned to Marvel in the 1980s with *What the—?!*, which featured a mixture of parodies of Marvel and DC characters and personalities. In 1995 a new publication featured a parody of the recent "Age of Apocalypse" crossover story line in the X-Men titles (*Marvel Riot* #1 [December 1995]). The comic recapitulates the series, making fun of its endless marketing, its indecipherable complexity, and its eventual pointlessness, even suggesting that the world would have been better off without "a line of X-books that seem to ramble on forever and ever without any hope of consistency and integrity regarding the storylines and characters who have since become soulless merchandising items dedicated to maintaining the stock prices of a megaconglomerate" (32).

The self-deprecating hipness of Marvel's parody comics suggests that readers are also hip and cool, that they were as in on the jokes as the writers and artists creating them. In "Marvel Comics and the Kiddie Hustle," Darcy Sullivan suggests that this practice encouraged readers to think of themselves as being part of Marvel's "in-group of hip-talking cognoscenti," a group of connoisseurs who were "too intelligent for comics" (33). The parody titles were at the forefront of this phenomenon, telling readers that superhero comics were silly and that Marvel's practices, such as those regarding reprints, were lazy at best and greedy at worst. Yet the parodies still allowed fans to take *Avengers* and *Invincible Iron Man* completely seriously. For Marvel, this strategy was amazingly effective in creating brand loyalty and legions of devoted comics fans.[1]

Since at least the 1970s, mainstream comic books have been filled with allusions and sly references to the work of famous creators, classic comics, and a variety of prominent and obscure characters. Putting comic books into a larger context can alleviate the problem of their lacking in power and depth, and patterns of allusions in mainstream comics help to provide this larger framework. Allusions can allow writers to tap into established continuity or to use classic archetypes while still creating original stories; allusions can allow artists to create a sense of tradition by imitating or echoing industry giants. For readers who recognize these allusions, comic books become filled with a greater importance, a larger web of significances, a longer tradition, a more developed history. The practice of reading comics can thus become more challenging and rewarding. Readers seem to become part of the creators' world, where all involved are working to build something bigger and better, something important.

Many of these allusions are primarily visual. Artists may purposefully alter their styles to echo that of an established master in the field. In mainstream comics, this technique is used most often when creators mimic Kirby's work. Active in comics from the late 1930s to the early 1990s, Kirby created or cocreated hundreds of characters, introduced entire genres of comics, and gave adventure comics the sense of dynamism that was central to their success. Because of his innovative work, he has been praised by all manner of comics artists, with some even choosing to do so in their published art. A perfect example is DC's *Mister Miracle Special* (1987). The title character—a super–escape artist who was part of a community of gods fighting to protect humans from the forces of evil—was one of Kirby's creations from his stint at DC in the early 1970s, and the story is clearly reminiscent of the character's earliest appearances. The art, by Steve Rude and Mike Royer, is a clear tribute to Kirby—it looks just like his work on the original series, especially in the battle scenes, where Miracle and his wife, Big Barda, seem almost to jump out of the panels to defeat the hordes of Darkseid. Another kind of tribute to Kirby appears in David Lasky's "Ulysses Unbound!" (*Boom-Boom* #2 [September 1994]) (see fig. 20). The story in this alternative comic explains how James Joyce came to write the classic novel *Ulysses*. Lasky copied the panel arrangements and character blocking from Kirby's work on the first issues of the earliest Marvel Comics, resulting in a twofold effect. First, the technique serves as a reminder that the writing of a novel such as *Ulysses* is, like a Kirby adventure story, a kind of epic in itself. Second, it suggests that Kirby's work, like Joyce's, is literature and is great in its own way.

Lasky's copying of Kirby in *Boom-Boom* is nearly what people in the industry call a swipe—copying of the basics of an image, changing some details to make it fit new characters and situations. Swipes are often signs of laziness, but sometimes they serve a particular purpose; if the purpose is clear, creators generally do not receive criticism for using them. Some swipes serve as a kind of signal, especially of a return to the values or tone of earlier comics. Beginning in the 1960s, DC's *Justice League of America* featured the collective adventures of that company's greatest superheroes. By the late 1980s, the publisher decided to change the comic's format to lighthearted superhero adventures. In response to fans' mixed reactions, the editors de-

Fig. 20 David Lasky pays tribute to Jack Kirby by copying some of his most famous pages (here, from the origin of the Fantastic Four) and transforming them into a retelling of James Joyce's life story (*Boom–Boom* #2 [September 1994]: 2; © David Lasky).

cided in 1992 to return to the original title's more serious traditions. To signal this change, the covers of the April 1992 issues of both *Justice League America* and *Justice League Europe* featured swipes imitating classic covers from the comic's early days.

Creators also allude to comic book history by imitating characters, especially central, archetypal superheroes. The most archetypal character of all is, of course, Superman, and an argument could certainly be made that he is the archetype for every superhero that followed him. Some superpowered characters are more clearly derived from Superman than others, however. In recent years, when publishers have wanted to create superhero universes (fully developed worlds where the adventures of groups of superheroes take place), the first step is to create Superman analogs. Some of these supermen include Icon (of the Milestone universe), Supreme (of the Image universe), Prime (of the Malibu Comics universe), and Samaritan (from Kurt Busiek's *Astro City*).

The other most commonly imitated archetype is that of Captain America. Created in 1941 by Joe Simon and Kirby, Cap was one of the first patriotic heroes to emerge during World War II. Just as every superhero universe needs its Superman, universes that assume a history going back to the 1940s need to have a superpatriot. The comic *1963* had USA, a costumed secret agent. Roy Thomas brought the late-1970s creation Steel, clad in red, white, and blue, into the *All-Star Squadron*. General Glory gave the Justice League of the late 1980s its patriotic hero. Byrne's Torch of Liberty took his *Danger, Unlimited* continuity back into the 1940s. Like Captain America, most of these characters have little going for them beyond their fighting ability, their dedication to American ideals, and their superstrength, which is often the product of some kind of government experiment.

Watchmen has most successfully echoed old comic book characters. Part of its power as a revisionist superhero comic arises through allusions to specific characters. In fact, Moore based the central characters on heroes from Charlton Comics, a small publisher in the 1950s and 1960s, to whose characters DC purchased the rights in the early 1980s. Dick Giordano, DC's vice president and executive editor at the time, had worked at Charlton, had a special affinity for these characters, and did not want them radically changed. Furthermore, DC was planning to reintroduce some of these characters in its own titles and in the upcoming crossover series *Crisis on Infinite Earths*. Consequently, Moore and Gibbons had to change direction.

This shift turned out to be a blessing for the series. When Giordano rejected the use of the Charlton characters, Moore and Gibbons developed new heroes based on their earlier plans but without the old continuity (Gaiman 97). This approach dictated the use of flashbacks and the appendixes at the end of each chapter that insured that all readers knew key characters' backgrounds. Had the creators gone with the obscure Charlton characters, fewer readers would have had the information necessary to understand the series. Although the characters' backgrounds are revealed in the series, they do resonate further, beyond the Charlton characters on whom they were based. Dr. Manhattan is more than just the molecule-manipulating Captain Atom; he also echoes every nearly omnipotent superhero from Superman to Miracleman to the Spectre. The Comedian refers more to patriotic heroes such as Captain America and superspies such as Marvel's Nick Fury than to Charlton's Peacemaker (a pacifistic diplomat who would take arms only as an absolute last resort and always in the name of peace). Rorschach is not just the Question; he is also every other obsessed vigilante from Batman to the Punisher. Nite-Owl is the Blue Beetle, but he is also other rich men — for example, Batman and Green Arrow — playing at heroism as a result of their money and inventions. More important, the Watchmen allude to all superheroes — their costumes, their separation from humanity, their motivations, their sexual predilections, their secret identities — making Moore and Gibbons's graphic novel one of the works that demands the most comics literacy from readers.

The epitome of literacy-intensive comics, though, might be those that depict the world of readers themselves. To understand all the nuances of these comics, readers need intimate knowledge of this culture. For that matter, to care about these stories — about losing a comic book collection or fantasizing about becoming a professional comics writer — readers are likely to need backgrounds similar to those of the main characters to identify with their particular problems. People involved in the comics industry can relate to fans, of course. Most contemporary professionals grew up reading comics and hence know a lot about fans, comic book conventions, comics shops, and the collectors' mentality that seems to fuel all of these phenomena.

Despite the fact that many writers and artists have created particularly fannish comics, many insist on distancing themselves from fans, portraying readers and their pastime very negatively. Because criticism of fans (or at least the comic-fan stereotype) could alienate readers from the mainstream companies, most of these critical texts appear in the industry's alternative publications. Despite their criticism, these alternative-comics creators still cannot escape the world of comics. Simply by focusing on this world, they limit their audience to people with enough comics literacy to understand these stories. In other words, the critiques of comic book readers can, for the most part, be read, understood, and fully appreciated only by the same readers.

The depictions of comic book fans themselves fall into two main categories, the direct and the metaphorical. Mainstream visions of comic book fans have usually been metaphorical. Some, such as Byrne's story, "Hero" (*Fantastic Four* #285 [December 1985]), have been sympathetic. Tommy Hanson, a devoted fan of the Human Torch, faces so much parental neglect and peer ridicule that he sets himself on fire in an attempt to become more like his hero. When the boy's parents blame the Torch for his death, the superhero briefly vows never again to use his powers. An omnipotent extradimensional creature named the Beyonder soon intervenes and shows the Torch the error of his ways by taking him back in time to see Tommy happy in his room, reading *Fantastic Four*. The Beyonder explains, "The death of this boy is not a burden for you to bear. He did not die because of you. It was through you that Tommy Hanson lived!" (20). It is not difficult to make the jump between Tommy, the fan of the "real" Human Torch, and fans of comic book superheroes, turning the story into commentary on the role of superheroes in fans' lives. Comics do not make fans' lives one dimensional or lacking in human contact; rather, says Byrne, comics provide fans an escape, an outlet.

The metaphorical fan is more sophisticated in Busiek's and Alex Ross's *Marvels* (#1–4 [January–April 1994]). The series's main character is Phil Sheldon, a freelance photographer working in New York City. The series shows everything from the birth of the original Human Torch to the death of Gwen Stacy, Spider-Man's long-time girlfriend, from Sheldon's perspective. Sheldon's (and all of New York's) reactions to the heroes and villains he calls Marvels is at the center of Busiek's and Ross's work. On another level, however, *Marvels* concerns the relationship between fans and Marvel. Artist Ross suggests that Sheldon's feelings about the Marvels work "as a metaphor for the fan's disillusionment with Marvel Comics" (Shutt 32).

The story begins with Sheldon — the Marvel fan — obviously fascinated by the Human Torch and the Sub-Mariner, two of the company's first characters. Just as superheroes needed World War II to really catch on with the public, patriotic heroes such as Captain America and their battles against the Nazis and Japanese encouraged people to support the Marvels. After the first issue, *Marvels* jumps to the 1960s, skipping over the 1950s — the period during which Marvel superheroes were not published. Over the next three issues, the Marvels are alternately praised and reviled by the American people (just as sales figures and publicity increased and decreased almost cyclically), but Sheldon remains a fan throughout. He gets angry when nonfans make fun of the Marvels, suggesting that these doubters do not understand the importance of heroes. Sheldon publishes a book that virtually deifies the Marvels, turning him into a true keeper of the flame, a proselytizer for the superheroes, like the fans urged to hook their friends on Marvel comics. When he realizes that the Marvels' battles never end and that the heroes can have little impact on the lives of "real" people, Sheldon abandons his devotion to them. Quitting his job taking photographs of and celebrating the Marvels, Sheldon returns to the family that he has neglected for years to live a normal life. Here, Busiek is also discussing how fans give up on Marvel — how they should give up on superhero comic books — to enter a world of reality, adulthood, and normality.[2]

The tone of the more direct depictions of fans ranges from the mocking to the vaguely sympathetic, but there have been few overtly positive views of them and their lives. Evan Dorkin's short stories about the "Eltingville Comic-Book-Science-Fiction-Fantasy-Horror and Role-Playing Club" are without a doubt the most negative. The four members of the club — Bill, Josh, Pete, and Jerry — are sexually frustrated adolescents whose entire lives revolve around comics, role-playing games, and science fiction, fantasy, and horror television and film. The first story featuring the group (*Instant Piano* #1 [August 1994]: 2–10) illustrates a typical meeting as it moves through the various items on the agenda, from new acquisitions to activism, from open debate to the viewing of bootleg soft-core pornography. Two members of the club subsequently hold a trivia competition to determine which one will have the opportunity to pay $250 for a twelve-inch Boba Fett action figure (*Instant Piano* #3 [February 1995]: 5–14]). Alternative-comics fans, generally critical of fanboys in the first place, laughed at the broad stereotypes that the club embodied, but fans also recognized people they knew, answered many of the trivia questions, and even saw a bit of themselves (or who they used to be) in the characters. Alternative fans probably saw even more of themselves in Dorkin's later attack in "The Northwest Comix Collective!" (*Dork* #6 [May 1998]: 19–inside cover) (see fig. 21). There, in a story similar to the first "Eltingville" installment, the group argues about the nuances of alternative comics and their creators, showing only a bit more intelligence than their mainstream counterparts.

Other comic book fans are depicted with more sympathy. Joe Matt's extended story "Fair Weather," from his autobiographical *Peepshow* (#7–10

Fig. 21 In mocking alternative-comics fans, Evan Dorkin shows that they can be as petty and narrow in their cultural choices as mainstream fans ("The Northwest Comix Collective," *Dork* #6 [May 1998]: 23; © Evan Dorkin 1998).

[March 1995–July 1997]), provides a glimpse of him as a young comic book fan (see fig. 22). The story illustrates the mania for comics experienced by many young fans and offers an understanding of what comics can mean to young people. In *Zot!* McCloud portrays the life of Ronnie, an adolescent comic book fan. Like his high school friends, Ronnie, an insecure African American, wants to escape from his supposedly boring life, and comic books are the tools that enable him to do so. He is actively preparing for a career with Marvel Comics, constantly jotting down ideas in a notebook devoted to comic books: "You need a lot of plot ideas if you want to break into the comic book industry. I have millions. Someday soon I'll go to New York and walk right into Marvel Comics and show them my stuff. I'll have so much they won't know what to do with it all," he thinks to himself on the way to school (*Zot!* #31 [May 1990]: 3). But deep down, Ronnie is plagued by self-doubt, feeling that no one understands him.

Comic book fans, especially those who grew up reading comics and dreamed on some level of becoming comic book professionals, identified with McCloud's story. Fans could see themselves deeply involved in role-playing games that merely emphasized aspects of the players' true selves; they could see themselves as teenagers worrying about how they could turn their passions into meaningful lives. Reader Gregory Greene commented on the similarities between his younger self and Ronnie: "I remember all the wonderful, fascinating (and, I'm sure, divinely inspired!) story ideas I had for comics when I was in high school. I also remember how nobody paid them any heed. I'm still not sure whether that was because the ideas really weren't so clever, or maybe because I was so weird they didn't want to deal with me" (*Zot!* #34 [December 1990]: 22).

Not surprisingly, most of the differences in the depictions of other aspects of comic book culture are consistent along mainstream-alternative lines. Most alternative visions of comic book conventions are negative, reflecting the feelings of those creators, who often feel out of place at such gatherings. Typical are the Harvey Pekar stories that show the author of *American Splendor* at Comicons, usually in some forgotten corner, ignored by most fans. A more positive vision of Comicons appears in a story in *Justice League America* in which Guy Gardner goes to the local convention to buy a copy of the first issue of *General Glory,* a comic from the 1940s about a patriotic hero. At first, Gardner thinks the fans are geeks who have taken their hobby too far: "Buncha losers, if ya ask me. Ain't got no lives, so they get lost in a buncha

Fig. 22 Young Joe Matt is shocked to find his comic book collection missing from his bedroom and quickly panics (*Peepshow* #8 [July 1995]: 6; © Joe Matt).

cartoon fantasies. Sure, when I was a kid, I read 'em, too. They helped me get through the hard times when my folks were goin' at it . . . when the other kids were bustin' my chops. Sure, they made me happy when everything else was makin' me miserable." Later, he reconsiders: "Y'know, now that I think of it, maybe they ain't geeks. Maybe they're as good a buncha eggs as yer ever gonna find! In fact, I'd rather be hangin' around with this bunch than those jerks in the League any day!" (*Justice League America* #46 [January 1991]: 12). So, while alternative comics creators are critical of Comicons, and especially the fact that the fans there do not seem interested in alternative work, the editors at DC Comics emphasize the superhero comics' positive effects on readers and the general goodness of those fans. Neither position is entirely surprising, and both are consistent with the attitudes of these different reading communities.

Specialty shops, too, appear in stories about comic book fans. With most of these appearances coming in alternative comics, it is not surprising for the shops to be portrayed in a negative light. Walking around New York City, Rob, the star of *Minimum Wage*, decides that he needs his comic book fix, but his girlfriend, Sylvia, is not very enthusiastic about going into the shop. Once inside, Rob has a hard time defending the industry in light of the proliferation of comics featuring cheap adolescent fantasies (Fingerman, *Minimum Wage* 62) (see fig. 23). In one of Matt Feazell's "Cynicalman" stories,

Fig. 23 Rob, a comic book creator, is embarrassed by the selection at his local comic book shop (*Minimum Wage, Book One* [1995]: 62; © Bob Fingerman).

the hero is in a comic shop after being fired from his job. While there, he samples a few issues but finds the comics to be truly awful. Then school lets out, and the shop fills with comics fans, rabid with the X-Men, the worth and condition of their comics, and a desire to buy multiple copies (Feazell 37–43).

Even mainstream comics mock the collectors' mentality. "The Collector," a story from *Simpsons Comics,* suggests that fans, obsessed with keeping their collection in perfect condition, destroy that which gave them pleasure in the first place (Vance and Roy). The cover of an issue of *Legion of Super-Heroes* (#49 [November 1993]) announced a special "enhancement," a common practice in the early 1990s to increase the collectibility — and hence, sales — of particular issues. The cover for this issue did not contain a hologram, foil, or even simulated bullet holes, all of which had been used in the past. Instead, it was "the world's 1st edible cover!" The small print added that it was edible only if the reader had the same superpower as Matter-Eater Lad, a superhero with the ability to eat and digest anything. Even ads refer to a market where comic books are for collectors' or speculators' rather than readers. An ad for DC's Vertigo imprint from 1993 urges, "Collect experiences. Speculate on Ideas. Vertigo. Suggested for readers" (*Black Orchid* #4 [December 1993]: inside back cover).

Many readers appreciate occasional criticism of their fellow fans. Few mainstream fans see themselves as part of the problems attacked in these stories. Stories that portray fans in a negative light are particularly important for readers of alternative comics, many of whom previously read mainstream books. Reading comics about how silly buying multiple copies of an issue is or about how fanboys flock to the latest hot superhero comic while ignoring quality publications reminds alternative fans of how they have changed as readers. Reading comics is still not entirely socially acceptable, but reading comics that mock comic book readers makes alternative fans (and creators) feel that they are somehow better than comics or above the industry's failings, just as Marvel's parody and salesmanship during the 1960s made the company's readers feel that they were too smart for most comics. This kind of self-reflexive move makes readers of alternative publications more a part of the comic book culture than they would have been otherwise.

The audience for comic books in the United States is limited by a number of factors besides comics literacy as discussed here. The subject matter of most comic books and the atmosphere of most comic shops discourage women's interest, as do social attitudes about comics (which also discourage men's curiosity). Such social attitudes constitute the broadest limitation on the comic book audience. For the most part, the American general public does not take comic books seriously, believing them to be primarily children's fare. Adults reading comics are seen as either socially or intellectually inept. The news media fail to report on comics aimed at mature readers or on increased academic interest in comics without opening with *Batman*-style sound effects. Consequently, there is a certain stigma attached to reading comics, and as a result people concerned about their public intellectual image avoid comic books. And because they do not read comics outside of childhood, many adults are unable to separate more serious fare from work aimed at children. Critic Gregory Cwiklik argues that something as basic as sound effects gives even serious stories an element of humor in the minds of the broader American readership: "No literate adult (outside of comicdom) is likely to take seriously any historical narrative with BWOWM!, SKREEEEEEEE, and BLAM! emblazoned all over it" (120).

Comics creators and readers respond to this attitude in part by turning inward, thereby encouraging more material dependent on comics literacy. This phenomenon occurs for the same reasons that any group that feels itself under attack by outsiders becomes more self-involved and insular. Creators and readers feel the need to defend the medium from critics, and their anger and resentment toward these people makes them less willing to produce stories that outsiders can appreciate. The use of the comics language itself limits the audience automatically, as do stories that violate many of these formal rules. The continuity that is important to long-running superhero universes and realistic narratives creates a body of knowledge that works as a barrier to new, inexperienced readers, as does mainstream comics' reliance on the conventions of the superhero genre. Frequent parodies and allusions demand readers familiarity with comics' history and current events. Stories that provide a behind-the-scenes look at comics — from both the creators' and the readers' perspective — demand perhaps the most comics literacy.

As the direct market for comics has grown, reducing the number of casual readers, the number of literacy-dependent comics has increased. Today, as speculators have begun to shift their interests from comics to other forms of popular culture, there are perhaps more longtime, devoted comics readers than ever before, which may help to explain the strong element of criticism in many literacy-dependent comics. Like any family or small group, comic book culture may be defensive about attacks from without but filled with venomous criticism from within. Criticism through parody or direct commentary may also serve as an intellectual justification for readers who want to make reading comics more acceptable to outsiders.

For readers who go to their neighborhood comics shops and buy the latest issue of *Radioactive Man*, laugh at the jokes about comic book readers in *Instant Piano*, or identify with the plight of fans such as Ronnie in *Zot!*, a comic book culture is created. The fact that thousands of Americans are making the same purchases for similar reasons and are laughing at the same jokes gives these comics readers a kind of kinship, a brotherhood. Buying literacy-dependent comics serves as a badge of membership, an announcement that readers are part of this culture. The act of buying certain comics also serves as a boundary between comic book culture and the outside world, which does not appreciate, enjoy, or understand comics.

5

From Comicons to Web Pages

The Origins of Comic Book Culture

Iowa City is considerably less crowded during the summer, when most college students return home. As a result, business at Daydreams slows down during June, July, and early August. But the regulars who stay in town continue their weekly treks to the comic book store. Some patrons even travel from their homes further away — from Cedar Rapids and the Quad Cities — just to visit Daydreams. Because the shop is less crowded, though, interactions during the summer can be more leisurely, as the clerks and others have more time to spend on individual customers and more time to chat.

Many summer conversations are the same as those during the rest of the year — the return of a fan-favorite artist to *Avengers* or the latest issue of *Hate.* A young reader might ask one of the clerks to recommend fun issues of *Incredible Hulk,* so the two of them might look through the back-issue bins for comics within the customer's price range. An older fan might ask the clerks which *Madman* trade paperback is the best or if they have seen a recently released Japanese *anime.* A group of fans might discuss the latest comic-inspired film.

In June some Daydreams customers also talk about going to the Chicago Comicon, usually held on or around the Fourth of July. For most fans, attending comic book conventions is a special treat, a once- (or twice-) in-a-lifetime event because of cost and distance constraints. But Iowa City's relative proximity to Chicago enables many Daydreams customers to attend the Comicon every year. These lucky fans might be talking about which back issues they hope to find, from which writers and artists they hope to get autographs, or how much money they plan to spend. Some fans might try to make arrangements to share rides or hotel rooms to save as much money as possible for comics, original art, videos, and action figures. A few might even hope to sell their own work, either directly to other convention-goers or to the editors and publishers who will attend.

Even fans who live close to the locations of major comic book conventions sacrifice, save, and make special arrangements for the occasions, much like holidays.[1] As such, comic book conventions have become an important part of many fans' lives. The conventions are also important as cultural events where fans get the opportunity to rub elbows with each other and with comic book professionals. Much of the interaction that helps to create comic book culture occurs over great distances, through the letters pages of comics, through fanzines, or through the virtual worlds of web pages, electronic zines, newsgroups, mailing lists, and chat rooms. Comic book convention interaction, though, is real and physical: fans get a chance to mingle, meet, and socialize with each other and with industry professionals. Regular convention-goers often start and renew friendships. The conventions, then, are important for how they illustrate the way in which interaction and the resulting boundaries work to create a specific comic book culture.

Comic book conventions began as an outgrowth of comics fandom in the early 1960s. Since many early fans had been active in science fiction fandom and its regular gatherings of fans, professionals, and dealers, the development of a comics-specific convention was natural. Informal gatherings of comics fans had begun as early as 1963, when Jerry Bails invited many of the most active fans to his home near Detroit to help tally the results of a comics poll, the annual Alley Awards. According to Bill Schelly, the ensuing party, "in some very important ways, bore many of the earmarks of later comicons: trading and selling of comics, an art show, a masquerade, a banquet (if one counts ordering out for pizza), celebrity artists, overnight accommodations, and fans from outside the immediate vicinity." Had it been open to the public, Schelly argues, the gathering could have been considered the first comic book convention. However, that honor goes to a meeting held in Detroit in May 1964 at which nearly seventy fans viewed science fiction films and more than a dozen dealers sold comics and other goods. Another meeting, held in New York City in July 1964 and attended by both fans and professionals, was the first to call itself a comic book convention. By 1965 comic book conventions were established as an integral part of fandom. Meetings were held that year in both Detroit (the Detroit Triple Fan Fair) and New York (the New York Comicon). Close to two hundred fans attended the New York convention (Schelly, *Golden Age* 65–79).

These early conventions established many of the traditions that would continue during subsequent events: dealers selling comics and related materials, socializing among comics fans and professionals, screenings of films, panel discussions devoted to comics, and costume contests. By the late 1990s such events were held all across the country, with most charging steep admission fees. The most important national convention is held in San Diego during the summer, but other important conventions take place in Chicago, Oakland, Detroit, Charlotte, Atlanta, and New York, with regional conventions in smaller cities throughout the year. The San Diego Comic-Con International is especially important to the industry for making deals and is clearly the most well attended by professionals. The 1998 convention attracted more than forty-two thousand people, an increase of four thousand from 1996 (Spurgeon, "San Diego Notebook" 17).

For comic book fans—especially fans of mainstream comics—Comicons can be overwhelming, a glorious excess of comics and comic art, much of it for sale in the densely packed dealers' room (see fig. 24). At most conventions, this area is the largest and most centrally located, literally the heart

Fig. 24 Bart Simpson and his friend, Milhouse (top right), enter the dealers' room at the Springfield Comics Expo (*Simpsons Comics* #13 [1995]: 8; By Gary Glasberg, Phil Ortiz, and Tim Bavington, © Bongo Entertainment).

of the event. At the 1995 Chicago Comicon, for example, the dealers' room easily took up as much space as the rest of the show combined. At the 1996 Mid-Ohio Con, held in Columbus the weekend after Thanksgiving, there were two large and overcrowded dealers' rooms. Most dealers sell comic books, but some also sell old paperbacks (usually science fiction); action figures; soft-core pornography; material related to multimedia phenomena, such as *Star Trek, X-Files,* and *Star Wars;* T-shirts, and bootleg videotapes.

Some diversity exists among the dealers selling comic books. Most are comic shop owners looking to sell their back-issue stock. Some bring recent issues that they have overordered; some bring new issues of hot comics, looking to sell multiple copies to speculators. Most of these dealers also sell collectible card games (for example, "Magic: The Gathering") and other items that appeal to the largely fanboyish customer base. Many larger dealers carry a wide variety of comics, from recent to silver age titles, including some relatively expensive individual copies. These types of dealers — the most prevalent at larger shows — also sell large quantities of inexpensive comics in "bargain bins" that often include 1970s and 1980s comics with little resale value, although this idea of value certainly varies among dealers and fans. Frequently placed on the floor, underneath the dealers' main tables, these comics might sell for as little as ten for a dollar. Dealers clearly do not want to bring these comics home, so they often reduce prices considerably at the end of conventions. It is common at conventions to see fans loading up on these cheap comics, with many creating collections from these unwanted issues.

Other dealers specialize. Each show has a dealer or two specializing in Japanese *manga* and *anime.* Bigger shows also feature a handful of dealers who specialize in alternative and/or underground comics, which most other dealers seem to ignore in favor of more traditional superhero comics. At bigger shows, there are also dealers specializing in golden age comics from the 1940s and early 1950s and more expensive silver age issues. These dealers' clientele — older fans and collectors with specific lists of issues and conditions — varies widely from that of other dealers. People buying and selling these types of comics value condition, so it is common to see buyers and sellers carefully going over forty- or fifty-year-old comics, with much haggling and comparison shopping. Some dealers sell original comic art and other one-of-a-kind items produced by writers, artists, and inkers. These items are among the most expensive sold at comic book conventions.

Most fans attending conventions buy comics. In addition to the bargain-hunting fans mentioned earlier, shop owners attempt to fill in their back stock with cheap comics to be resold for a couple of dollars each. Some fans looking at big-ticket items are also dealers, looking for specific issues for regular patrons. Other fans — usually middle-aged men carrying locked brief-cases — sell expensive comics or original art to dealers. At typical comic book conventions, dealers and convention-goers exchange large amounts of both money and comics. In some ways, comic book conventions are all about commerce.

This commerce also takes place outside the dealers' room. Big conventions have large spaces devoted to comics publishers, many of whose displays involve multimedia presentations designed to sell products. At the 1995 Chicago Comicon, for example, the DC Comics display included a huge video monitor and stereo speakers playing music from the upcoming film *Batman Forever.* The company's installation created the sense of different rooms devoted to different categories of DC products — Batman titles, Vertigo books, Legion of Super-Heroes, Howard Cruse's graphic novel *Stuck Rubber Baby.* Each separate area was stocked with previews, excerpts, or entire photocopied comics that had not yet been released. Nearby were vast piles of free posters and pins that enthusiastic convention-goers snatched up regardless of content. (Getting free things is one of the favorite occupations of comic book convention attendees, and many come home with enough posters to wallpaper their apartments or dorm rooms.) Although Marvel's display lacked music, it was similar and even included an actor dressed as Spider-Man who posed for pictures with fans.

More than freebies attract fans to publishers' displays. Throughout the conventions, comic book professionals sit at their publishers' tables to sign autographs and talk to fans. The creator's autograph increases a comic book's value, so many convention-goers come with piles or even large boxes of comics that they hope to have signed. The lines to get autographs or even sometimes quick sketches from the most popular writers and artists can be very long, and many fans consequently spend much of their time at conventions waiting. For most, this waiting is worthwhile, as it results in a chance to talk to a creator or get a signature that can make a comic more valuable either as a keepsake or as an investment.[2] Some convention-goers bring their own artwork and use these occasions to get feedback — or, they hope, job offers—from professionals. This kind of business has become so important, especially at large conventions such as those in Chicago and San Diego, that publishers such as Marvel, DC, and Dark Horse set aside specific times for prospective artists (and, to a lesser degree, writers) to meet with editors to review portfolios. At big conventions (again, especially in San Diego), advanced freelance artists make contacts that result in job offers. As Lurene Haines explains in *Getting into the Business of Comics* (1994), "attending a convention is one of the most important methods of securing work in the comic industry" (31). Some promising young artists are asked to leave samples with editors. Others hopefuls get specific advice about how to improve their work. These meetings have become so important that many conventions also include special presentations on all aspects of creating comics.

Other writers and artists come to conventions independent of publishers. Usually in a separate room or section (nicknamed Artists' Alley), these creators number in the hundreds at the Chicago and San Diego conventions. Some of these creators are published mainstream artists selling their original art and on-the-spot sketches. (Many fans bring small sketchbooks for this purpose.) Other attendees are independent writers and artists selling self-published comics or minicomics. Some creators are local artists selling unauthorized artwork starring their favorite characters. Much of this work borders on the pornographic, as the illustrations often depict superheroines in various states of undress. Artists whose work focuses on superheroes and/or sexist representations of women are often among the most common in Artists' Alley, and because this work is grouped with the alternative comics, fans of that genre are often disconcerted and feel out of place. Their searches for obscure minicomics or new works from their favorite creators entail wading through tables of Todd McFarlane imitators producing sketches of Wonder Woman in lingerie. Furthermore, some alternative artists and fans argue that they are ghettoized by being shunted into separate areas.

Conventions also feature a variety of other activities that give fans a break from the commerce of the dealers' room, Artists' Alley, and publishers' area. Most conventions include panel presentations where fans can hear professionals talking about their work, the history of the industry, or their plans for their current comics. At the 1997 San Diego Comic-Con, for example, DC writers and editors participated in a panel discussion about the future of the Justice League, giving fans some inside information about new members and different directions the series might take (Stratton). The 1995 Chicago Comicon featured a presentation that supposedly allowed fans the opportunity to "Decide the Future of Marvel Comics" or at least to help decide which characters might get their own titles. At the beginning, the host (an anonymous publicity representative) announced, "Some of the information I'll be telling you, I'll probably get in trouble for." This statement was likely more than a bit of an exaggeration, but some fans probably felt that they were getting the scoop on future events in various Marvel titles.

Other panel discussions have a broader appeal. Some feature golden or silver age writers and artists talking about what it was like to create comics in those eras. Other panels focus on genres (for example, superheroes or Westerns) or on particular audiences (children or women). The 1997 San Diego Comic-Con included panel discussions about on-line comics and the future of the medium, both attended by Scott McCloud, author of *Understanding Comics* (Stratton). Highlights of the 1998 Comic-Con included panels on political correctness in comics and (again) "The Future of Comics as an Art Form" (Spurgeon, "San Diego Notebook" 19). A number of panels usually focus on small-press comics, the creation of minicomics, or various legal issues. Some such sessions are obviously aimed at the professionals in attendance, but, with the permeable boundaries between them and fans, many attract a broader audience. Sometimes it is hard to tell the difference between participants and attendees. At a presentation on small-press comics at the 1995 Chicago Comicon, Greg Hyland, one of the creators of *Lethargic Comics,* suggested, "The audience should be up" on the panel along with the participants.

A variety of other activities fill up the rest of the convention schedule. Trivia contests (often focusing on the superhero comics of the silver age) are popular, often pitting a team of professionals against a team of fans, sometimes in a game-show format. Other media are also important, as many conventions include rooms devoted to role-playing games, Japanese *anime,* or science fiction films. Television shows such as *Babylon 5* and *Buffy the Vampire Slayer* often make their presence known at comic book conventions, with writers, directors, and actors giving talks or hosting video presentations. Many shows also include efforts for charity. The Comic Book Legal Defense Fund, dedicated to helping creators and retailers with censorship-related issues, is a ubiquitous presence at conventions, selling original art, buttons, T-shirts, and comics. The organization has recently raised

funds at the Chicago Comicon through a dunk tank that allowed participants to try to soak industry professionals for a small donation. Many conventions also include blood drives, and charity auctions are also common.
For example, all proceeds from the 1996 River City Comics Convention in
St. Louis went to the St. Louis Effort for AIDS. Costume contests are still a
traditional part of many comic book conventions, especially in the evenings
as part of social events.

For many fans, the opportunity to socialize with other fans and professionals makes comic book conventions special: they offer a chance to meet
people known only through E-mail, to renew acquaintances made at earlier
conventions, or to meet people (and professionals) with similar interests.
Many of the reports about the 1997 San Diego Comic-Con posted on the alternative-comics electronic mailing list comix@world.std.com featured stories about parties and trips to Tijuana more prominently than accounts of
events at the convention itself. For creators, conventions are like a family
reunion, a chance to spend time with people they may see only a couple of
times a year. One of fan Michael J. Vasiliou's best experiences at the 1996
Chicago Comicon happened when he was "walking home about 11:00 after
the [*Babylon* 5] reception and checking out the late-night panel and finding
about 30 or so people sitting around the corner of the lobby discussing the
Legion [of Super-Heroes]. Well, [I] couldn't resist joining THIS group" (rec.arts.
comics.misc newsgroup, June 27, 1996).

Given the crowds and the amount of money changing hands, comic book
conventions are surprisingly peaceful places, which is not to say that they
are solely friendly places, with comics fans of different sorts all happily enjoying their hobby. There are two important conflicts among convention-
goers. The first is between the more traditional fans, interested in silver age
comics and similar expensive publications, and younger (or less mature) fanboys interested in hot titles, grim and gritty violence, and soft-core pornography manifested in 1990s trends such as "bad girl" comics. People interested in buying the big-ticket items such as golden age comics and original
art would clearly rather not have these kids running around the convention
floor. Older fans bringing their families would rather not see the pornography or the casual glorification of violence found at nearly every convention. Many convention-goers would clearly prefer comics that can be enjoyed by both children and adults. At the 1995 Chicago Comicon, Stan Lee
and Julius Schwartz (a longtime editor at DC Comics) both expressed dis-

may at current comic book trends. Schwartz said, "I shudder at what I see" of contemporary comics, and the audience applauded. Lee explained that he was not "that violently against censorship" and that he would be happier if comics were less violent and less dark, and the audience liked this idea. Other presentations at the same convention emphasized the need for comics that parents could feel safe about giving to their sons and daughters and for comics that featured single-issue stories, just like those from the silver age.

The second conflict is between mainstream readers and creators and their alternative counterparts. Many alternative fans feel very out of place at a typical comic book convention. Explains Tom Spurgeon, an editor at the *Comics Journal*, "San Diego with its attention on spandex and boobies can be very wearying for alternative or seriously-intended cartoonists" (comix@world. std.com, July 22, 1997). Aside from the ghettoized Artists' Alley, finding alternative and underground comics — even by someone as prominent as Robert Crumb — at most comic book conventions can almost be impossible. This kind of division caused Joe Chiapetta, author of the alternative and anticorporate *Silly Daddy*, to announce at a panel discussion at the 1996 River City Comic Book Convention, "Most comic book fans are idiots." Chiapetta knew that, apart from the fifteen or twenty people attending his presentation, his audience was not at the comic book convention. Many alternative artists and writers have begun to stop attending these mainstream conventions, to focus their energies and limited funds on more worthwhile outlets, such as new conventions devoted to alternative comics, including the Alternative Press Expo (APE) and the Small Press Expo (SPX). The 1998 SPX, held in Bethesda, Maryland, brought three hundred creators and 1,200 readers and retailers together to talk about the alternative end of the industry (Oarr 2). Such conventions reflect a growing split — and growing awareness of it — in the comic book market and audience.

For now, though, mainstream and alternative creators and readers can be found at most large conventions, making these events some of the few sites where all of comic book culture comes together to interact. Still, conventions are special, and most of the interaction that helps to create comic book culture takes place more regularly and on a smaller scale. The rest of this chapter will focus on these interactions and the resulting boundaries. In many ways, letters pages are the most basic building blocks of interaction in comic book culture. They are also among the most specific, attracting correspondents and readers devoted to particular titles. Professional magazines devoted to comic books — *Comics Journal, Comic Buyers' Guide,* and *Wizard*—include broader interaction, but they too have their specific audiences and specific boundaries surrounding them, as do self-published fanzines. Electronic forums such as web pages and multiuser dungeons (MUDs) offer a new kind of interaction but reflect boundaries similar to those that have shaped comic book culture for decades. These boundaries — and those built around it from the outside — have created comic book culture.

Comic books may be a marginalized form of popular culture, but their fans have one distinct advantage over those of other forms of popular culture. In comic books, there is always the potential for fans to interact in sites published, and hence made official, by the creators responsible for the production of the texts themselves. This kind of interaction takes place in letters pages (also called letters columns or lettercols) included in most regularly published comic books. These letters pages can be an important source for research into the culture of comic book readers, but they must be approached with care.

As Martin Barker warns in *Comics: Ideology, Power, and the Critics* (1989), "Letters are selected, and often for early editions solicited or ghostwritten. They are not produced by some 'natural sampling' of readers' responses" (47). This manipulation by publishers makes letters pages so useful: "They are a part of the self-image of the comic. They present that self-image, and help to encourage the right kind of future response from readers" (47). Letters thus can reveal editors' ideas about a comic's intended audience and about how it will be read. These pages are also important because they allow fans to interact with creators, content, and other readers. This is one of the most basic levels of interaction in comic book culture, where participation is so widespread that it helps to make it unique among popular media cultures.

As comic books grew in popularity in the early 1950s, publishers began to transform a text page mandated by postal regulations from an infrequently read short story to a compilation of readers' comments. William Gaines's EC Comics was one of the first companies to prominently feature these letters pages on a regular basis. In its horror comics of the early 1950s, these pages were "hosted" by that title's narrator: the Crypt-Keeper, the Vault-Keeper, or the Old Witch. Fans could make announcements about clubs, advertise for pen pals, comment on stories, argue with other fans, and participate in contests to see who could invent the most disgusting pun along the lines of those offered at the end of the stories. Along with the "Fan-

Addict Club," the lettercols were crucial in creating the brand loyalty—and the sense of community—common among EC's fans.

By the early 1960s, letters pages had become a central part of comic book culture and constituted a crucial ingredient in the origins of an organized comics fandom. The practice of printing writers' complete addresses enabled fans to communicate directly with fellow aficionados and to compile mailing lists of people who might be interested in fanzines. Publishers also used the letters pages to mobilize fans. Marvel Comics in particular used the lettercols to create a sense of community and loyalty among its fans. Letters columns in *Fantastic Four,* among others, were filled with in jokes, praise for fans, and, most important, a sense of shared adventure that made early Marvel readers feel like participants in the company's success. Fans were proud to say that they were "True Believers," and the letters pages were important in creating this feeling.

By the 1970s, nearly all mainstream comics included letters. There were, however, important differences between the lettercols published by DC and Marvel. In many DC comics, letters were shortened, excerpted, or compiled into lists of suggested guest stars. Marvel letters pages, conversely, often contained very long letters in which fans praised, criticized, or offered detailed suggestions. Unlike DC editors, who referred to readers as "them," the editors of Marvel's letters pages frequently directly addressed their fans, often using the inclusive "we" or "us." The letters page in *Captain America,* for example, was called "Let's Rap with Cap"; in *Daredevil,* it was called "Let's Level with Daredevil." This phrasing suggests a kind of mutual participation among creators, editors, readers, and even the characters themselves. Around this time, DC featured lettercol mastheads depicting some of its characters reading fan letters. The contents of the letters pages, however, contradicted these visual messages, as editors often deliberately separated creators from readers. Marvel's readers were encouraged to suggest story ideas, as editors emphasized the close ties between the audience and the creators. The idea that fans—as editors in absentia—and professionals were creating the comics together was central to Marvel's rhetoric. Many fans undoubtedly believed they had a role in shaping their favorite comics and, perhaps as a result, the company became the most successful American comic book publisher by the late 1970s.

Along with this variation in tone and strategy, there were also important differences between Marvel and DC letters in terms of subject matter. In the 1970s fans writing to one of the DC titles would almost always comment on a previous issue's story, either praising or panning it. Fans writing to Marvel comics would do the same, but substantial numbers of people also examined comics' content by offering interpretations of long story lines or explanations about the powers and abilities of various supercharacters. Negative letters were common in both Marvel and DC letters pages, especially in the 1970s, but the criticism often differed. While Marvel fans' criticism could be very pointed, focusing on the work of particular writers and artists or even the company's whole output, negative letters from DC fans were usually mild, comparing a weak story to a stronger one a few issues earlier. Very rare were wholesale attacks on the company or even a particular series. By the early 1980s, though, DC letter columns began to become more like Marvel's, with longer letters that privileged content and commentary over simple reaction. By the late 1980s and early 1990s, Marvel letters pages had lost much of their critical edge, with DC lettercols taking up the slack.

Letters pages can also be found in contemporary independent and alternative comics. There, they often serve different purposes than in mainstream comics. The letters pages in *Hate* and *Naughty Bits* both establish and nurture a sense of community among readers based on generation and gender, respectively. Letters can fill up nearly half of each issue of Dave Sim's *Cerebus* because of fans' long-winded responses to his stories and their political implications. Dan Clowes uses his occasional letters pages in *Eightball* to mock his less psychologically stable fans and mirror the comic's sense of irony and weirdness. Other alternative creators use lettercols to rant about their lives, political and cultural issues, and the comic book industry.

Lettercols in all sorts of comics encourage interaction between fans, content, and creators. On the most basic level, this interaction occurs in the letters of commentary, the most prevalent type of fan correspondence. Readers are clearly not afraid to shower their favorite creators with effusive praise. *Sandman* fan Cris T. Halverson of Minneapolis wrote, "Thanks to all of you [involved with the comic] for bringing to us the most artistic and profound thought-provoking comic ever (and the only one to hold my attention). Special thanks to [the creators] for unsurpassedly bringing such life and depth to characters that have existed before and beyond humankind and [the] comics realm. My wholehearted agreement with all those impressed and obsessed who have praised you in the past, and I'll leave it to those yet to come to voice the rapture in my marrow each time I pick up or set down yet another issue" (*Sandman* #32 [November 1991]: 30). This kind of praise could be found in Marvel comics of the 1960s and early 1970s, too, where creators had become heroes themselves. Writer Steve Englehart was a favorite of many Marvel fans, especially for his work on *Dr. Strange* and *Captain America*. One reader, Thomas Holaday of Wellesley, Massachusetts, was so excited by Englehart's work that he declared that the writer "is scripting the most *contemporary* fiction in America," adding that the details "convince the reader that he is in the midst of a special kind of genius, the kind that knows the roots, stems, leaves, and blossoms of the Tree of Popular Knowledge" (*Captain America* #183 [March 1975]: 18). Fans also get excited about the kinds of stories that a writer or artist tells. Readers of Terry Moore's *Strangers in Paradise*, for example, have praised his depiction of women. Fan Debbie Byrd enthusiastically announced that this is "a comic for women!" filled with authentic images of women's lives (see fig. 25): "You won't find any triple-E silicone-filled busts bursting from a shredded t-shirt conveniently torn to reveal just enough flesh to get a guy breathing hard here," she writes. "What you will see are sweat pants and tousled hair, sagging breasts and bulging bellies" (*Strangers in Paradise*, v2 #1 [April 1994]: 23).

Laudatory letters in Marvel comics have traditionally gone beyond praising the creators to celebrating the publisher as well, especially for its supposed courage and relevance. These letters often mimic Marvel's own self-congratulatory prose. One fan applauded a handful of creators for "daring

Fig. 25 Because of troubles with her roommate, Katchoo, Francine has a midnight snack (*Strangers in Paradise* v2 #2 [November 1994]: 6; © 1998 Terry Moore).

to be different, daring to experiment, daring to be GREAT. THEY ARE DAR-
ING TO BE MARVEL!" (*Alpha Flight* #16 [November 1984]: 30). Dwight Hal-
berstam of Denver waxed philosophically about the upcoming death of a
member of the team: this event and other Marvel births and deaths "show
us what it is that makes Marvel so special: change. . . . As in real life, nothing
is constant in the Marvel Universe. . . . It is wrong to think of the Marvel
Universe as somewhere else, somewhere governed by different rules, different causes and effects. The Marvel Universe is OUR universe. Those heroes
live HERE, on OUR earth. It is OUR lives they protect, our values they represent" (*Alpha Flight* #16 [November 1984]: 30).

The lettercols include more than just praise, though, as fans have often
seen through the lack of quality in their reading. Particularly during the
1970s it would not have been difficult to find negative responses in comics'
letters pages. Some are simple complaints about a story or art (see fig. 26).
Other letters can involve a great deal of anger, especially when fans believe
that a character is being mishandled. Writer Denny O'Neil's infusion of "relevance" into DC's *Green Lantern* was generally praised, but some readers
were angry about the comic's new political emphasis. "Surely *Green Lantern*
deserves a better fate than to be made the tool of an ideological extremist,"
one fan wrote. "Just as I would not have William Buckley write *Green Lantern*,
so too do I object to Mr. O'Neil's opinionated, fustian rhetoric. His gall seems
to know no bounds. The decade-long work of [writers John] Broome, [Gard-
ner] Fox, and others in establishing *Green Lantern* at the pinnacle of comic
magazine perfection has been completely nullified in three short issues by
Mr. O'Neil's propagandistic extravaganza" (*Green Lantern* #81 [December
1970]: 30).

The murder of Spider-Man's girlfriend, Gwen Stacy, in the early 1970s
prompted some bitter and angry letters from fans. J. M. Black of Alameda,
California, wrote, "How DARE you kill Gwendolyn Stacy!? You are a pack of
soulless, mercenary sadists. I am no longer a True Believer." Sergio J. Andrade,
of Roselle, New Jersey, was perhaps even angrier, addressing his letter "to
whomever had the idea of killing off Gwen Stacy": "You rattlesnake, you
buzzard, you large red insect, you worm, you cockroach, you lizard, you
skunk, you tapeworm in the digestive system of humanity: why is it when a
superhero and his girl finally seem to be getting it together, you kill off the
girl? May you lose every tooth in your head but one, and in that one may
you have a toothache; may someone put arsenic in your midnight cocoa;

Fig. 26 Bob Brown and Don Heck were among *Avengers* fans' least-favorite artists and hence were the frequent subject of letters (*Avengers* #119 [January 1974]: 2; by Steve Englehart, Bob Brown, and Don Heck, © Marvel Comics).

may you be struck down by a spirit of justice and be reincarnated as an amoeba!" (*Amazing Spider-Man* #124 [September 1973]: 31).

Fans of alternative comics sometimes react angrily, too. Many readers of *Hate* were dismayed, to say the least, by Peter Bagge's decision to print the series in color. Some suggested that it was a sign that he was selling out, while others claimed it was no longer as "edgy" as it once was. One fan explained, "I used to love the visual aspects of [Bagge's] comix, it created the perfect atmosphere, and indulged my eyes. Now *Hate* looks like a piece of shit, like something that should be in the Sunday comics. BRING BACK THE REAL DRAWING AND PUT AN END TO THIS CRAP! I am (or was) a faithful reader of *Hate*. . . . Now you have lost me" (*Hate* #19 [June 1995]: inside back cover).

In the 1970s Marvel editors frequently tried to placate angry readers by explaining how important their letters were to the company. Some reiterated Lee's notion that readers' letters were important as guidelines for the creators. Responding to complaints about *Power Man*, one editor explained,

"We don't score hits with every issue. Sometimes, a story has flaws or just doesn't come up to snuff. Which is why your letters are so valuable to us in producing these comments.... So don't let anybody tell you your letters aren't important, people. They are vital to these magazines" (*Powerman* #24 [April 1975]: 18). Fifteen issues later, the message was the same. "We actually *do* read every letter you send," the editor claimed. "We listen to your comments. We write and draw our books according to what you—the *real* editors of Marvel Comics—want to see. How else do you think we became the number one comics company today?" (*Powerman* #39 [January 1977]: 18). The emphasis on this kind of relationship in 1970s letters pages differed greatly from Marvel's approach in the preceding decade. During the company's early years, Marvel created a sense of camaraderie in the pages of its stories. By the 1970s, though, whether because of bad or overly serious comics or because the comics failed to reach the anticipated audience, that kind of rapport—or the illusion of that rapport—had to be established in the letters pages, subtly changing their purpose in Marvel's overall strategy regarding its readership.

Creators involved in independent and alternative comics often explain their goals for their letters pages at the beginning of a new series. Some artists and writers are clearly interested in creating accurate samplings of feedback from readers. In the second volume of *Strangers in Paradise*, Moore announced, "I will make a point to run all kinds of comments [on the letters pages], not just the lovey stuff. Since *SIP* is a story about the good and bad in life, it only follows that the letters column should read the same way and not like a lettercol from a fanboy magazine" (*Strangers in Paradise*, v2 #2 [November 1994]: 24). Other creators are less hospitable. Martin Wagner, author of *Hepcats*, declared, "It's my humble opinion that if you don't like me or my work you don't have to be [in the lettercol]" (*Hepcats* #0 [November 1996]: 23). Some independent creators are committed to putting together an interesting read: "As for the letters column, I think I will be working it a different way from your average letters page," explained Zander Cannon, creator of the epic fantasy *Replacement God*. "I don't know about anyone else, but as a comics- and letters page-reader, I get kind of bored reading letters that all say the same thing. 'Dear So-and-So, I love your comics. They are great. Did I mention that I love them? You should be in color. Why aren't you monthly? You should have a cross-over. Please send me a free sketch. I love your comics. I am in love with one of your characters. And don't you think that your handling of the democratic overthrow of the military junta in issue 304 was from a blindly socialist perspective, and should possibly have taken in some points of view of other political groups to provide a compelling argument? I want to see Rocket Girl naked. Etc., etc., etc.'" (*Replacement God and Other Stories* #1 [May–June 1997]: 23).

Questions from readers and the resulting responses from creators or editors are essential for the development of a unique letters page. Most of these questions focus on a handful of themes. Many fans try to point out mistakes or logical incongruities within stories. Other mainstream readers ask about continuity, especially where a story fits into the overall history of a superhero universe. Some want more details about characters: for example, the letters pages of Kurt Busiek's *Astro City* are filled with questions about characters of whom readers get only a tantalizing glimpse. Busiek refuses to answer, urging his readers to be patient and wait for the story that will resolve their questions. The letter pages, then, give readers a forum for discussing their theories about his often mysterious characters.

Discussions such as these shift reader interaction on letters pages to the realm of content. Often, these missives are very specific, centering on events themselves. Other letters focus on the intricacies of plot, with writers sometimes offering their own ideas for where a particular story line should go or suggesting scenarios for new stories. Some reader interaction with content focuses on characters. Fans of comics that combine two or more heroes flood the letters pages with suggestions for costars, while team comics attract letters filled with ideas about new members. Many fans are particularly sensitive about a character being portrayed accurately, prompting letters filled with tips for writers and artists on how to depict the "real" hero.

Some interaction with the content of comics functions on a broader level, though, when readers offer their own interpretations of stories or use them as inspiration for discussion of other topics. Some reader interpretations are simple analogies, finding parallels between comics events and those in the real world. Fan Greg Jones, of Houston, Texas, for example, saw the Galactus story[3] as a symbol for American involvement in Vietnam, with the Silver Surfer representing the United States (*Fantastic Four* #54 [September 1966]: 31). Other interpretations are more like literary analysis, especially in DC's Vertigo comics, where complex systems of symbols and multiple layers of meaning inspire readers. This phenomenon began with Alan Moore's run on *Swamp Thing*, a series about a walking plant creature—at times, the embodiment of all plant life on the earth — infused with the spirit of a dead scientist. Moore used the character to create didactic horror stories that readers loved trying to decipher. Fan Jillian Beifuss, of Charlottesville, Virginia, argued that one story illustrated the loss of grace in the contemporary world (*Swamp Thing* #42 [November 1985]: 31). Robert Jeschonek of Johnstown, Pennsylvania, offered a quasi-feminist reading of "The Curse," a story about menstruation and werewolves (*Swamp Thing* #45 [February 1986]: 31).

Political issues are among the many topics fans address in letters pages. Paul Chadwick's 1996 miniseries, *Concrete: Think Like a Mountain*, involves the encounter between the title character, a former political speechwriter whose brain was transplanted by aliens into a nearly indestructible body, and members of the environmental group Earth First! By the end of the six issues, Concrete has joined their organization and helped to save a virgin forest in the Pacific Northwest from loggers. Taking a cue from the content of the story — and from the creator's announcement in the first issue — the letters pages were filled with a conversation between Chadwick and his readers about the morality of Earth First!'s tactics and environmentalism in general (see fig. 27). Not surprisingly, a vigorous debate ensued, with some readers announcing that the series had actually politicized them to the point of action (*Concrete: Think Like a Mountain* #4 [June 1996]: 25).

Letters pages also give fans an opportunity to interact with each other. Some of this interaction involves debates between fans over content. For example, Dave Olsen of Santa Barbara, California, wrote "an open letter" to a number of prominent Legion of Super-Heroes fans whose correspondence had been urging more developed relationships between members of the group. "If you want ROMANCE, why don't you stick to romance comics?" he asked. "Personally, I appreciate it when a comic is what it claims to be; and after all, this *is* ADVENTURE *Comics*. Please remember that" (*Adventure Comics* #353 [February 1967]: 15). In the 1970s, a lettercol debate raged among fans about the fate of the Captain America/Falcon team. The editors encouraged this controversy by soliciting readers' opinions and frequently reminding them that the fate of the Falcon "depends on the reaction of Marveldom Assembled" (*Captain America* #176 [August 1974]: 18).

Bagge's decision to use color in *Hate* prompted angry letters from fans but also an even angrier backlash. D. Mueller of Raleigh, North Carolina, wrote, "I just finished reading *Hate* #19 and the letters page pissed me off. Why is everybody bitching? I'm goddamn sick of the bitching." The writer

Fig. 27 Concrete debates politics with members of the Earth First! movement, mirroring the debate taking place in the comic's letters pages (*Concrete: Think Like a Mountain* #4 [June 1996]: 10; © Paul H. Chadwick).

ended by addressing fellow readers: "If you don't like what's in *Hate*, then shut the fuck up and buy something else." An anonymous "sincerely pissed reader" from Cumberland, Maine, wrote, "Hey all you whiny tight ass hole alterna-huggin' palsys—There's *nothing* wrong with *Hate* or Peter Bagge's writing/art/etc. It's *you*—you dumb unappreciative goons" (*Hate* #20 [September 1995]: 21).

Other fans have come together in support of their favorite titles through letters pages. In the mid-1970s, Marvel's *Amazing Adventures*, starring a swordsman named Killraven in an apparently hopeless battle against an invasion from Mars, always seemed to be under the threat of cancellation. As part of a campaign to save the comic, fan Mason Aldrich urged his fellow readers to "get off your tails and write today! Or the next copy of *Amazing Adventures* you receive may feature Millie the Model" (*Amazing Adventures* #36 [May 1976]: 19). The campaign was short-lived, however; the comic was canceled three issues later. According to his letter printed in the final issue, Aldrich received seventy letters in the span of a week and a half supporting his effort to save the publication, with many thanking him directly for his efforts (*Amazing Adventures* #39 [November 1976]: 19).

Happier interaction also takes place in the letters pages, as fans share their own creations. One issue of *Astro City*, for example, contains a photograph of fan Paul Saint-Laurent's homemade action figure of Busiek's hero, Jack-in-the-Box (*Kurt Busiek's Astro City*, v2 #6 [February 1997]: 26). *Strangers in Paradise* (v2 #1 [April 1994]: 22) ran a contest in which readers were asked to send their portraits of the main characters, Katchoo and Francine, with the best poetry and artwork published in subsequent issues. In the letters pages of *Hate*, Bagge ran contests that awarded readers dates with characters and special appearances in the comic (for example, the "Win a Date with Stinky" contest [*Hate* #3 (fall 1990): 23]). A different kind of creativity could be found in Bongo Comics's *Radioactive Man*. Some fans developed their own scenarios to fill gaps in Radioactive Man's past, while other readers strove to point out "continuity errors" within the existing issues (*Radioactive Man*, v3 #216 [August 1994]: 30). This interaction helped to expand the mythos of the series and make the humor, at least in the letters pages, a collaborative effort.

Fans of the Legion of Super-Heroes also worked with creators through lettercols to construct a fantasy world. Readers chose team leaders in letters, and some suggested new characters appeared in the comics. Other readers simply had questions about the futuristic universe where the Legion's adventures take place. The answers from editors and creators helped to make that universe more realistic and three-dimensional for fans. As Legion fan Mike Flynn explained, "[Editor Mort] Weisinger and his readers were shaping the Legion together." In fact, Flynn argued, "What was said in the letter column was just as canonical as what was within the panels" (*Legion Outpost* 10 [spring 1981]). By contributing to the construction of the series's continuity, fans appearing in the lettercols also helped to establish the unique fandom surrounding the Legion. Across the industry, this kind of dialogue helps to keep fans interested in comics, thereby helping to create distinctive reading communities.

Because of all of this interaction, letters pages occupy an important place in comic book culture. Lettercols exist at the boundary between fans and creators, readers and content; the fact that it is an official and public forum makes the interaction there unique. Television programs and movie stars receive mail from fans, but those letters rarely become public. With comic books, though, fans interact in the publications themselves. This interaction may occur in isolation from the rest of the media world, but it only helps to intensify the boundaries created in the process. Fans gain an identity and have it strengthened through awareness of others involved in similar activities. This awareness—and the feeling of fellowship it creates—begins in the letters pages.

Still, it is important to remember that the letters pages offer readers a site for *mediated* (if not manipulated) interaction. Editors decide which letters to publish and which to ignore; some editors create their own letters to serve their own purposes. Without further research, it is impossible to tell how much of the interaction is real and how much is a kind of public relations effort on the part of comic book publishers to educate their audience about how the comics should be read. The reality of letters pages is most likely somewhere in between authentic expressions and cynical manipulations. Even if the lettercols are based primarily on the imaginations of comics readers, the communities that result are important, as is cultural participation through letters pages. Without lettercols, comic book culture might not exist at all. For some fans, however, they are not enough.

Because of the specificity of letters pages, readers and fans interested in broader conversations—about the entire industry or trends in particular comic books—have turned to other publications. Until the 1970s no major independent magazines featured in-depth discussions of comic books, so fans started their own publications. Defined by Fredric Wertham as "uncommercial, non-professional, small-circulation magazines which their editors produce, publish, and distribute" (*World* 33), fanzines devoted to comic books began appearing in the 1950s, in part because of the popularity of EC comics, and peaked in the late 1960s and early 1970s as comic fandom grew into maturity. As the fanzines grew, they evolved into professional publications less concerned with the comings and goings of fandom and more concerned with the work of writers and artists employed by the major comics publishers. Fanzines persisted into the late 1990s, but comic book culture became dominated by professional magazines. Both professional and amateur publications are important to the culture, though, because of the fan interaction in them.

Three professional magazines — *Comics Journal, Comic Buyer's Guide,* and *Wizard: The Guide to Comics* — constitute the trinity of contemporary comics conversation, but each one serves a different audience. *Comics Journal,* published by Fantagraphics, is furthest toward the alternative end of the spectrum, attracting a small but loyal audience of alternative creators and readers along with a smattering of older, well-respected comics artists. *Comics Journal* also contains a strong academic element, as the magazine is one of the few periodicals that includes serious criticism and analysis of comic books. *Comics Buyer's Guide* (or *CBG*), edited and published by longtime fan Maggie Thompson, is aimed at an audience of fans and retailers that is slightly older than the average for comic book culture. The preponderance of advertisements, especially for back issues, suggests that *CBG* is targeted at serious collectors, especially of silver and golden age comics. Ads are a common element of *Wizard* as well, but this publication focuses on hot comics, recent titles that speculators believe will become important (and expensive) commodities in the future. The magazine also includes a price guide that is updated monthly, along with lists of the highest selling comics and the hottest artists and writers. Because of its focus on comics that are particularly popular with adolescent males, *Wizard* is often considered a fanboy magazine.

All three of these publications share audiences that are thoroughly devoted to comics — albeit often to very different kinds of comics. This difference is often exhibited in the magazine's letters pages. *Wizard's* lettercol, "Magic Words," is the least acerbic of the three, with generally friendly and fun letters from the magazine's regular readers. Little biographical information about these readers is included, but the magazine also runs a pen pal column that suggests that most of its readership is typical fanboys. The journal's correspondents, however, do not fit the image of the nondiscriminating fanboy, interested only in the comics that are supposed to be quick collectors' items. In fact, many writers are quick to criticize the mainstream comics that they read every month. At the beginning of every new year, *Wizard* asks readers to focus their letters on the best and worst of the previous year and to include suggestions about what they would like to see in the coming year. The 1995 edition of the survey includes criticism of gimmick covers, the Spider-Clone saga, increasing prices, Marvel's saturation of the market, and crossover series in general (*Wizard: The Guide to Comics* #42 [February 1995]: 8–15). These readers clearly do not merely accept everything that the publishers throw out at them; at the least, they criticize what they read.

Many *Comics Buyer's Guide* readers are also critical fans. This weekly newspaper of the comic industry is filled primarily with advertisements and feature articles that read like advertisements, but it also contains a vigorous lettercol. Writers to *CBG* comment on the business side of the industry, comic book conventions, particular titles, and the work of specific artists, among other topics. Many of these fans are highly critical of what they perceive as destroying the industry: the lack of children's comics, the overreliance on crossover stories that are so complex that they automatically limit the series' audiences, the high price of comic books, and the abandonment of accessible, non–comic shop retail outlets. As befits an older audience, the people writing to *CBG* often base their commentary on a sense of history or nostalgia. Many write about discovering comics as children at the local drugstore or flea market and about how sad they are that many of these outlets no longer exist. These fans clearly criticize an industry (and especially Marvel Comics and Image Comics) that they see as having abandoned the kind of values and fun that epitomized comics a generation ago. These fans are devoted to comics but are angry about publishers' lack of vision and the industry's lack of direction.

Angry letters are a common occurrence in the *Comics Journal's* lettercol, "Blood and Thunder," but every correspondent supports comics on some level. Debates about comics make the letters pages a significant part of an already very substantial magazine. Many of these debates can last for months, with answers and responses flowing back and forth from reader to author to second reader to author and so on. One recent essay that spawned a vigorous debate was Gregory Cwiklik's "The Inherent Limitations of the Comics Form as a Narrative Medium." Cwiklik argued that the comics medium is doomed to be inferior (in terms of both popularity and critical respect) to film and text-based literature because of various inherent limitations: the necessity of sound effects and word balloons and the time it takes to produce quality comics. The essay was as close as the publication perhaps has ever come to criticism of the comics medium (although criticism of the comics industry is very common), and readers were quick defend comics. Many correspondents objected to Cwiklik's direct comparison of different storytelling media, while other writers pointed out the large number of person-hours needed to produce a typical motion picture, comparing it to the time needed to produce graphic novels. These responses continued for more than a year after Cwiklik's article appeared.

If the *Comics Journal* has a particular editorial philosophy, it celebrates an alternative-comics ethos and valorizes raw, do-it-yourself, "honest," often obscure works. As a result, almost everything published by a large company will be criticized, as if the magazine was set on a kind of automatic pilot that produces negative reviews at the merest approach of a mainstream series. News about publishers like Image, Marvel, and DC is always included in the magazine but is often written with such a jaundiced eye that the information often leaves a bad taste in some readers' mouths. Although the magazine has recently been providing more coverage and analysis of mainstream comics, this change has met with resistance from readers. Ray Mescallado's column "Fanboi Politik," devoted to applying literary theory to contemporary superhero comics, has not been well received by many alternative fans, who dismiss the mainstream as worthless trash. Reader David Auerbach called the column "pseudo-literate academic pablum," suggesting that the initial essay praised comics (such as *Astro City*) that "are the same old garbage with pretty, stilted pictures" and that "maintain a facade of highbrow intelligence while playing to the same old puerile lusts for violence and power." The magazine allows columnists to respond directly to angry readers, and Mescallado explained that Auerbach's (and the *Journal's* own) "knee-jerk anti-superhero (and often anti-mainstream) comics myopia" constitutes an important element in his reasons for writing the column (*Comics Journal* #196 [June 1997], 2–4).

The *Comics Journal* was not always apparently opposed to mainstream comics. As a youth, executive editor and publisher Gary Groth was active in superhero comics fandom. In the late 1960s, Groth published *Fantastic Fanzine*, which focused on Marvel Comics. In 1976 he took over the struggling *Nostalgia Journal* and quickly shifted its emphasis away from advertisements and toward features. He also changed the name to *Comics Journal* and adopted the current magazine format (Schelly, *Golden Age* 129–30). For many years, the periodical continued to focus on contemporary mainstream comics as well as comics of the golden and silver ages. Even into the mid-1980s, the *Comics Journal* featured detailed news and reviews of mainstream superhero comics. Shortly thereafter, though, the magazine's promise to cater to discerning fans meant an increasing focus on independent black-and-white comics, the emerging alternative-comics scene. By the 1990s, the *Journal* had become a magazine almost snobbishly devoted to alternative comics. Its article "The Best Comic Shops in North America," for example, clearly emphasized selection of alternative, small press, and minicomics over (mainstream) back issue collections. The alternativity of the *Comics Journal* is now taken for granted, but occasional interviews with artists such as Joe Kubert, Gil Kane, Carmine Infantino, and Barry Windsor-Smith continue to reveal Groth's roots in older, mainstream fanzines.

The history of these fanzines goes back to 1952, when young fan Ted White published *The Story of Superman* on a small postcard mimeograph machine. Filled with information about the Man of Steel, the one-shot publication had a very limited distribution, perhaps fewer than fifty copies (Benson 39). According to historian and fanzine editor John Benson, the first regularly published comics fanzine was Bhob Stewart's *EC Fan Bulletin.* Inspired by science fiction fanzines, Stewart announced the debut of his publication in a lettercol in *Weird Science* (#20 [July–August 1953]: 18); shortly thereafter, the eighty people who responded to his letter received the first issue of his fanzine. The small mimeographed magazine included editorial comment and brief news notes about the doings at EC Comics. Stewart even provided a map of the EC offices, giving fans a unique insight into how writers and artists functioned. *EC Fan Bulletin* ended after the second issue, but other fanzines took its place, including *Potrzebie,* the *EC Fan Journal, Hoohah!,* and EC's house publication, the *EC Fan-Addict Club Bulletin* (Benson 40–46). Many devoted fanzine creators even continued their publications after EC's 1955 demise, helping to keep interest in EC titles alive.

EC's fans constituted a small, concentrated group, so these fanzines reached a very limited audience. Wider distribution for comics fanzines happened slowly, but the inclusion of comics-related articles in Dick and Pat Lupoff's science fiction fanzine *Xero* (premiering in 1960) began to rekindle interest in comic books of the 1940s (Schelly, *Golden Age* 19). The revival of DC superheroes such as the Flash and Green Lantern inspired Jerry Bails and Roy Thomas to publish *Alter-Ego*, featuring articles about characters, creators, and comic book publishers. The first issue, from the spring of 1961, included previews of upcoming DC comics, articles about the Wizard (a 1940s villain) and Wonder Woman, fiction about the Spectre (a 1940s creation of Jerry Siegel), brief ads listing comics wanted for trade, and a parody of DC's new *Justice League of America*. In many ways, the triple focus of the first issue of *Alter-Ego*— articles on golden age characters, news and features about the revived superheroes of the silver age, and amateur comic strips—directed the content of fanzines throughout the 1960s and into the 1970s.

Fanzines quickly proliferated in the 1960s. Explains Schelly, "A teenage comic fan would see his or her first fanzine, and instantly become seized with the compulsion to publish" his or her own (*Golden Age* 99). Through the amateur comic strips, the fanzines served as an important creative outlet for fans. During a period when breaking into the professional ranks was difficult, the fanzines were important as a proving ground for young writers and artists. Also, in an era without professional publications about comic books, the fanzines whetted appetites for facts and information. Previews of upcoming comics and gossip about what was happening at Marvel or DC gave fans inside information that they could share with (or withhold from) their fellow readers. Articles about golden age characters offered information that was otherwise unavailable to fans because of cost or scarcity.

To be sure, the fanzines had varying degrees of quality. Some were poorly printed, and many were filled with typos and other mistakes, often because of the technological limitations of typewriters and mimeograph machines. Many such publications were written by children or teenagers. Called "crudzines" by critics, many of these particularly amateurish magazines lasted only a few issues as fans quickly began to focus their energies on the more successful, well-respected publications. The Academy of Comic-Book Fans and Collectors sponsored the *Comic Reader*, giving that fanzine, filled with news and previews, a great deal of authority and a circulation of one thousand (Schelly, *Golden Age* 58). *Rocket's Blast–Comicollector* (or *RB-CC*) was originally two fanzines, one focusing on advertisements and the other on news, previews, and reviews, but when the publications combined in 1964, they gave fandom one of its longest-running fanzines, with a peak circulation of 2,500 per issue (Schelly, *Golden Age* 93). *Alter-Ego* also remained well respected, especially for articles, interviews, and comic strips by some of fandom's most prominent creators. Schelly reports that "an estimated *eight to ten thousand copies* of *Alter-Ego* #4 through #9 were probably distributed" (*Golden Age* 91). By October 1966 there were an estimated 192 different comics fanzines totaling 724 issues (Schelly, *Golden Age* 89). By October 1971, similar estimates showed there to be 631 fanzine titles and 2,730 individual issues (Schelly, *Golden Age* 130).

Fanzines of the 1960s and '70s fell into a handful of different categories. Most common were general fanzines, or gen-zines, that featured advertisements, articles, and amateur comic strips. Other fanzines specialized, sometimes in advertisements (ad-zines), articles (article-zines) or news and previews (news-zines). Published eight times a year by 1969, the *Comic Reader* was one of the longest running and most popular news-zines. Each issue included information on new books (especially science fiction and fantasy) and on comics, including descriptions of guest stars, artists, villains, and plot synopses. Some issues included reproduced cover art and advertisements for specific issues of certain comics. The article-zines were often further specialized (Schelly, *Golden Age* 90). Fanzines specializing in amateur comic strips were also important. The first was G. B. Love's *Fighting Hero Comics* (debuting in 1963), but more important was *Star-Studded Comics*, published by the Texas Trio—Howard Keltner, Larry Herndon, and Buddy Saunders. According to Schelly, "Within a short period of time, *Star-Studded Comics* established itself as virtually the 'official showcase' of the amateur superhero strip" (*Golden Age* 49).

Like other fanzines, *Star-Studded Comics* relied on a number of different contributors. Most had official rules that encouraged the submission of articles, comics, and advertisements from readers. Bails explained that *Alter-Ego* would be printed according to demand for advance sales: "No subscriptions will be sold, but I will reserve a copy of the next issue for any reader in return for: 1) an article, feature, ad, news, or comments that I accept for publication; or 2) 24¢ in postage stamps" (*Alter-Ego* #1 [spring 1961]:

3). Bails later took this philosophy — widely adopted by other fanzine publishers — a step further in a new fanzine, *Capa-Alpha*. Common in science fiction fandom was the amateur press association (APA), in which a central mailer would assemble preprinted contributions from a variety of participants, each of whom would then receive a complete set of material. Adapting this idea to comics fandom, the first issue of the comics amateur press association (CAPA) publication appeared in October 1964 (Schelly, *Golden Age* 62). As of October 1994, *Capa-Alpha* had passed its 360th mailing after thirty years of continuous monthly issues (Schelly, *Golden Age* 133).

Another APA, *Interlac*, began in 1976 and is devoted to the Legion of Super-Heroes. An April 1977 mailing included thirty-four different contributors and 285 pages of material. Because it comes from so many different sources, *Interlac*'s quality varies. Some of the individual fanzines that constitute it are mimeographed, while others are photocopied. Some are filled with typos and grammatical mistakes, while others are impeccably written and typed. Most of the components include stories, news, previews, commentary, and gossip somehow focusing on the Legion of Super-Heroes and its current (and former) creators, but there is also a great deal of material on other comics, too. Not surprisingly, all the mailings include talk about the group itself, especially its direction and rules. To join the *Interlac* club, a fan needs to first join the waiting list, which requires submitting an application and purchasing copies of the mailing. To become a member, people on the waiting list must submit forty-five copies of a zine of at least four pages. Regular members must also donate money to pay for covers, mailing, and special printing costs. All of these rules are spelled out in the "*Interlac* Constitution," included in every mailing as part of the "Legion Bulletin," which is filled with club business information (*Interlac* #6 [April 1977]: 3–4). For the most part, *Interlac* contributors are critical fans, poking fun at silly comics trends, attacking unpopular Legion creators, and expressing their opinions about the business of the comics industry. *Interlac* reached its tenth anniversary in 1986 with its sixty-first mailing, complete with 1,028 pages of material from ninety-eight contributors.

Fanzines are much less common in the 1990s than they were in the 1960s and 1970s. There is some continuity between the publications of the two periods, though. Some contemporary fanzines still maintain the traditional fanzine practice of encouraging and rewarding contributors. Jim Kingman, editor and publisher of *Comic Effect*, explained his method of promoting readers to submit reviews of and articles about comic books: "And if your article is printed, you get the issue you're in free" (*Comic Effect* #1 [n.d.]: 2). The same policy is followed by the *Jack Kirby Collector*, a highly professional looking publication devoted to the examination of the history of one of the central figures in the evolution of comic books in America, and by the new *Comic Book Artist*, a fanzine that celebrates the work of writers, artists, and editors throughout comics history.

The widely distributed (but nonprofit) *Jack Kirby Collector* is one of the many contemporary fanzines that are easily confused with professional magazines. With the ubiquitous presence of photocopiers and desktop publishing, many contemporary fanzine editors can easily lay out and print high quality publications. Many issues reproduce artwork at a level the earlier fanzines could not have approached. Some fanzines, such as Scott Saavedra's *Comic Book Heaven*, Jeff LeVine's *Destroy All Comics*, and Peter Bagge's *I Like Comics*, are produced by professional comic book artists and prominently feature their creators' visual styles. Conversely, professional magazines such as the *Comics Journal* and *Comics Buyer's Guide* sometimes feel like traditional fanzines. The *Comics Journal*, with articles, reviews, and letters seemingly written by a very specific (and relatively small) group of people with similar tastes in comics, suggests the kind of fan club that would have been common in the pages of fanzines of the early 1970s. *CBG*'s numerous advertisements suggest a traditional ad-zine. However, because the *Comics Journal*'s Groth and *CBG*'s Thompson have roots in this older fandom, the resemblances to the earlier forms are not surprising.

Most contemporary fanzines serve somewhat different purposes from those of older fanzines. Many 1990s fanzines are clearly nostalgic. *Comic Effect*, for example, seeks to rekindle the simple joy children find in reading comics. The fanzine is filled with reviews in which Kingman and his fellow contributors explain why they love the comics they read as children: "Maybe," he adds, *Comic Effect* "will tempt you to sift through those back issue bins and buy and read them for yourself" (*Comic Effect* #1 [n.d.]: 1). There is also a strong element of nostalgia in Gene Kehoe's *It's a Fanzine*, a publication filled with articles about a wide variety of old-time comics, from *World's Finest* to *Shock Suspenstories*. Kehoe even admitted to being out of touch with contemporary comics: "Let me know if I'm missing much," he asked his readers (*It's a Fanzine* #44 [summer 1996]: 3). In *Comic Book Heaven,* Saavedra illuminates some of the weirdness — and fun — of the comic books he grew up reading.

Saavedra's fanzine is also clearly personal, coming out of the desire to recapture the "giddy pleasure" in comics he lost as he became a professional (*Comic Book Heaven* #1 [May 1995]: 1). He wants to share his vision of comics with his readers. The same is true of Chris Staros's *Staros Report,* an thick annual fanzine. The heart of the *Staros Report* is its list of the best comic books ever published. The articles and interviews are also substantial, but they are definitely secondary to the list, in which Staros explains what is good and why. As of 1996, Staros's list contained 121 items. LeVine also offers explanations about good and bad comics in *Destroy All Comics,* a fanzine filled with reviews of recent comics and minicomics (see fig. 28). Whereas Staros writes only about comics that he likes ("everything on this list is worth reading," he explained [Staros 2]), LeVine seems to most enjoy savaging the comics that fail to meet his personal (if rather vague) aesthetic criteria.

The articles and interviews featured in most of these fanzines are very specific, often focusing on a cohesive readership or branch of comics. *Destroy All Comics* is clearly farthest to the alternative side, as demonstrated by his inclusion of comics by and interviews with often obscure creators. Furthermore, LeVine privileges minicomics over the output of traditional publishers. The *Staros Report* is also dedicated to alternative comics, albeit to more prominent titles and creators. The 1996 edition, for example, includes a *Love and Rockets* character index and bibliographies for both Alan Moore and Neil Gaiman. Other fanzines, though, are more specific. The *Jack Kirby Collector* focuses on Kirby's work and long career, with individual issues narrowing that focus to such topics as his work at DC, women in Kirby comics, and his villains. The first issue of Daniel K. Raeburn's zine *Imp* (1997) is an extended analysis of Clowes's work in *Eightball* and other alternative comics.

Most of these contemporary fanzines do not differ greatly from their traditional counterparts. However, few old-style fanzines continue to exist in the late 1990s, for a number of reasons. First, professional magazines have taken on many of the tasks performed by the older fanzines. For news about comics, fans can easily turn to the *Comics Journal, CBG,* or *Wizard,* all of which are widely available and usually reliable, as are publications such as

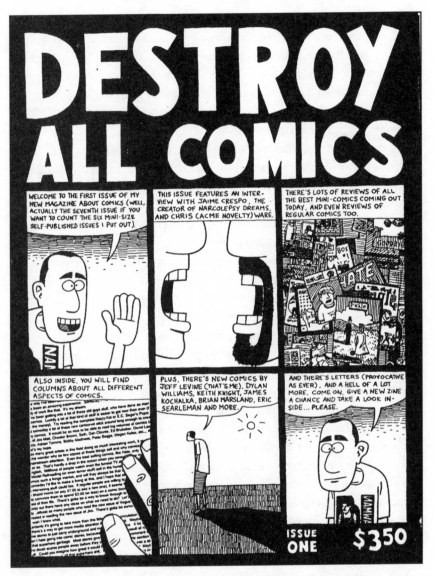

Fig. 28 Jeff LeVine's *Destroy All Comics* is one of a new breed of comics fanzines. LeVine is a published comics creator, and the fanzine focuses on mini– and alternative comics (*Destroy All Comics* #1 [November 1994]; © Jeff LeVine).

Comic Shop News, a small newspaper with listings of new comics and industry gossip that is commonly given away at specialty shops. Many comics fans also purchase publications such as *Previews,* a catalog from Diamond Distribution that readers use to order comics through shops. All of these publications have taken on an official status in the industry, so their writers and editors have access to material much more quickly than almost all amateur fanzine publishers.

As the number of comic book publishers has increased, the need for fanzines that publish amateur comic strips has decreased. It is now relatively easy for ambitious writers or artists to publish their own comic books or to find professional publishers. Minicomics have become a viable (if not lucrative) format, giving alternative-minded creators the sort of training ground that might previously have existed in fanzines. Breaking into the industry might be harder for a superhero writers or artists, interested more in doing stories starring the X-Men or Gen-13 than in creating a realistic comics story, but mainstream publishers in the late 1990s seem go through "hot new" artists at an incredible pace, suggesting that it has become easier to break into comics than it was in the late 1960s. The bottom line is that the direct market, expanding number of publishers, and the advent of black-and-white independent comics have made unnecessary fanzines featuring amateur strips.

There is also a new threat to the fanzine: electronic interaction found on the Internet. Instead of publishing fanzines, comics readers now can easily create home pages and use them to publish reviews of comics. Reviews can be sent by E-mail to create a kind of virtual APA, in which all the recipients can also be contributors. Web-page hosts can post an exhaustive list of the all the best comics ever published—just like Staros. Comics art can be easily downloaded or scanned in. Interviewers can solicit questions from other fans on the Internet and create ongoing dialogues with creators in newsgroups or chat rooms. Web-page hosts do not need to worry about page length, printing, or mailing, only about learning the programming software to allow the creation and maintenance of the sites. Because of their ease of use, these and other electronic interactions have become integral parts of comic book culture.

Beginning in the summer of 1997 the door of Daydreams Comics and Cards featured a small note urging customers to visit the shop's new home page on the World Wide Web. Virtual customers could find a place very much like the real store on College Street in Iowa City. The website is filled with humor, in jokes, and a lighthearted, if cynical, approach to comics. In 1997 it featured a photo of clerk Adam Mix surrounded by four chimpanzees shaking their heads, reminding visitors not to take the site too seriously. The site offers a great deal of information about Daydreams' stock and other shop-related facts, but a little further exploration yields more examples of its staff's wit and knowledge. One section includes brief (and often hilarious) summaries of some of the shop's odd, expensive back issues. Another area includes a quiz, with questions ranging from mainstream comics to alternative classics, Japanese *manga,* and European graphic albums.

By creating a web presence, Daydreams offers facilities to the increasing number of people devoted to comic books who have begun interacting not only in the physical world but also in the virtual one. In many ways, comic books (especially mainstream ones that require a readership knowledgeable about characters and continuity) are a natural for web pages, with their potential for housing vast amounts of information and ease of reproducing graphics. Hypertext links enable fans to easily find images and ideas. Broad access to web pages has combined with their technological advantages to enable Internet-based information sources largely to replace fanzines, giving groups and individuals relatively easy ways to narrowcast comic book preferences to others with similar likes and dislikes. Newsgroups and listservs have taken up the slack of everyday conversation, giving comics fans an outlet unlike any that previously existed. Role-playing games such as MUDs and multiuser simulated environments (MUSEs) give fans a chance to play the roles of characters about whom they have read for years. For many comic book readers, isolated from fellow fans and perhaps even buying their comics through one of many mail-order houses, these new electronic, computerized media products are their only forays into this culture.

Fans discovering computerized interaction will be amazed at the amount and variety of material on comic books. Newsgroups, chat rooms, superhero-based MUDs, and electronic zines offer scholars unique challenges, not the least of which is the volume of data. Using any World Wide Web search engine results in literally thousands of hits that in one way or another include comic books. Another difficulty involves the web's fluid nature. Addresses change frequently; sites disappear without warning. Many listservs archive their posts, but on others, messages disappear (either literally or through the volume of material) shortly after they appear. The conventions of electronic communication also contribute to the difficulties. As Mark Rogers suggests in "Virtual Fans, Virtual Ethnography: The Culture of Comics Fans On-Line," the immediacy of E-mail and the ability to quote specific sections of an analysis result in often superficial arguments and little thoughtful conversation. This electronic interaction, though, remains important, particularly as the most contemporary manifestation of comic book culture.

Pages on the World Wide Web are perhaps the most accessible of the new forms of computer-assisted communication. Despite the number of comics-related web pages, most fall into one (or more) of a handful of categories, from personal pages devoted to one individual's vision of comics to clearinghouses that collect links to other sites. In many ways, all comics-related web pages resemble old fanzines. Websites involve a narrowcasting of information and opinions to a relatively small, select group of people devoted to the medium. Having a web page simplifies the process of distribution, making it easier for writers and editors in part by eliminating the need for a printing budget. At the same time, the dissemination of information on a website is almost infinitely broad, as virtually any plugged-in member of Western society is a potential part of the audience. Thus, web pages have much larger potential audiences than did old-style fanzines. Easy accessibility has not, however, encouraged the inclusion of noncomics content or specific explanations for nonreaders of comic books. Like fanzines, websites' real audiences are still very specific.

Publishers of E-zines are among the most aware of their ties to the older publications. One electronic journal calls itself the "DC Fanzine," and all of them change their content at regular intervals. David LeBlanc, editor of the "Comic Book Network," calls his virtual publication an "electronic magazine" and has an edition available through E-mail, much like a traditional magazine is distributed through the physical mail. The home page contains both previous and current issues, offering visitors more than what would be available with a traditional publication. There are also various supporting materials, including reviews, convention reports, graphics, and links to other comics-related sites. "DC Fanzine" is an extensive E-zine filled with feature articles and reviews. As with the "Comic Book Network," the editors of "DC Fanzine" maintain a separate weekly mailing list, called the "Daily Planet" for news about DC comics. Visitors to "DC Fanzine" can take part in polls, contests, and chat rooms (available through DC Comics Online), or browse its repository of comics-related links.

These links to other sites are a common element to almost all comic book web pages. Some such sites have become clearinghouses for other websites. One of the most extensive is "Jonah Weiland's Comic Book Resources," where web surfers can find hundreds of different pages through an easy-to-use topic index. These links are updated regularly, and Weiland selects a "site of the week," making his page an excellent starting place for comics fans. In many ways, "Comic Book Resources" is also an E-zine, offering visitors news, graphics, interviews, chat rooms, and message boards on a variety of topics.

"Comic Book Resources" clearly has a mainstream focus, but other clearinghouses focus on alternative comics. One example was Mike Fragassi's "Alternative Comics: A WWW Guide" (no longer extant). He divided his long list into two parts, pages that feature comics images and pages about comics. Fragassi also included short essays to explain what alternative comics were. These pieces helped to show visitors what kinds of web pages would be featured on Fragassi's lists, but mainstream comics fans looking for a page about *Spawn* or *Superman* might not have read these pieces after failing to find anything of interest in the list of links. Fragassi's and similar pages offer alternative fans directional buoys that simplify the process of searching through oceans of mainstream comics web pages.

Other web pages pay tribute to their creators' favorites. Most mainstream tribute pages are devoted to particular titles and characters, with subjects ranging from major characters such as Batman and Superman to relatively minor ones such as Adam Strange, a DC science fiction superhero from the 1960s. Teams of superheroes in particular have inspired numerous tribute pages. "Avengers Assemble!," a page devoted to Marvel Comics's superteam, is among the most detailed tribute pages on the web. Visitors were previously greeted by head shots of older Avengers scrolling across the top of the screen; however, the page was revised so that the word *Avengers,* filled with comics images, introduces visitors to the page. They can then read the long news section, including an interview with Busiek, the new *Avengers* writer, or get information on the Avengers mailing list, the source of much of the page's material. Results of polls about fans' favorite team members are posted, as is an archive of the best conversation threads from the mailing list. There is even a glossary to help newcomers understand the special terms used by members of the mailing list, providing a sense of the group's rules and expectations. A *war,* for example, is explained as what happens when "one list member engages another in an intense war of words," but the definition also adds that "the war focuses on an Avengers topic, and does NOT become too personal." Another term, *fanboy argument*, is defined as one that focuses on which character could defeat another in a fight. But these *Avengers* fans emphasize, this kind of argument is "not exactly smiled upon on the list."

The "Uncanny X-Page" is another mainstream tribute page that offers visitors many opportunities for interaction. Like "Avengers Assemble!" there are links to a related newsgroup and archives containing classic posts, some of which have their own space on the page, suggesting that they have become important parts of the X-Men fan culture. For example, Jennifer Vodvarka's "Pissed-Off X-Fan FAQ" demonstrates her love/hate relationship with the X-Men comic books. She praises the people who established the series in the late 1970s and 1980s, especially writer Chris Claremont. At the same time, though, Vodvarka attacks those whom she believes responsible for the decline of X-Men comics: the Marvel executives who appeal to the fanboy ethos that emphasizes marketing schemes over story content, and editor Bob Harras, whom Vodvarka calls, "AN IDIOT WHO NEEDS TO GET HIS DIRTY LITTLE HANDS OFF OF THE X-BOOKS!" The presence of her comments on the web page suggests that they are more than merely the rantings of a single fan and perhaps represent a common sentiment among the comic's readers.

People also use comics-related web pages to tell the world about their favorite comics. These sites are often part of larger home pages filled with a variety of personal information, from family histories to résumés. For example, Bob Hegwood's home page is essentially an advertisement for his business, but there is also a section called "Literary Works: A Tribute to Stan Lee and Jack Kirby" about his favorite childhood comics. Hegwood explains, "These pages are simply my way of fondly remembering the good 'ol days, and all the joy that King Kirby and Stan the Man brought to me in my younger days. Since many of the really good Marvel epics cannot be appreciated nowadays unless you have lots of money for really expensive back-issues, I thought I'd display some of the better ground-breaking issues for all to see." Each set of three covers is accompanied by a paragraph in which Hegwood relates how he got hooked on these Marvel comics. Another personal page, "Aardvark's Comic Book Madness," is part of Kevin Newburn's larger home page. On "Comic Book Madness," Newburn has posted his

Image-influenced sketchbook, his hall of fame (including creators such as Rob Liefeld and Todd McFarlane), and the covers of and information about his collection of issues of *Marvel Team-Up,* starring Spider-Man. A more interesting personal page is Steve Conley's "SuperMarketing: Ads from the Comic Books," a collection of images from advertisements from comics from the 1940s through the early 1970s. The page also includes "Testimonials," a section where visitors can contribute stories about buying the products advertised in the comics.

A handful of academics working in the field of comic book studies also have their own personal web pages. Gene Kannenberg, a graduate student at the University of Connecticut, for example, maintains the "Comix Scholarship Annotated Bibliographies" web page, where scholars can find a long list of academic and nonacademic works about comic strips and books. Kannenberg is adding book reviews to his bibliography, and visitors are encouraged to submit them. Rogers, a 1997 Ph.D. from the University of Michigan, formerly had a web page where he posted a syllabus for a class he taught on comic books and various comics-related scholarly papers. Other scholars have established the "Grand Comic-Book Database" to create a catalog of every comic book ever published, listing story and creator information that would be useful to fans and scholars alike.

Creators often maintain personal web pages as well. Shannon Wheeler's "Too Much Coffee Man Page" is relatively simple. It contains an archive of weekly comic strips that originally appeared in the on-line magazine *Mania* and links to E-mail Wheeler. The site also contains what Wheeler's calls "Stuff to Download" (including a pattern for a Mac desktop and a Windows screen saver) and "Crap to Buy," which is virtually the same as the ads included in the *Too Much Coffee Man* comics. Wheeler's home page seems aimed at self-promotion, but other creators offer more to their visitors. Sarah Dyer's "Action Girl Online" is a virtual expansion of her *Action Girl Comics,* an anthology devoted to all-ages, "girl-centered but boy-friendly" comics. "You'll find stuff here that won't be anywhere else, from additional articles . . . to Internet-specific stuff like Action Girl-approved Web pages and resources," Dyer explains. As with Wheeler's page, there are items for sale, but there are also links to other web pages (comics related and otherwise), a list of recommended zines, information on the creators whose work appears in the current issue, and even "Go Figure," Action Girl's guide to female action figures. Whereas Wheeler's page is almost exclusively commercial, Dyer also offers her fans a particular vision of popular culture that is meant to help empower women and girls.

Still, making money has become an important function of the World Wide Web, so it is not surprising that publishers and retailers have established their presences there. Publishers such as Marvel, DC, Dark Horse, and Fantagraphics all have home pages where readers can get information about upcoming issues and new titles; however, all of this information does not mean that these pages do not contain promotional materials and advertising. Retailers, too, have created websites. "Comics 2000," for example, offers "savings, selection, and service for comic book collectors around the world." This service includes the opportunity for fans to send lists of desired back issues. Comics 2000 will then forward the list to more than two hundred shops that are part of its nationwide network. Many of these shops also maintain web pages (often through Comics 2000) that offer additional services to their virtual customers.

Although many web pages offer visitors the chance to interact with creators and other fans, most of this interaction is delayed, or even passive, requiring a gap in time between interactions or directly involving only the reader of the posted material. Other sites for electronic communication offer more opportunities for active interaction, among them Usenet newsgroups and listservs. The newsgroups are bulletin boards where users post articles, reviews, and commentaries at a central virtual site. Other users can respond by posting their own messages or by E-mailing the original author. Hence, many conversation "threads," or sequences of a particular discussion, can last for weeks, with multiple layers of posts, as users respond not only to the original but also to other responses. Listservs achieve similar kinds of interaction, but E-mail subscribers to a particular listserv receive a copy of every contribution to it. Because subscriptions are required, listservs tend to attract hard-core participants, while newsgroups, with less of a commitment required from users, attract casual users.

The simplicity of both formats has helped to create literally thousands of different listservs and newsgroups, with many focusing on very specific cultural products, comic books among them. Comics-related listservs focus on alternative comics, European comics, comic book scholarship, the business of comics, the writing of comics, Superman, *Astro City,* the X-Men, and comics-related fan fiction, among other topics. Newsgroups with comics discussions began as rec.arts.comics, but the number of participants forced it to split up — into four in 1992, seven in 1994, and fifteen by the summer of 1997.[4] Rogers reports that in 1994 the largest comics newsgroup, rec.arts. comics.misc, attracted between 250 and 400 new posts every day, prompting one of these splits ("Virtual Fans"). Longtime newsgroup participants are especially sensitive about the boundaries between the different groups. As explained in the rec.arts.comics FAQ (frequently asked questions, a document designed to explain the newsgroup's basics to newcomers), "Certain areas are designated for certain things, and it impedes the enjoyment of others if you post in the wrong areas." Particularly important are the boundaries around rec.arts.comics.marketplace, where fans buy and sell comics, and rec.arts.comics.other-media, where film and television adaptations are discussed: "You think it's neat to discuss casting the *Sandman* movie? So did I, the first fifteen or so times," the moderator explained. "The fifteenth time was back in 1991, however, and it's starting to wear a bit thin. However, in rec.arts.comics.other-media, you will find people who *want* to discuss this type of thing."

These rules and boundaries are important to many people participating in listservs or newsgroups. After listing all of the different newsgroups, the "Guide to Posting on Rec.Arts.Comics.*" explains some of the conventions governing subject headings and "spoilers," the revealing of crucial plot points that might ruin the story's impact on new readers. Many conventions are linguistic, teaching newcomers about the language the group has developed to make reading through dozens of posts more efficient. Not knowing this language has an important effect on communication, or, rather, on who communicates. According to Rogers, "those posters who properly employ the jargon get more response to their posts, while others, perhaps those who only read the newsgroup occasionally or those seeking a particular piece of information, get relatively little response, unless they post something inflammatory. Hence, most of the discussion takes place among those who are already linguistically in the culture" ("Virtual Fans"). These conventions help to define the newsgroups' boundaries, limiting access of a presumably permeable group to those people who know its rules. Posts, then, concern not only comics but also the kinds of communication that take place between participants. Therein lies the main difference between newsgroups and lettercol correspondence. Newsgroups also have more open criticism, less flattery of creators, and frequent explorations of tangents to the subjects at hand.

Territory, then, is one of the most important topics where conventions and protocols are emphasized. Many listserv and newsgroup members want to limit posts that are off topic, or do not fit into the accepted intellectual territory. When a new listserv is formed, for example, one of the first actions is the creation of a charter that spells out what can be talked about and, often, by whom. A recently formed listserv devoted to the academic discussion of comic books featured long debates about the individuals who would serve as moderators and about whether anyone outside of the university setting would be allowed to participate. The boundary between mainstream and alternative comics and their fans is often particularly important in newsgroups and listservs, with some formed with the explicit desire to escape from the other branch of comics. In an August 1995 post on the comix-alternative listserv, comics scholar Joseph Witek asked, "Does anyone remember back in the Charter Wars when I proposed that we should talk about all comics as long as we weren't being stupid about it and bunches of people said, 'No, no — we came here to get away from mainstream comics; any mention of longjohns and we're off to form me-and-my-friends-minicomix-l'?" For some fans, including Witek, boundaries of subject matter are not as important as boundaries of how subject matter is discussed. "Now," he continued, "we debate the continuity forms of DC vs. Marvel and groove on *Kamandi* nostalgia and nobody bats an eye. All to the good, says I." Most posters are not as open-minded as Witek, though, and many newcomers who do not quite fit are openly mocked by more experienced members. Others, as Rogers suggests, are simply ignored and eventually move on.

Other forms of electronic interaction occur in real time. Many on-line services offer chat rooms where users can "meet" other fans of their favorite comics and sometimes even creators. Both DC and Marvel Comics maintain chat rooms through America Online. Most such chat rooms are devoted to particular titles, and at different times, different creators will visit to talk about upcoming events in their titles. Of course, fans also interact with each other in chat rooms. Another kind of real-time interaction can be found in MUDs, which Howard Rheingold defines as "imaginary worlds in computer databases where people use words and programming languages to improvise melodramas, build worlds and all the objects in them, solve puzzles, invent amusements and tools, compete for prestige and power, gain wisdom, seek revenge, indulge greed and lust and violent impulses" (145). Comics fans involved in MUDs can immerse themselves in superhero universes and play as members of the X-Men or Justice League.

Although based on superheroes such as the X-Men characters, most of these simulations take place in a universe slightly different from the one featured in the comics, suggesting that the players of these simulations use the games not just for entertainment but also for the kind of active production of culture that has been attributed to fans by scholars such as Henry Jenkins. His "textual poachers," struggling to possess and control their favored media products, eventually begin creating their own products through their own imagination and by assembling bits and pieces of their cultural raw materials into something new and unique. Comic book fans involved in these computer-based simulations partake in the same sorts of activities as do *Star Trek* and other media fans writing slash fiction or producing fan videos. Together, as a community of game players, comic book fans create new fictions about characters they have known for years.

In this way, most of the people involved in computer-mediated communication about comics have centered themselves in one or more specific communities. The conventions and specificity of newsgroups and listservs clearly suggest the classic interpretive communities of Stanley Fish and other literary theorists. These groups contain people who read the same material, laugh at the same jokes, and very often make consistent aesthetic judgments about what they read. The people subscribing to or regularly visiting a particular electronic magazine are a kind of community, too, with similar preferences and attitudes toward the comics they read. The communities surrounding web pages suggest a new kind of group organization that uses a virtual site instead of a real one as a meeting place. Visitors to the site may never meet, but they do maintain important cultural ties by reading the same comics, by remembering the same trivia, and by speaking the same language—the language of comics, whether mainstream or alternative, silver age or contemporary. These, then, are some of the ways in which comic book culture is created and maintained. In the past, this culture was constructed out of letters pages and fanzines. Those phenomena still exist, but some of the new bricks and mortar holding the culture together consist of virtual material such as web pages and newsgroups.

In the future, perhaps this virtual material will change comics fandom, just as hypertext and digital technology have the potential to change both the comics format and the comics industry. A web page's potential to reach millions of people might make it easier to become a fan, to learn the information and language that are necessary for interaction within this community. Perhaps the web will make it easier once again to be a casual comics fan by breaking down the boundaries formed by the direct market. The web's wider access to comics information (and perhaps someday comic "books" themselves) may expand fandom while making it less devoted. More likely, though, only established comics readers will find the websites and newsgroups that will be a necessary part of participating in future comics culture, thereby maintaining the borders between comic book fans and the rest of the American popular culture audience.

6

Conclusion

Creating Comic Book Culture

For a number of years, I did not tell anyone I read comic books. Whether this was the fault of the comic books or my own insecurities, I am not sure, but during my four years as an undergraduate, I kept my comic book–reading past a secret from my classmates. Sometimes, I would sneak off to a bookstore near campus to check out what was happening in the latest issue of *Avengers* or *Justice League*, but I did so only when I knew no one would see me. "It's time to be an adult," I must have thought to myself, ashamed of my continuing need to look at the latest issues. "It's time to get rid of this nasty habit." And so I did, selling most of the comic books I accumulated over the course of the previous twelve years and storing the rest in a dark corner of my closet.

Up until that time, comic books — especially superhero comics — had been a central part of my identity. To this day, I can vividly (if not necessarily correctly) remember the first comic book I ever owned and, like many fans, I can fondly recall the first time I entered a comic book shop, amazed at the boxes and boxes of back issues, shocked to find not one but two new issues of *Uncanny X-Men*. Despite social skills which truly left something to be desired, my childhood was never boring because of the comic books I could read over and over again. I filled my spare time categorizing my collection by character, back cover advertisement, date, or title, tracing comic book images, drawing comic book characters, and, with a little help from a couple of my cousins and one of my sisters, acting out comic book stories as little radio plays that the four of us would tape on our family's cassette recorder. My grandmother once even sent me a card suggesting that I have a happy birthday "with my comic book friends." By junior high school, I had become a discerning comic book reader, writing the titles of my recommended reading list on my lunch bags, hoping someone would be so interested, so overwhelmed by my good taste that they would instantly decide to be my friend. I took comic books seriously, once even writing a fan letter to Marvel's *Avengers,* asking the creators to do more with the character Wonder Man (an insecure strongman plagued by self-doubt, especially in the midst of battle) and questioning the editors' choice of artists. For a time, I even had hopes of being a comic book writer. Using my various superhero, *Star Trek,* and other action figures—okay, dolls—I would create convoluted stories that resembled those in my favorite titles. A couple of times, I even photographed some of the action, resulting in my own homemade photo-comics.

But after my junior year of high school, I stopped. The titles and creators in which I had been interested were changing, and moving from the Chicago suburbs to a small Illinois town suddenly made comics much harder to find. One day, I decided to stop reading comics—something I never thought I would do. And, for a number of years, I was happy with my decision. I was almost completely oblivious to what was going on in the publishing format that had been so important to my childhood, but it did not seem to matter.

In his introduction to *Textual Poachers,* Henry Jenkins writes that his love for the media fandom surrounding *Star Trek* and other science fiction programs inspired him to go to graduate school and work to become a credentialed academic (4–5). For me, the process worked in the opposite direction: graduate school brought me back to comic books. I took a course in applied ethnography for which I interviewed an Iowa City comic book writer and artist. Of course, I said to myself, to write about this subject, I need to familiarize myself with what is happening in comics. Soon, I found myself in the local comic book store, buying new issues of old friends (like *X-Men*) and comics I could not have even imagined in 1985 (such as *Hate* and *Eightball*). I found a world with which I had lost touch, a world that I realized I liked a lot. Naturally, what I liked had changed (Harvey Pekar's autobiographical *American Splendor,* for example, was a new favorite), but it was still comics. Five comics quickly became ten, then twenty, then thirty, until now I probably own more comic books than I did when I was seventeen years old, before I began selling my first collection.

So, yes, I am a comic book reader. Like Scott Bukatman in "X-Bodies: The Torment of the Mutant Superhero," I feel the need to admit to my comics-reading past. Part of the reason for doing so is to establish the source of some of my authority, at least among other comics fans. From my own experience, reading something about comics by someone with limited knowledge of or experience in the field automatically turns off comic book fans. I hope that my admission here and everything written up to this point will secure the validity of my work, at least among comics fans.

The other reason for explaining my history with comics is more important. "Writing as a fan about fan culture poses certain potential risks for the academic critic," Jenkins explains, "yet it also facilitates certain understandings and forms of access impossible through other positionings" (*Poachers* 6). Being a fan has helped me establish trust with correspondents and interview subjects who would probably be more willing to share fan perspectives with someone like me than with someone from outside the culture. Conversely, there is the danger of getting too close to the material about which I write, of being too far inside the culture to write about it fairly. In many ways, comics culture is a closed system with firm boundaries between itself and the rest of the world. This system influences how comic books can be studied. The standard narrative of the history of the format is based primarily on the work of fans, and that perspective has been hard to escape. The demonization of Fredric Wertham in histories and in the comics themselves is one example. Scholars such as Amy Kiste Nyberg are now beginning to reevaluate his work and its impact on the industry, but the fan-scholar must first overcome a lifetime of negative portrayals of the psychiatrist. Wertham is truly more complex than fans believe, with his often progressive politics and frequent criticism of mass culture. Fan histories do not or cannot examine these aspects of his work. Even the periodizing of comics history — into nostalgic "golden" and "silver" ages — emerges from fan traditions. In fact, these terms seem to describe the monetary value of old comics to collectors more than to make a statement about quality.

Of course, comics scholars could develop alternate periodizations, but even such divisions would come out of the experience of longtime readers, such as those more familiar with the brief renaissance of the late 1980s than with the superhero comics of the 1940s. This reimagining might involve a new "golden age" in which revisionary superhero comics such as *Watchmen* were central works, but again, such periodization emerges from fans' familiarity with the genre and the literate awareness of how these comics work as critiques of their predecessors. The fan-scholar must be aware of these kinds of issues and the inevitable risks that are involved with coming from inside comics culture. But there is also the danger of being too far outside to be able to see the culture's nuances or to understand and sympathize with how comic book readers use their cultural products. Insider interpretations of this culture may be problematic and subjective, but the few outsider perspectives on comic books — Wertham's *Seduction of the Innocent* is a classic example — are perhaps even more flawed by denying consumers the power to explain how they use their favored texts. Other outsiders seeking to write about comics culture may simply be overwhelmed by it, while an insider — or someone like myself trying to walk the line between insider and outsider — should be able to negotiate its complexity to focus on what is important.

The truth of the matter is that there really is no objective insider or outsider view of comics culture. In a situation such as this one, being in between — being a fan-scholar with an understanding of the worlds both within comics culture and outside of it — might be the best alternative. These boundaries have caused some problems, however. Just as comics culture is a closed system, so too is the comics industry, a phenomenon that explains the general lack of economic and marketing data in this work. At the same time, my desire to maintain some semblance of objectivity meant that I could not establish the contacts with writers and artists that would have allowed me to include their perspectives on comics culture.

Evaluating this culture, however, remains difficult. As a fan, I know that comic book culture can enrich the lives of the people involved in it. For myself, coming back to comics and discovering communities of people with whom I could talk about comics — whether those communities are made up of fellow Daydreams customers or academics interested in the format and its meanings — has added something to my life. Comic book culture has given me a sense of belonging and even a desire for activism, to persuade more Americans to take comic books seriously. As a scholar, though, I realize that this culture might not be seen as being as authentic as, for example, an ethnic culture with a long history. In fact, comics culture might be seen as superficial or even troubling. Critics might point to comics culture as part of a larger trend toward communities based on affinity groups or the "lifestyle enclaves" described in Robert Bellah and his coauthors' *Habits of the Heart*. Some critics might argue that these close-knit groups contribute to American society's movement away from more traditional cultures or represent a shift toward selfish individualism and away from community values. Some commentators have asserted the opposite, that affinity groups are not a cause but rather a symptom of a larger problem. James Fallows, for example, in his 1996 book *Breaking the News: How the Media Undermine American Democracy*, argues that communities organized around the Internet, talk radio, or even comics suggest a loss of engagement with public life on the part of the general populace. These new communities, Fallows writes, "allowed people to think that they could play some part in a larger activity. . . . They made people believe that the outcome of this activity would make some difference in their lives" (242). According to this view, being involved in comic book culture, talk radio culture, or the home-schooling movement is a way to make up for what is missing in national public life.

Critics might contend that this phenomenon makes Americans narrow their vision of life. Now, such critics argue, Americans are more interested in finding fellowship with people who share religious beliefs or political persuasions or who maintain common musical or cultural preferences and less interested in interacting with society as a whole. These new kinds of Americans would rather participate in a forum on the Internet about their favorite television program than in a political debate or campaign. The communities with which they are concerned are national, not local, but are also isolated, with members scattered throughout the country. Unfortunately, critics say, these affinity group members have little concern for people outside their own group.

To be sure, this argument has some validity. Alternative comic books in particular are not really part of mass culture and could more accurately be described as artisanal or folk culture. Many alternative creators are not interested in communicating with the general American audience and instead are content to tell stories to the small numbers of people who have access to and interest in their comics. At the same time, though, these people are not interested only in comics; they have lives and interests outside of comics culture, sometimes including American public life. I find myself in a similar situation as I want to relate comics culture to American culture but still look at it as a unique entity. As a scholar of America, I want to look critically at comic book culture and see how it represents larger trends that can be applied to the world beyond the comic book shop. At the same time, though, I also want to respect the ways in which comics readers use their medium, which means not judging them or their culture by some sort of outside criteria of value. In trying to walk the line between insider and outsider, I have strived to do both. Americans can learn important lessons from comic book culture, in part because it has an authenticity that can be seen as long as scholars are willing to judge it on its own terms. The main purpose of this project, though, is descriptive, as I work to demonstrate how a relatively long-lived affinity group — readers of comic books — has developed into an authentic and complex culture of its own.

A basic division between mainstream and alternative comic readers — and their particular aesthetic standards — helps to create different reading communities, but others also exist within the culture. Many readers openly call themselves fans and are devoted to particular titles, companies, genres, or creators. Other readers are best characterized as collectors or speculators, with many of the latter derisively called fanboys. The presence of these different reading communities and the relatively impermeable boundaries between them begs the question of whether there is something that can actually be seen as comic book culture. There are certainly some important differences between alternative fans and mainstream speculators, between snobbish readers of the *Comics Journal* and fanboys who gobble up *Wizard* every month. But there are also some important similarities, especially in terms of their understanding of the language of comics. Like the larger American culture, though, comics culture is a multiculture — an amalgamation of different cultures and communities that is unified by something fundamental, either from within or from without. In comic book culture, that fundamental something is a devotion to and appreciation of the comics medium, which nearly all Americans outside of this culture lack.

The diversity of comics culture means that individual readers and reading communities can be positioned at different locations within it. At the center are longtime readers, men or women who have spent most of their lifetimes reading comics, from the most mainstream superhero books to the most alternative minicomics. These readers have the critical language to talk about comics in the same way that others talk about film or traditional fiction, but these ideal comics readers also remember what it was like to read comics as a child. Nearby are the fans turned professionals, who have turned their hobby into a life's work. Other reading communities can be positioned moving away from this core, where comics have saturated fans' lives, to the periphery, where comics are just another form of entertainment. In the world of comics, though, the periphery is narrow and the core is deep. This arrangement differs greatly from that of the audiences of other culture-forming media, where many, if not most, of those involved are fans only during the act of consumption.

On the most basic level, comic books help to define and limit this culture. All of them use the particular language of comics that Scott McCloud began to chart in *Understanding Comics.* This comics literacy is limited to comic book readers, automatically turning away potential readers unfamiliar with this language. Other comics rely on readers' knowledge of the superhero genre for their impact. Some books allude to or parody other well-known comics, demanding that readers have some knowledge of the original referent. Other comics comment on the world of comic book fans: the collector mentality, comic shops, and comic book conventions. Nearly all comics, both mainstream and alternative, from *X-Men* to *Love and Rockets,* rely on a readers' knowledge of past continuity, without which many stories can be completely incomprehensible. In many ways, these fannish comics flatter their readers by reminding them that they hold this special knowledge lacked by most of the population. This flattery then helps to cement the devotion to comics while giving readers a common culture.

Fan involvement is also central to this culture (see fig. 29). Comic book conventions give fans and collectors a chance to find fellowship with like-minded compatriots. Conventions offer fans a setting where they can feel comfortable indulging their love of comics, where they are praised instead of mocked for their knowledge of the culture. Letters pages give readers an official place for debate and discussion where fans can praise or criticize titles and creators, involve themselves in events of or issues raised by stories, and even find outlets for their creative ambitions. Fanzines have allowed readers the same kinds of outlets, albeit in a nonofficial venue. These publications demonstrate comics fans' passion for their favorite media products. Most fanzines are not published to make a profit but to allow editors, writers, and publishers to share their love of comics. This motivation also leads to comics-themed pages on the World Wide Web. Other forms of electronic interaction, such as chat rooms and newsgroups, provide readers opportunities to converse with their fellows, occasionally in real time. As always, though, the boundaries between different kinds of fans, and especially between fans and nonfans, have central importance.

These boundaries, in fact, have helped to create comic book culture and the specific reading communities within it. One of the most important of these boundaries remains the one between mainstream and alternative readers. Most alternative readers are simply not interested in mainstream stories of superheroes, and many alternative fans do not want to support cor-

Fig. 29 Ronnie, Spike, and the rest of Zot's friends participate in comic book culture by creating their own stories and by engaging in superhero role-playing games (*Zot!* #31 [May 1990]: 9; © and ™ 1998 Scott McCloud).

porate products—Marvel's and DC's comics. Fans of self-published comics, especially minicomics, believe that there are important differences—both aesthetic and ideological—between the mainstream and the alternative (Doherty 27). Mainstream, fanboyish readers might value a comic book for the fight scenes or for the hero's ingenuity or bad attitude. Older mainstream fans might be interested in a comic that turns the superhero genre on its head or might favor a clear art style or one that emphasizes bodies in action over emotional subtlety. Alternative fans might prefer a comic that speaks to them personally, that achieves the creator's individual vision, or that features a challenging art style (much in the way a reader of contemporary postmodern literature might value an enigmatic writing style). Alternative readers do not appreciate the qualities of the *Avengers* or *Aquaman,* but mainstream readers do.

In fact, for many die-hard alternative-comics readers, the mainstream is a source of humor, an easy target for mockery. This kind of attitude can even be found on occasion in the *Comics Journal.* A column called "Viva La Comix!" frequently pokes fun at the silliness, bad writing, and dishonesty of mainstream comics and their publishers. Sometimes, the *Journal* aims at its more mainstream competitor, the *Comics Buyer's Guide,* for example, printing four pages of fake letters meant to mimic and parody those commonly found in the *Guide* ("Oh, No!"). The snobbishness that this feature epitomizes is one of the reasons why many mainstream and independent comics readers avoid the *Comics Journal.* The magazine's publishers and editors have created a boundary that is difficult to cross.

To be sure, mainstream fans have also erected walls between themselves and alternative comics. Sometimes, this process happens with little consideration, as some mainstream readers (and apparently the people who manage the shops they patronize) are simply oblivious to the existence of other kinds of comics. For others, reading mainstream comics is a conscious choice. Many mainstream readers are devoted to their favorite comics out of nostalgia, because the publications elicit memories of childhood that *Hate* or *Minimum Wage* do not conjure. Other readers do not want to be challenged by alternative comics' adult images and themes. All of these phenomena help to create a divided culture, with mainstream and alternative readers in opposite camps and fans of independent comics (and those willing to read any kind of comic) caught in the cross fire. The two groups do have some common knowledge and skills (that is, the basics of comics literacy), but the very different reasons for reading comics and the different kinds of comics they read have created these distinctive reading communities.

Even more central, though, is the boundary between comics readers and people who do not read comics. Most estimates claim between five hundred thousand and two million regular comic book readers in the United States. Some of the millions of Americans this figure does not include simply do not understand comics: "It's sometimes amazing to hand a comic page to someone who doesn't read them and watch what they do with it," artist David Mazzuchelli explained in a *Comics Journal* interview. "I've known people to take what we would think of as a standard six-panel-grid page, two, two, and two, read the upper left-hand panel, finish that, and go down to the middle left-hand panel, and then want to go down from that, and then up to the right-hand side" (Brayshaw 62–63).

Beyond this basic problem of lack of experience, many people simply do not understand fans' desire to purchase, read, and collect comics. Fan Richard Lupoff's novel, *The Comic Book Killer* (1989), relies for suspense in part on the main character's ignorance of comic book culture. Throughout the beginning of the novel, insurance investigator Hobart Lindsey encounters a variety of different kinds of fans, but he still does not understand why they are interested in comic books. Finally, he asks comic shop owner Jack Glessner and his partner about the phenomenon: "What's so interesting about comic books? I've looked at some. I used to read 'em when I was a little kid, and that makes sense to me, but why should grown adults care about them? They're garbage! Kids like 'em because they're colorful and exciting, but you're two intelligent men. Why?" Glessner answers, "I guess it only matters if you grew up on comics, like I did. Jesus, I used to wait for the new *Justice League* and *X-Men* like they were the word of God. I knew every character, every story. I could tell you who wrote and drew every adventure, what villains they fought. Everything. Everything. . . . They're my past, do you see that Lindsey? . . . I don't want those old comics to go on the junk heap. I want kids to get 'em and save 'em and love 'em. I don't want 'em to go extinct. If they do, my past is gone" (124–25).

One reason Lindsey might not understand the culture of comic books is the boundary formed by its bad reputation. Quite frankly, most Americans view comic books with contempt, especially when read by adults. Adult fans and collectors are seen as geeks and worse. Reading material supposedly aimed at children is somehow seen as a sign of psychological maladjustment or arrested development. And reading comics clearly aimed at adults does not sit any better with the noncomics segment of the population. Images that would be fine in a contemporary novel (such as sexual relations between consenting adults) often shock novice comics readers, sometimes even prompting cries of pornography. Truly pornographic comics can even result in imprisonment for creators and/or retailers selling the comics, even though video stores with X-rated films are tolerated. Going back at least as far as Wertham's *Seduction of the Innocent,* comic books' negative connotations in society at large have helped to isolate readers and mold the culture.

The comic book industry is not blameless, however. The rise of the direct market for comics in the 1980s has helped to remove them from the daily lives of most Americans by taking comics out of drugstores and off newsstands. As a result, some Americans are probably only dimly aware that comic books still exist, let alone continue to represent an industry worth hundreds of millions of dollars per year. For fans, though, the direct market and the specialty shops brought comic books to a central location where devoted readers could find all the titles they wanted. It also helped to facilitate the growth of alternative comics and the increase in adult comic readership. According to comics scholar Mark C. Rogers, though, the direct market and the comic shops meant an end to comic books as a mass medium. Publishers now sell their products to a narrow fan audience made up of devoted readers, turning comic books into a niche medium focused on mainstream readers and collectors ("Silver Age"). Thus, in turn, comics are kept away from the general public, adding to the boundary between readers and nonreaders.

Although some people in the industry (especially alternative creators and publishers who believe, with good reason, that their products can appeal more to an intelligent, literary audience than to fans of superhero comics) are trying to break down this comics-noncomics boundary by bringing their books out of the direct market and into traditional bookstores (Morales 50), the fact remains that comics fans and comic book culture are isolated from the rest of American culture. The impermeable boundaries between those inside and outside of comic book culture are clearly different from the boundaries around other forms of popular culture. The boundaries around baseball culture, for example, are extremely permeable and allow for different levels of involvement. Casual fans might watch a few games and know a few players but still get excited about the play-offs and World Series. More involved baseball fans might follow their favorite teams in the paper, watch numerous games on television, and attend a few games a year. Another level of fan might have season tickets; scout the team's minor league prospects; participate in a fantasy baseball league; make regular pilgrimages to the National Baseball Hall of Fame in Cooperstown, New York; and/or belong to the Society for American Baseball Research. The same is true for other forms of popular culture, from *Star Trek* to punk rock, but comic book culture is different. The impermeable boundaries make it hard for potential casual readers to become interested. As a result, comic book culture is filled with devoted but isolated readers. Their sense of being under attack, of the industry struggling in comparison to everything from motion pictures to computer games, leads to the construction of even stronger boundaries between fans and nonfans as a kind of defense mechanism.

Many fans, to be sure, prefer the situation as it is and enjoy being misunderstood. Many Americans find a certain pleasure in obscurity, whether it is finding a secret fishing hole or collecting every compact disc released by an obscure Los Angeles punk band. Some indie rock fans have been known to end their relationship with an artist or band once a certain level of popularity or mainstream acceptance has been achieved. Some of this behavior results from a fear that the performers will sell out, but another cause is the loss of the feeling of personal connection that obscurity brings. Comic book fans thus have feelings of ambivalence. Many fans simply like doing something that relatively few Americans do and enjoy the challenges of trying to collect their favorite comics. Some even like the fact that reading comics is often seen as vaguely transgressive. At the same time, though, many of these same readers would like to see comic books (especially their favorite titles) achieve wider acceptance in American culture. Alternative fans debate how comics such as *American Splendor* and *Naughty Bits* can be sold in bookstores with other examples of contemporary literature so that intelligent readers might be interested enough to pick up an issue or a graphic novel. Mainstream fans debate whether the latest comics-themed film project will bring masses of Americans back to comic books. At the same time, though, these fans often criticize newcomers attracted to comic books because of a film or animated television series who lack the necessary background and have not paid their comics dues.

Efforts to create a general public acceptance of comic books have been unsuccessful, leading to continued isolation and the continued creation of comic book culture by fans and professionals. Fans have developed their own languages, mythology, and jokes. "Can you speak fanboy?" asks Ray Mescallado. "If I make a joke about Herb Trimpe or Alex Saviuk, or refer to the Ice Cream Soldier or Willie Lumpkin, would you laugh or nod your head?" ("Riddle"). Fans have demonized Wertham and valorized William Gaines, making them into Manichaean figures, battling for the future of comics. Fans have helped to create the future of the Legion of Super-Heroes and to inspire the revival of some of DC's golden age characters. Fans have developed their own interpretations of *Watchmen, Sandman, Cerebus,* and *Love and Rockets.* Fans have made their own superhero costumes and altered store-bought action figures to depict their favorite characters rather than the ones the toy manufacturers created. Fans have written, edited, and published fanzines, complete with amateur comic strips, and created web pages devoted to their favorite characters and creators. Fans and collectors have developed their own often very different measures of what is important or good, and many have refused to buy ill-conceived or badly produced comics. Fans talk about these aesthetic standards everywhere — in comic shops, at conventions, in newsgroups and chat rooms, in letters pages. Fans have become professionals and in that position have created stories and characters of particular interest to members of the culture. Fans have created reflexive comics about the business of comics, their history, and their fans (see fig. 30). In fact, the only type of fan that has not taken part in this active creation of culture has been fanboys, which is why the rest of comic book culture has viewed that type (its handful of positive associations notwithstanding) with such derision.

I have described the elements important to the uniqueness of this culture, but the element of participation that pervades it is most central. Participation in comic book culture begins early, as even the youngest readers find themselves playing superheroes, imagining themselves as the Hulk, Batman, or Wonder Woman. Young fans read with a sense of identification, seeing themselves as the heroes. Eventually, as comics fans age, they put these fantasies down on paper as short stories, role-playing game scenarios, or actual comics. Some fans satisfy their impulse to participate in comic book culture through fanzines, which might publish amateur comics or reviews. Other fans write letters to their favorite titles; if published, the letters become part of the comic book itself. Some fans take participation so far that they begin publishing their own comics, often as minicomics. Many creators

Fig. 30 Reflexive stories and art are important parts of comic book culture. Top: Artists Greg Hyland and Brian LeMay allude to the cover of the first issue of *Fantastic Four* and parody John Byrne's repeated use of it (*Lethargic Comics* #3 [March 1994]; by Greg Hyland and Brian LeMay, © 1998 Lethargic Comics); bottom: Dan Clowes mocks Stan Lee and the Marvel rhetoric about the importance of the company's comics ("Young Dan Pussey," *Eightball* #1 [October 1989]: 25; © Daniel G. Clowes).

actively encourage this undertaking: Matt Feazell's *Understanding Mini-Comics: The Art and Science of Stick Figures* (1993) shows readers how easy it is to tell stories through comics. Writer/artist/editor Sarah Dyer urges her readers to lead active lives with a do-it-yourself ethos: "It's great to read/listen to/watch other people's creative output, but it's even cooler to do it yourself. Don't think you can do comics? Try anyway, even if they're just for yourself!" (*Action Girl Comics* #1 [October 1994]: inside cover). This kind of grassroots participation can lead comics fans to become professional writers, artists, critics, or even scholars.

This book begins an analysis of comic book culture. Future research will focus on specific reading communities, from fans of *Legion of Super-Heroes* to homosexual comic book readers, from serious comic book collectors, investing thousands of dollars on an issue from the 1940s, to prospective creators hoping to produce the masterpieces of the twenty-first century. Another project might compare comic book fans to those of *Star Trek*, science fiction, role-playing games, or sports teams. More thorough analyses of letters pages and fanzines are needed, as are interpretations of reflexive comics that utilize new literary and cultural theories. Other scholarship will focus on production and distribution, the aspects of commodity culture not examined in depth here. But most future directions of comics scholarship, like those of the comic books themselves, are still uncharted. Faced with challenges such as a shrinking market, competition from computer games, the possibilities of digital comics, consolidation of distributors, and others, the comic book industry is on the verge of changes that could alter it and its audience forever. As these changes take place, what needs to be studied will change, too.

All of these projects will teach something, not just about comic books and their readers but also about American life in general—just as this book does. The fact that this comics culture is unique to the United States (and Canada) is certainly significant. In Japan and Europe, where the medium is much more widely accepted, comics culture is very different, with its members experiencing much less of a sense of embattlement. Perhaps in these countries, comics culture does not even exist as a distinct entity, having been integrated into the broader popular culture. The study of American comic book readers, then, can illustrate the importance of cultural hierarchies, the role of commodities in the creation of culture, and the ways in which different kinds of cultural texts are evaluated by critics, scholars, and the public at large in the United States. On the most basic level, this work can demonstrate how important popular culture can be to its devoted consumers. Comics culture demonstrates how media audiences do not merely interact with their favored texts to create interpretations. At the center, active participation creates worlds where fans and readers can feel at home and among friends, complete and fulfilled. For comic book readers, these texts and the culture and people surrounding them are important: fans truly care about the medium and the industry. It might be easy to dismiss comic books as escapist trash beneath the notice of most scholars and critics, but it is certainly harder to dismiss the sincere and very active culture surrounding comics. For good or bad, comics culture has become a part (albeit a small part) of American culture, but what is most significant is that the people involved find it personally satisfying.

Another important lesson of this work is that cultural formations or "scenes" can evolve out of almost anything. Judging these cultures can be tricky, but if evaluations are based on participation, comics culture is indeed healthy. In some ways, the productivity of comics culture — with fans helping to create the culture through web pages, fanzines, letters to the editor, amateur comics, and becoming professionals — makes it a model for cultures in general. Perhaps American culture would be healthier if more Americans felt that they were active participants and not merely consumers of it. As Fallows argues, American public, political culture would be more vibrant if more people were encouraged to participate and fewer were lulled into a superficial cynicism by the media. The culture of comics in the United States may not be diverse, and it may be plagued by an important conflict between mainstream and alternative readers, but it has encouraged multiple levels of cultural engagement. If the broader American culture could do so, perhaps there would be no need for lifestyle enclaves and affinity groups. Perhaps, then, comics culture can teach Americans ways to reintegrate cultural life into an active, participatory whole.

Notes

Chapter 1

1. Nearly every comic book shop offers regular patrons a reservation service through which the customers' favorite titles — their "pull lists" — are saved when each week's delivery of new comics arrives. This practice benefits both the shop and the readers. Every month, regular patrons receive catalogs from the shop's distributors. The customers can then pick out what they want from the catalog and make any changes to their pull lists. (Comics appear in catalogs months before becoming available and sometimes even months before being completed.) Pull lists give shop owners a good idea of how many copies of a particular comic book to order, which is important because shop owners pay for the comics they order, albeit at a substantial discount. In exchange for the discount, shop owners keep every copy they order, unlike unsold magazines, which can usually be returned to distributors. Accurate ordering based on pull lists and knowledge of patrons results in less difficult-to-sell overstock. Consumers receive two primary benefits. First, avid readers or collectors are assured of getting every issue of their favorite publications. Second, most shops pass along part of their discount, thereby saving regulars as much as 25 percent on their purchases. The practice also makes the regular customers feel well treated and special, which, in turn, also benefits the shop through loyalty and continued patronage.

2. Although readers can still subscribe to their favorite titles, the convenience of comic shops and even specialty mail-order houses (and the proliferation of limited series and specials) has certainly made subscriptions less important for all concerned. However, companies like DC still advertise subscriptions. One such advertisement, published in the first issue of the Vertigo series *Terminal City* (#1 [July 1996], after p. 19), says that "all comics are mailed in weather-resistant polybags with protective backing boards" and that subscribers will receive "special discounts on hardcover books, trade paperbacks and other DC Comics merchandise."

3. Authorities on comic book collecting are very specific about the proper way to handle and store comics. The *Overstreet Comic Book Price Guide,* for example, includes a paragraph explaining the four steps for properly handling comics and specifies strategies for their preservation: "Store books in a dark, cool place with

relative humidity of 40–75% and a temperature as cool as possible.... Air conditioning is recommended. Do not use regular cardboard boxes, since most contain harmful acids. Use acid-free boxes instead. Seal books in Mylar or other suitable wrappings or bags and store them in the proper containers or cabinets to protect them from heat, excessive dampness, ultraviolet light (use tungsten filament lights), polluted air, and dust.... Plastic bags should be changed every two to three years, since most contain harmful acids" (Overstreet A-28).

Chapter 2

1. The most prominent example of these attacks on Wertham and the other critics is the December 1949 special issue of the *Journal of Educational Sociology*, which was devoted entirely to comic books and their much-discussed effects. The same journal also devoted its December 1944 issue to comic books.

2. Unlike the romance comics published by DC, Charlton, and other companies, *Our Love Story* and *My Love* were filled with advertisements that were exactly the same as those found in other comics. Whereas issues of DC's *Falling in Love* (#129 [February 1972], #140 [March–April 1973]) included ads for an advice book written by *Partridge Family* star Susan Dey, exercise equipment that promised to "add alluring curves to skinny legs," and aids for "long, beautiful nails," Marvel's *My Love* (#29 [July 1974]) included ads for Charles Atlas (the famous "Insult That Made a Man out of Mac") and karate self-defense systems along with the traditional fan features like the "Bullpen Bulletins."

3. These new titles also flooded the market, something that many fans then and since have accused Marvel of doing. In fact, some scholars have suggested that in the mid-1970s Marvel engaged in this practice to squeeze a new company, Atlas Comics, out of the market. Atlas had attracted some prominent creators, like Archie Goodwin, Wally Wood, Steve Ditko, and Howard Chaykin, and the company had been started by Lee's former boss at Marvel, Martin Goodman, and Lee's brother, Larry Leiber. After a few issues of standard adventure comics, Atlas Comics went out of business, perhaps because of Marvel's actions.

4. Those nine titles were *Fantastic Four, Amazing Spider-Man, The Avengers, Thor, Tales to Astonish* (first starring Ant-Man and the Wasp, later the Hulk and the Sub-Mariner in separate features), *Tales of Suspense* (starring Iron Man and Captain America), *The Uncanny X-Men, Strange Tales* (starring the Human Torch and Dr. Strange, with Nick Fury later taking the Torch's place), and *Sgt. Fury and His*

Howling Commandos. In 1968, a new arrangement with DC (which had previously distributed Marvel comics) allowed Marvel to "publish as many books as the market would bear" (Daniels 1991, 139), and the number of titles the company published quickly jumped to twenty-two.

Chapter 3

1. Amos and Gaiman apparently have a close friendship. The collection *Sandman: A Game of You* is dedicated to her, and lyrics from her song "Tear in Your Hand" (from her 1991 disc *Little Earthquakes*) are included in a chapter of *Sandman: Brief Lives*. There, Amos sings, "Me and Neil'll be hangin' out with the Dream King." The credits for that song include one for "Ranz" as "Sandman Comic Supplier." Fans have also speculated that Amos might have been the model for Delirium of the Endless. On her disc *Boys for Pele*, Amos gives special thanks to Neil Gaiman. While promoting that album, she mentioned *Sandman* during interviews on MTV's *120 Minutes* and Public Radio International's *World Cafe*.

2. A letter from Eric Reynolds of Fountain Valley, California (*Cerebus* #112–13 [July–August 1988]: 19), perfectly expressed this view: "Dear Mr. Sim, I like your book. I dislike you. I really like your book. I dislike you even more. In fact, I think you're such an asshole that I have stopped reading *Cerebus*. Now, 'big fucking deal,' you might say, 'I lost a shithead reader.' Unfortunately, I am but one of many. I manage a comic book shop, and I know of at least ten people who boycott your book, a book they once enjoyed, because they know what a true fuck-up you are. Now you know why *Cerebus* sells like shit."

3. Beginning in the mid-1970s, toy manufacturer Mego began producing eight-inch-tall superhero dolls. The company started with the DC characters from the *Superfriends* animated television series (Superman, Batman and Robin, Aquaman, and Wonder Woman), as well as Tarzan, but later the line of toys expanded to include Marvel characters (at first Spider-Man, the Hulk, and Captain America and later the Fantastic Four, Thor, Conan the Barbarian, Iron Man, and the Falcon), villains, and other DC characters (including Shazam!, Green Arrow, and the Teen Titans). The company also produced figures based on *Planet of the Apes, Star Trek,* the *Wizard of Oz,* and *Ivanhoe*. All the dolls were made of molded plastic, with most having the same bodies but different heads. Their costumes were removable, meaning that the smaller parts—gloves and boots especially—would inevitably get lost. Some figures, including Thor, Captain America, and Conan, even had the

same weapons as their comic book counterparts. The Mego superheroes are now collectors' items, with mint versions still in their boxes worth substantial sums.

Chapter 4

1. Perhaps because of DC's traditionally very different strategies for attracting readers, parodies were never as important to that company. DC's attempts at parodies were usually mild or ineffective. In the mid-1960s, the *Inferior Five* was clearly meant to mock Marvel's *Fantastic Four,* but the parody never went much beyond the title. In the mid-1980s, DC transformed its long-running *Justice League of America* into a lighthearted superteam comic. Fans were divided about whether the comic was an appropriate place for humor, but the series provided readers an alternative to the always serious, constantly universe shaking adventures of groups such as the Avengers, X-Men, and New Titans. Another series from around the same time, *Ambush Bug,* was a more Marvel-style parody, but the character was limited to a miniseries, a handful of specials, and a few guest appearances.

2. The last page might work slightly against this reading. When Sheldon asks his assistant, Marcia, to photograph him and his wife, he also asks the local newspaper boy to appear in the picture. The boy — Danny Ketch — is reluctant but finally agrees. Sheldon calls him a "nice, ordinary boy," but devoted Marvel fans know that when he grows up he becomes the superhero Ghost Rider. Perhaps Busiek's point is that fans can never totally escape the world of superheroes, comics, and Marvel (*Marvels* #4 [April 1994]: 45).

Chapter 5

1. As of this writing, I have attended three comic book conventions: the 1995 Chicago Comicon, the 1996 River City Comic Book Convention in St. Louis, and the 1996 Mid-Ohio Con in Columbus. Much of the convention descriptions that follow is based on these experiences, along with reports of other conventions published in comics magazines such as *Comics Journal, Comic Buyers' Guide,* and *Wizard.* Accounts of trips to conventions also appear regularly on the World Wide Web, especially in newsgroups and mailing lists.

2. Professional writers and artists are often ambivalent about this process of getting signatures and meeting fans. William Messner-Loebs's *Bliss Alley* (#1 [July 1997]: 29–31) includes a "Guide to Convention and Signing Etiquette" in which he

advises fans to "think about what you are doing" when asking for autographs and conversing with pros. Professionals, he explains, are often not paid to attend conventions and frequently have a lot on their minds while signing books and talking to fans. As a result, he suggests, fans should not try to be cute by verbally attacking or teasing writers or artists. Heeding this and other similar advice would certainly help interactions between fans and pros, which can, on occasion, be less than friendly. Some artists and writers are well known among fans for being rude, while other creators are famous for their willingness to do specific sketches and their general amiability. Messner-Loebs (a writer and artist who has worked in both mainstream and independent comics) explains that he likes conventions, but many professionals clearly do not and attend only out of a sense of obligation or because of contractual requirements.

3. Appearing in Lee, Kirby, and Sinnott's *Fantastic Four* #48–50 (March–May 1966), the Galactus saga is one of the most beloved story lines in mainstream comics. Galactus is a cosmic entity who devours planets for his sustenance, and Earth is next in line. Galactus sends his herald, the Silver Surfer, to Earth to prepare the world for its destruction. The Fantastic Four try to fight the Surfer, but Galactus arrives and begins assembling his machines that will suck the life energy out of the planet. As the group gradually realizes there is no way to stop Galactus, Silver Surfer meets the Thing's blind girlfriend, Alicia Masters, and begins to learn about humanity's inherent nobility. Another cosmic being, the Watcher (a member of a race of cosmic beings devoted to observing the development of intelligent races across the universe) uncharacteristically gets involved, sending the Human Torch to get the only weapon that will destroy Galactus. Because of Alicia, the Surfer has decided that humanity and the Earth must be allowed to live, so he attacks Galactus. Meanwhile, the Torch returns with the Ultimate Nullifier, a handheld weapon with enough power to destroy the galaxy and Galactus with it. Mr. Fantastic threatens to use the weapon, and Galactus gives up. He and the Watcher briefly debate the fate of the Earth, with the Watcher urging Galactus to see "the seed of grandeur within their frail, human frames." He agrees to find another world to devour, but before he leaves he exiles the Silver Surfer to the Earth and warns the Fantastic Four that humans must "be ever mindful of [their] promise of greatness!" (*Fantastic Four* #50 [May 1966]: 9, 10).

4. As of the summer of 1997, the comics-related newsgroups were as follows: rec.arts.comics.alternative, rec.arts.comics.creative (devoted to fan fiction about original characters), rec.arts.comics.dc.lsh (about the Legion of Super-Heroes), rec.arts.comics.dc.universe, rec.arts.comics.dc.vertigo, rec.arts.comics.elfquest, rec.arts.comics.

european, rec.arts.comics.info (for news and FAQs), rec.arts.comics.marketplace, rec.arts.comics.marvel.universe, rec.arts.comics.marvel.xbooks, rec.arts.comics.misc, rec.arts.comics.other-media (about comic books transformed into television programs, films, music, computer games, and so forth), rec.arts.comics.reviews, and rec.arts.comics.strips. For a history of these groups, see Rogers, "Virtual Fans."

Bibliography

Abbott, Lawrence L. "Comic Art: Characteristics and Potentialities of a Narrative Medium." *Journal of Popular Culture* 19 (spring 1986): 155–76.

Action Comics #1 (June 1938), Detective Comics [DC Comics].

Bacon-Smith, Camille. *Enterprising Women: Television Fandom and the Creation of Popular Myth.* Philadelphia: University of Pennsylvania Press, 1992.

Bagge, Peter (w, a). "Follow That Dream." *Hate* #8 (spring 1992), Fantagraphics.

Bails, Jerry. "It's a Matter of Policy" [column]. *Alter-Ego* #1 (spring 1961), Jerry Bails: 3.

Barker, Martin. *Comics: Ideology, Power, and the Critics.* Manchester and New York: Manchester University Press, 1989.

Barker, Tom, and Gary M. Carter, producers. *The Overstreet World of Comics.* Overstreet Productions/Threshold Home Video, 1994.

Bellah, Robert, Richard Madsen, William M. Sullivan, Ann Swindler, and Steven M. Tipton. *Habits of the Heart: Individualism and Commitment in American Life.* New York: Harper and Row, 1985.

Benson, John. "The EC Fanzines: Part One: The Gelatin Years." *Squa Tront* [fanzine] #5 (1974), Jerry Weist: 38–46.

Benton, Mike. *Superhero Comics of the Golden Age: The Illustrated History.* Dallas: Taylor Publishing, 1991.

———. *Superhero Comics of the Silver Age: The Illustrated History.* Dallas: Taylor Publishing, 1991.

"The Best Comic Shops in North America." *Comics Journal* #151 (July 1992), Fantagraphics: 89–96.

Bloom, John Douglas. "Cardboard Images of the Past: Baseball Card Collecting and the Politics of Sport." Ph.D. diss., University of Minnesota, 1991.

Braun, Sol. "Shazam! Here Comes Captain Relevant!" *New York Times Magazine,* May 2, 1971, 32, 36–50, 55.

Brayshaw, Christopher. "Mazzuchelli." *Comics Journal* #194 (March 1997), Fantagraphics: 62–63.

Broertjes, Harry. *The Legion Outpost* [fanzine] #9 (1975), Little Brother Publications.

Brown, Chester. *Ed the Happy Clown: The Definitive Ed Book.* Toronto: Vortex, 1992.

Bukatman, Scott. "X-Bodies: The Torment of the Mutant Superhero." In *Uncontrollable Bodies: Testimonies of Identities and Culture,* edited by Rodney Sappington and Tyler Stallings, 92–129. Seattle: Bay Press, 1994.

Busiek, Kurt (w), and Alex Ross (a). *Marvels* #1–4 (January–April 1994), Marvel Comics.

Byrne, John (w, a). "The Doctor Is In!" *Sensational She-Hulk* #5 (September 1989), Marvel Comics.

———. "Hero." *Fantastic Four* #285 (December 1985), Marvel Comics.

———. "Interrupted Melody." *Sensational She-Hulk* #31 (September 1991), Marvel Comics.

———. "Tall Disorder." *Sensational She-Hulk* #4 (August 1989), Marvel Comics.

Captain America Comics #2 (April 1941), Timely Comics [Marvel Comics].

Chadwick, Paul. "Author's Forum" [column]. *Concrete: Think Like a Mountain* #1 (March 1996), Dark Horse Comics: 23–26.

Claremont, Chris (w), and Jim Lee (a). "Rubicon." *X-Men* #1 (October 1991), Marvel Comics.

Clowes, Dan (w, a). "The Death of Dan Pussey." *Eightball* #14 (1994), Fantagraphics: 21–26.

———. *Ghost World.* Seattle: Fantagraphics, 1998.

———. *Like a Velvet Glove Cast in Iron.* Seattle: Fantagraphics, 1994.

———. "On Sports." *Eightball* #14 (1994), Fantagraphics, 10–14.

———. "Young Dan Pussey." *Eightball* #1 (October 1989), Fantagraphics: 23–32.

"ComiCon." *New Yorker,* August 21, 1965, 23–24.

Coupland, Douglas. *Generation X: Tales for an Accelerated Culture.* New York: St. Martin's, 1991.

Crumb, Robert (w, a). "Joe Blow." In *The Complete Crumb,* edited by Gary Groth with Robert Fiore and Robert Boyd, 6:34–39. Seattle: Fantagraphics, 1991.

———. "Uncle Bob's Mid-Life Crisis." *Weirdo* #7 (1993), Last Gasp Eco-Funnies: 6–13.

Cruse, Howard. *Stuck Rubber Baby.* New York: DC Comics, 1995.

Cwiklik, Gregory. "The Inherent Limitations of the Comics Form as a Narrative Medium." *Comics Journal* #184 (February 1996), Fantagraphics: 117–20.

Daly, Steven, and Nathaniel Wice. *alt.culture: An A-to-Z Guide to the '90s — Underground, Online, and over-the-Counter.* New York: HarperCollins, 1995.

Danet, Brenda, and Tamar Katriel. "No Two Alike: Play and Aesthetics in Collecting." *Play and Culture* 2 (1989): 253–77.

Daniels, Les. *Comix: A History of Comic Books in America.* New York: Outerbridge and Dienstfrey, 1971.

———. *Marvel: Five Fabulous Decades of the World's Greatest Comics.* New York: Harry N. Abrams, 1991.

Dauphin, Gary. "To Be Young, Superpowered, and Black." *Village Voice*, May 17, 1994, 31–38.

David, Peter. "Ain't a Library!" *Overstreet's FAN*, June 1995, 31.

Davis, Alan (w, p), and Mark Farmer (i). *Justice League of America: The Nail*. New York: DC Comics, 1998.

Doherty, Brian. "The Embarrassment of Riches." *Reason*, August–September 1997, 21–27.

Dorkin, Evan (w, a). "Bring Me the Head of Boba Fett!" *Instant Piano* #3 (February 1995), Dark Horse Comics: 5–14.

———. "The Eltingville Comic-Book-Science-Fiction-Fantasy-Horror- and Role-Playing Club!" *Instant Piano* #1 (August 1994), Dark Horse Comics: 2–10.

———. "The Northwest Comix Collective!" *Dork* #6 (May 1998), Slave Labor Graphics: 19–inside cover.

Dyer, Sarah. "Introduction" [column]. *Action Girl Comics* #1 (October 1994), Slave Labor Graphics: inside cover.

Eco, Umberto. "The Myth of Superman." In *The Role of the Reader: Explorations in the Semiotics of Texts*, 107–24. Bloomington: Indiana University Press, 1979.

Eisner, Will. *The Dreamer*. Northampton, Mass.: Kitchen Sink Press, 1986.

Englehart, Steve (w), Sal Buscema (p), Frank Robbins (p), Vince Colletta (i), Joe Giella (i), Frank Giacoia (i). "Nomad: The Man without a Country." *Captain America* v1 #176–83 (August 1974–March 1975), Marvel Comics.

"Escapist Paydirt." *Newsweek*, December 27, 1943, 55–56.

Estren, Mark James. *A History of Underground Comics*. Berkeley, Calif.: Ronin, 1993.

Evanier, Mark (w), Steve Rude (p), and Mike Royer (i). "No Escape from Destiny!!!" *Mr. Miracle Special* #1 (1987), DC Comics.

Falling in Love #129 (February 1972), National Periodical Publications [DC Comics].

Falling in Love #140 (March–April 1973), National Periodical Publications [DC Comics].

Fallows, James. *Breaking the News: How the Media Undermine American Democracy*. New York: Vintage, 1996.

Famous First Editions #C-26: *Action Comics* #1 (1974), National Periodical Publications [DC Comics].

Feazell, Matt (w, a). *Cynicalman . . . The Paperback!* Baltimore: Thunder Baas Press, 1987.

———. *Understanding Mini-Comics: The Art and Science of Stick Figures* (1993), Not Available Comics.

Feiffer, Jules. *The Great Comic Book Heroes*. New York: Bonanza, 1965.

Feldstein, Al (w), and Wally Wood (a). "EC Confidential." *Weird Science* #21 (September–October 1953), EC Comics: 1–8.

Fine, Gary Alan. *Shared Fantasy: Role-Playing Games as Social Worlds.* Chicago: University of Chicago Press, 1983.

Fingerman, Bob (w, a). "Conventional Behavior." *Minimum Wage* #4 (1996), Fantagraphics.

———. *Minimum Wage, Book One.* Seattle: Fantagraphics, 1995.

Fish, Stanley. *Is There a Text in This Class?: The Authority of Interpretive Communities.* Cambridge: Harvard University Press, 1980.

Fiske, John. "The Cultural Economy of Fandom." In *The Adoring Audience: Fan Culture and Popular Media,* edited by Lisa A. Lewis, 29–45. New York and London: Routledge, 1992.

Flynn, Mike. "Xanthusian Eyes and Trommite Hearts." *Legion Outpost* [fanzine] #10 (spring 1981), Mike Flynn and Harry Broertjes: n.p.

Gaiman, Neil. "Interview with Alan Moore and Dave Gibbons." In *The New Comics,* edited by Gary Groth and Robert Fiore, 94–104. New York: Berkeley, 1988.

Gaiman, Neil (w), Chris Bachalo (p), and Mark Buckingham (i). *Death: The High Cost of Living.* New York: DC Comics, 1994.

———. *Death: The Time of Your Life.* New York: DC Comics, 1997.

Gaiman, Neil (w), Mike Dringenberg (p), and Malcolm Jones III (i). *Sandman: The Doll's House.* New York: DC Comics, 1990.

Gaiman, Neil (w), Mark Hempel (a), Richard Case (a), D'Israeli (a), Teddy Kristiansen (a), Glyn Dillon (a), Charles Vess (a), Dean Ormston (a), and Kevin Nowlan (a). *Sandman: The Kindly Ones.* New York: DC Comics, 1996.

Gaiman, Neil (w), and Dave McKean (a). *Death Talks about Life* (1994), DC Comics.

Gaiman, Neil (w), Shawn McManus (a), Colleen Doran (a), Bryan Talbot (a), George Pratt (a), Stan Woch (a), and Dick Giordano (a). *Sandman: A Game of You.* New York: DC Comics, 1993.

Gaiman, Neil (w), Jill Thompson (p), Vince Locke (i), and Dick Giordano (i). *Sandman: Brief Lives.* New York: DC Comics, 1994.

Gaiman, Neil (w), and Charles Vess (a). "The Tempest." *Sandman* #75 (March 1996), DC Comics.

Gaiman, Neil (w), and Michael Zulli (a). "The Wake: An Epilogue." *Sandman* #70–73 (September–December 1995), DC Comics.

Gaines, William (w), and George Evans (a). "An Ample Sample." *Vault of Horror* #32 (August–September 1953), EC Comics: 17–22.

Gaines, William (w), and Graham Ingels (a). "Dying to Lose Weight." *Vault of Horror* #18 (April–May 1951), EC Comics: 23–30.

Giffen, Keith (w), J. M. DeMatteis (w), Linda Medley (p), and Jose Marzan (i). "Old Glory." *Justice League America* #46 (January 1991), DC Comics.

Gilbert, Scott. "'He Said to Tell You He Had a Real Good Time': Acme Novelty Library, Vol. 1–3." *Comics Journal* #174 (February 1995), Fantagraphics: 47–48.

Gimple, Scott M. (w), and Phil Ortiz (a). "Sense and Censorability." *Simpsons Comics* #39 (1998), Bongo Comics.

Gitlin, Todd. *The Sixties: Years of Hope, Days of Rage.* New York: Bantam, 1987.

Gomez, Jeff. *Our Noise.* New York: Simon and Schuster, 1995.

Green, Robin. "Face Front! Clap Your Hands! You're on the Winning Team!" *Rolling Stone,* September 16, 1971, 29–34.

Gregory, Roberta (w, a). *A Bitch Is Born.* Seattle: Fantagraphics, 1994.

———. "Crazy Bitches." *Naughty Bits* #1 (March 1991), Fantagraphics: 1–4.

Griffith, Bill (w, a). "Pinman and the Chastiser." *Zippy Quarterly* #12 (December 1995), Fantagraphics: 1–11.

Groth, Gary. "Comics: The New Culture of Illiteracy, or Why the World Is Turning to Shit, Part 563." *Comics Journal* #152 (August 1992), Fantagraphics, 3–6.

———. "The Straight Dope from R. Crumb." *Comics Journal* #121 (April 1988), Fantagraphics: 49–120.

———. " . . . That's the Spice of Life, Bud." *Comics Journal* #152 (August 1992), Fantagraphics, 45–70.

Groth, Gary, and Alan Moore. "Mainstream Comics Have, at Best, Tenuous Virtues." *Comics Journal* #152 (August 1992), Fantagraphics: 89–100.

"A Guide to Posting on Rec.Arts.Comics.*." Website (www.bonner.rice.edu/morrow), August 1997.

Haines, Lurene. *Getting into the Business of Comics.* Livonia, Mich.: Stabur Press, 1994.

"The Hallowed Ranks of Marveldom" [column]. *Amazing Spider-Man* #68 (January 1969), Magazine Management [Marvel Comics]: 24.

Harker, Jean Gray. "Youth's Librarians Can Defeat Comics." *Library Journal* 73 (December 1, 1948): 1705–7, 1720.

Harvey, Robert C. *The Art of the Comic Book: An Aesthetic History.* Jackson: University Press of Mississippi, 1996.

Hernandez, Gilbert. *Poison River: A Love and Rockets Collection.* Seattle: Fantagraphics, 1994.

Hopkins, Mariane S., ed. *Fandom Directory* #16. Springfield, Va.: Fandata Publications, 1996.

Howe, Neil, and Bill Strauss. *13th Gen: Abort, Retry, Ignore, Fail?* New York: Vintage, 1993.

Howell, Richard, ed. *Real Love: The Best of the Simon and Kirby Romance Comics, 1940s–1950s.* Forestville, Calif.: Eclipse, 1988.

Hutcheon, Linda. "Discourse, Power, Ideology: Humanism and Postmodernism." In *Postmodernism and Contemporary Fiction,* edited by Edmund J. Smyth, 105–22. London: B. T. Batsford, 1991.

Hyland, Greg (w, a), and Brian LeMay (w, a). *Lethargic Comics* #3 (March 1994), Alpha Productions.

Immonen, Stuart (p). *Legion of Super-Heroes* v4 #49 (November 1993), DC Comics: cover.

Inge, M. Thomas. "A Chronology of the Development of the American Comic Book." In *The Overstreet Comic Book Price Guide,* 26th ed., compiled by Robert Overstreet, A96–102. New York: Avon, 1996.

"In Memoriam" [column]. *Tales from the Crypt* #46 (February–March 1955), EC Comics: inside cover.

Interlac [fanzine] #6 (April 1977), Amateur Press Association.

Interlac [fanzine] #61 (August 20, 1986), Amateur Press Association.

Jacobs, Will, and Gerard Jones. *The Comic Book Heroes from the Silver Age to the Present.* New York: Crown, 1985.

Jenkins, Henry. "'Strangers No More, We Sing': Filking and the Social Construction of the Science Fiction Fan Community." In *The Adoring Audience: Fan Culture and Popular Media,* edited by Lisa A. Lewis, 208–45. New York and London: Routledge, 1992.

———. *Textual Poachers: Television Fans and Participatory Culture.* New York and London: Routledge, 1992.

Jurgens, Dan (w, p), and Brett Breeding (i). "Doomsday!" *Superman* v2 #75 (January 1993), DC Comics.

Karasik, Paul (w), and David Mazzuchelli (a). *Paul Auster's City of Glass.* New York: Avon, 1994.

Kehoe, Gene. *It's a Fanzine* [fanzine] #44 (summer 1996), Gene Kehoe.

Kennedy, Jay. *The Official Underground and Newave Comix Price Guide.* Cambridge, Mass.: Boatner Norton Press, 1982.

Kingman, Jim. *Comic Effect* [fanzine] #1 (n.d.), Paloma St. Publications.

Kraft, David Anthony, ed. *FOOM* [fanzine] #20 (winter 1978), Marvel Comics.

Kurtzman, Harvey (w), and Wally Wood (a). "Superduperman!" *Mad* #4 (April–May 1953), EC Comics: 1–8.

Larew, Eric J. "New Comics: The Medium Done Well." *River Cities' Reader,* July 31–August 6, 1996, 9.

Lasky, David (w, a). "Ulysses Unbound!" *Boom-Boom* #2 (September 1994), ÆON.

Lee, Stan. *The Origins of Marvel Comics*. New York: Simon and Schuster, 1974.

———. *Son of Origins of Marvel Comics*. New York: Simon and Schuster, 1975.

Lee, Stan (w), and Steve Ditko (a). "Spider-Man!" *Amazing Fantasy* #15 (August 1962), Marvel Comics: 1–11.

Lee, Stan (w), and Gil Kane (a). "—And Now, the Goblin!" *Amazing Spider-Man* #96 (June 1971), Marvel Comics.

———. "The Goblin's Last Gasp!" *Amazing Spider-Man* #98 (August 1971), Marvel Comics.

———. "In the Grip of the Goblin!" *Amazing Spider-Man* #97 (July 1971), Marvel Comics.

Lee, Stan (w), and Jack Kirby (a). ". . . To Wake the Mangog!" *Thor* #154 (July 1968), Atlas Magazines [Marvel Comics].

Lee, Stan (w), Jack Kirby (p), and Dick Ayers (i). "The Return of Doctor Doom!" *Fantastic Four* #10 (January 1963), Marvel Comics.

Lee, Stan (w), Jack Kirby (p), and Joe Sinnott (i). "The Coming of Galactus!" *Fantastic Four* #48 (March 1966), Vista Publications [Marvel Comics].

———. "If This Be Doomsday!" *Fantastic Four* #49 (April 1966), Vista Publications [Marvel Comics].

———. "The Startling Saga of the Silver Surfer!" *Fantastic Four* #50 (May 1966), Vista Publications [Marvel Comics].

LeVine, Jeff. *Destroy All Comics* [fanzine] #1 (November 1994), Slave Labor Graphics.

Lobdell, Scott (w), Hilary Barta (p), and Rurik Tyler (i). *Marvel Riot* #1 (December 1995), Marvel Comics.

Lukin, Josh. "Childish Things: Nostalgia and Guilt in Grant Morrison's Comics." *Comics Journal* #176 (April 1995), Fantagraphics: 83–87.

Lupoff, Richard A. *The Comic Book Killer*. New York: Bantam, 1989.

MacDonald, Heidi. "Alas, Poor Claremont, I Knew Him Wolverine . . ." *Comics Journal* #99 (June 1985), Fantagraphics: 53–56.

———. "Triumph and Despair in the Temple of Elitism." *Comics Journal* #100 (July 1985), Fantagraphics: 182–87.

Mann, Ronn, producer/director. *Comic Book Confidential.* Sphinx Productions, 1988.

Marcus, Greil. "Notes on the Life and Death and Incandescent Banality of Rock 'n' Roll." *Esquire,* August 22, 1992, 67–71, 73, 75.

"Marvel Comics Demands an End to *Megaton Man* Marvel Parodies." *Comics Journal* #104 (January 1986), Fantagraphics: 12–14.

Massara, Jim. "Fan on the Street: Ed Thomas." *Comics Interview* #6 (August 1983), Fictioneer Books: 59–61.

Matt, Joe (w, a). "Fair Weather." *Peepshow* #7–10 (March 1995–July 1997), Drawn and Quarterly Publications.

———. *Peepshow: The Cartoon Diary of Joe Matt.* Northampton, Mass.: Kitchen Sink Press, 1995.

McCloud, Scott (w, a). "Clash of Titans." *Zot!* #31 (May 1990), Eclipse Comics.

———. *Destroy!* (1988), Eclipse Comics.

———. "The Great Escape." *Zot!* #36 (July 1991), Eclipse Comics.

———. *Understanding Comics: The Invisible Art.* Northampton, Mass.: Kitchen Sink Press, 1993.

Mescallado, Ray. "A Day in the Life: *Death: The High Cost of Living* and *The Death Gallery.*" *Comics Journal* #169 (July 1994), Fantagraphics: 49–52.

———. "Everything Old Is New Again." *Comics Journal* #190 (September 1996), Fantagraphics: 109–12.

———. Review of *Kurt Busiek's Astro City* #1. *Comics Journal* #179 (October 1995), Fantagraphics: 38.

———. "The Riddle of the Runaway Cultural Capital: Pierre Bourdieu and Barry Allen." Discourse on the Fanboi Politik Website (www.avalon.net/~fanboi).

Messner-Loebs, William. "Guide to Convention and Signing Etiquette" [column]. *Bliss Alley* #1 (July 1997), Image Comics: 29–31.

Michelinie, David (w), John Romita Jr. (p), and Bob Layton (i). "Demon in the Bottle." *Iron Man* #128 (November 1979), Marvel Comics.

Miller, Frank (w, p), and Klaus Janson (i). *Batman: The Dark Knight Returns.* New York: DC Comics, 1986.

Miller, John Jackson. "State of the Industry 1995: The Year Everything Changed." In *The Comics Buyer's Guide 1996 Annual,* edited by Maggie Thompson, Michael Dean, Brent Frankenhoff, Joyce Greenholdt, and John Jackson Miller, 51–69. Iola, Wis.: Krause Publications, 1995.

Moore, Alan. "An Ecstatic Effluence of Enjoyment and Erudition, Effortlessly Erupting from the Epicenter of Egotism!" [column] *1963* #5 (August 1993), Image Comics: 10.

Moore, Alan (w), and Brian Bolland (a). *Batman: The Killing Joke.* New York: DC Comics, 1988.

Moore, Alan (w), and Dave Gibbons (a). *Watchmen.* New York: DC Comics, 1987.

Morales, Robert. "That's Entertainment: Telling New Stories with Comics." *Publishers Weekly,* June 30, 1997, 49–55.

Morrison, Grant (w), and Dave McKean (i). *Batman: Arkham Asylum.* New York: DC Comics, 1989.

Morrison, Grant (w), Chas Truog (p), and Mark Farmer (i). "Deus Ex Machina." *Animal Man* #26 (August 1990), DC Comics.

———. "Monkey Puzzles." *Animal Man* #25 (July 1990), DC Comics.

Morrison, Grant (w), Chas Truog (p), and Doug Hazelwood (i). "A New Science of Life." *Animal Man* #19 (January 1990), DC Comics.

Muhlen, Norbert. "Comic Books and Other Horrors." *Commentary* 7 (1949): 80–87.

My Love #29 (July 1974), Marvel Comics.

"Newswatch." *Comics Journal* #97 (April 1985), Fantagraphics: 14–16.

Not Brand Ecch #1 (August 1967), Canam Publishers Sales [Marvel Comics].

Nyberg, Amy Kiste. "Seal of Approval: The Origins and History of the Comics Code." Ph.D. diss., University of Wisconsin-Madison, 1994.

Oarr, Chris, ed. *Small Press Expo '98.* Bethesda, Md.: Small Press Expo, 1998.

"Oh, No!" *Comics Journal* #190 (September 1996), Fantagraphics: 11–14.

Oldenburg, Ray. *The Great Good Place: Coffee Shops, Community Centers, Beauty Parlors, General Stores, Bars, Hangouts and How They Get You through the Day.* New York: Paragon, 1989.

Overstreet, Robert. *The Overstreet Comic Book Price Guide,* 24th ed. New York: Avon, 1994.

Parsons, Patrick. "Batman and His Audience: The Dialectic of Culture." In *The Many Lives of the Batman: Critical Approaches to a Superhero and His Media,* edited by Roberta E. Pearson and William Uricchio, 66–89. New York and London: Routledge, 1991.

Pekar, Harvey. "Rapping about Cartoonists, Particularly Robert Crumb." *Journal of Popular Culture* 3 (spring 1970): 677–88.

Pekar, Harvey (w), Greg Budgett (a), and Gary Dumm (a). "Awaking to the Terror of the New Day." *American Splendor* #3 (1978), Harvey Pekar: 6–14.

Pekar, Harvey (w), and Robert Crumb (a). "*American Splendor* Assaults the Media." *American Splendor* #8 (1983), Harvey Pekar: 29–32.

Pound, John (w, a). "Ronald Rabbit." *Death Rattle* #1 (1972), Kitchen Sink Press: 6–10.

Priore, Frank V. "Why Do People Collect Comics?" In *Fandom Directory*, vol. 1, no. 2, edited by Harry A. Hopkins, 262–64. N.p.: Fandom Computer Services, 1980.

Radway, Janice. *Reading the Romance: Women, Patriarchy, and Popular Literature.* Chapel Hill: University of North Carolina Press, 1984.

Raeburn, Daniel K. "The Fallen World of Daniel Clowes." *Imp* [fanzine] #1 (1997), Daniel K. Raeburn.

Reidelbach, Maria. *Completely Mad: A History of the Comic and Magazine.* Boston: Little, Brown, 1991.

Reynolds, Eric. "Pro/Con Politics." *Comics Journal* #178 (July 1995), Fantagraphics: 1–2.

Reynolds, Richard. *Superheroes: A Modern Mythology.* Jackson: University Press of Mississippi, 1992.

Rheingold, Howard. *The Virtual Community: Homesteading on the Electronic Frontier.* New York: HarperCollins, 1994.

Robbins, Trina (w, a). *It Ain't Me Babe* (July 1970), Last Gasp Eco-Funnies.

Rodi, Robert. *What They Did to Princess Paragon.* New York: Dutton, 1994.

Rogers, Mark C. "The Silver Age and the End of Comics as a Mass Medium." Paper presented at the annual meeting of the Popular Culture Association, San Antonio, Texas, March 26–29, 1997.

———. "Virtual Fans, Virtual Ethnography: The Culture of Comics Fans On-Line." Mark Rogers Home Page (www-personal.umich.edu/~cmarx/home.html), August 1997.

Rose, Margaret A. *Parody: Ancient, Modern, and Postmodern.* New York and Cambridge: Cambridge University Press, 1993.

Saavedra, Scott. *Comic Book Heaven* [fanzine] #1 (May 1995), Scott Saavedra.

———. *Comic Book Heaven* [fanzine] #4 (April 1996), Scott Saavedra.

Sabin, Roger. *Adult Comics: An Introduction.* New York and London: Routledge, 1993.

———. *Comics, Comix, and Graphic Novels: A History of Comic Art.* London: Phaidon, 1996.

Sacco, Joe (w, a). "How I Loved the War." *Yahoo* #5 (December 1991), Fantagraphics.

Sanders, Clinton R. "Icons of Alternate Culture: The Themes and Functions of Underground Comix." *Journal of Popular Culture* 8 (spring 1975): 836–52.

Savage, William W., Jr. *Comic Books and America, 1945–1954.* Norman: University of Oklahoma Press, 1990.

Schelly, Bill. *Fandom's Finest Comics: A Treasury of the Best Original Strips from the Classic Comics Fanzines, 1958–1975.* Seattle: Hamster Press, 1997.

———. *The Golden Age of Comic Fandom.* Seattle: Hamster Press, 1995.

————. *Labors of Love: The Classic Comic Strips of the* 1960s Fanzines. Seattle: Hamster Press, 1994.

————. *Labors of Love* 2: Classic Ama-Strips of the Ditto Fanzines. Seattle: Hamster Press, 1996.

Schmitt, Ronald. "Deconstructive Comics." *Journal of Popular Culture* 25 (spring 1992): 153–61.

Schoenberg, Tom. "Comic Book Store Is Daydream Come True." *Daily Iowan*, April 5, 1995, 2A.

Scott, Naomi, ed. *Heart Throbs: The Best of DC Romance Comics*. New York: Simon and Schuster, 1979.

Server, Lee. *Danger Is My Business: An Illustrated History of the Fabulous Pulp Magazines*. San Francisco: Chronicle Books, 1993.

Shutt, Craig. "Art Imitates Life." *Wizard: The Guide to Comics* #42 (February 1995), Wizard Press: 26–32.

Siegel, Jerry (w), and Joe Shuster (a). "Superman." *Action Comics* #1 (June 1938), Detective Comics, Inc. [DC Comics]: 1–13.

Simon, Joe (w), and Jack Kirby (a). "Different." *Young Romance* v4 #6 (1950), Prize/Headline Publications.

————. *Boy Commandos* #2 (November–December 1973), National Periodical Publications [DC Comics].

————. *Young Allies* #1 (Summer 1941), Timely Comics [Marvel Comics].

Simpson, Don (w, a). "News of the World." *Megaton Man* #4 (June 1985), Kitchen Sink Press.

"Special Editorial" [column]. *Vault of Horror* #40 (December 1954–January 1955), EC Comics: inside front cover.

Spiegelman, Art. *Maus: A Survivor's Tale*. New York: Pantheon Books, 1986.

Spurgeon, Tom. "Watch Out, Here Comes a Metaphor: Kurt Busiek and Mainstream Comics, 1996." *Comics Journal* #188 (July 1996), Fantagraphics: 85–94.

————. "San Diego Notebook 1998: A View from the Floor." *Comics Journal* #207 (September 1998), Fantagraphics: 17–20.

Staros, Chris. *The Staros Report—1996*. Marietta, Ga.: Chris Staros, 1995.

Steranko, Jim. *The Steranko History of Comics*. 2 vols. Reading, Pa.: Supergraphics, 1970.

Steumpfig, Julie. "State of the Industry." In *Comic Buyer's Guide 1994 Annual*, edited by Maggie Thompson, 35–47. Iola, Wis.: Krause Publications, 1993.

Stratton, Jerry. "Fear and Loathing in San Diego '97—Weekend." Negative Space Website (www.hoboes.com), August 1997.

Sullivan, Darcy. "Marvel Comics and the Kiddie Hustle." *Comics Journal* #152 (August 1992), Fantagraphics: 30–37.

———. "More from the Moolahverse: The Case against Bookstores." *Comics Journal* #178 (July 1995), Fantagraphics: 4–5.

"Superfans and Batmaniacs." *Newsweek*, February 15, 1965, 89–90.

"Superman's Other Life!" *Superman* v1 #132 (October 1959), National Periodical Publications [DC Comics].

Superman vs. the Amazing Spider-Man (1976), National Periodical Publications [DC Comics]/Marvel Comics.

Tebbel, John, and Mary Ellen Zuckerman. *The Magazine in America, 1741–1990.* New York: Oxford University Press, 1991.

Thomas, Roy (w, a). "The Bestest League of America." *Alter-Ego* [fanzine] #1 (spring 1961), Jerry Bails: 17–21.

Thomas, Roy (w), Jim Craig (p), and Pablo Marcos (i). "What If Spider-Man Joined the Fantastic Four?" *What If* #1 (February 1977), Marvel Comics.

Thrasher, Frederic M. "The Comics and Delinquency: Cause or Scapegoat." *Journal of Educational Sociology* 23 (December 1949): 195–205.

Tomine, Adrian (w, a). "The Author Addresses the Audience." *Optic Nerve* v1 #7 (summer 1994), Adrian Tomine: back inside cover.

Tulloch, John. "'But He's a Time Lord! He's a Time Lord!': Reading Formations, Followers, and Fans." In *Science Fiction Audiences: Watching* Doctor Who *and* Star Trek, edited by John Tulloch and Henry Jenkins, 125–43. New York and London: Routledge, 1995.

———. "'We're Only a Speck in the Ocean': The Fans as Powerless Elite." In *Science Fiction Audiences: Watching* Doctor Who *and* Star Trek, edited by John Tulloch and Henry Jenkins, 144–72. New York and London: Routledge, 1995.

U.S. Senate Committee on the Judiciary, Subcommittee to Investigate Juvenile Delinquency. *Hearings,* 83d Cong., 2d sess., 1954.

Valentino, Jim. "What If We Had Imaginary Stories?" *Amazing Heroes* #29 (August 15, 1983), Redbeard: 46–69.

——— (w, a). "Birthday." *Touch of Silver* #1 (January 1997), Image Comics.

Valerio, Mike, and Ken Gale. "The Legion Bulletin." *Interlac* [fanzine] #6 (April 1977), Amateur Press Association: 2–3.

Vance, Steve (w, p), Tim Bavington (p), and Bill Morrison (i). "Who Washes the Washmen's Infinite Secrets of Legendary Crossover Knight Wars?" *Radioactive Man* #679 [#5] (1994), Bongo Comics.

Vance, Steve (w, p), and Bill Morrison (i). "The Origin of Radioactive Man!" *Radioactive Man* #1 (1993), Bongo Comics.

———. "See No Evil, Hear No Evil!" *Radioactive Man* #216 [#3] (1994), Bongo Comics.

Vance, Steve (w, p), and Sondra Roy (i). "The Collector!" In *The Simpsons Comics Extravaganza*, 34–38. New York: HarperCollins, 1994.

Veitch, Rick (w, a). *Brat Pack* #1–5 (August 1990–May 1991), King Hell Press/Tundra Publishing.

Waid, Mark (w), and Alex Ross (a). *Kingdom Come* #1–4 (1996), DC Comics.

Ware, Chris (w, a). *Acme Novelty Library* #1 (winter 1993), Fantagraphics.

Warshow, Robert. "Paul, the Horror Comics, and Dr. Wertham." *Commentary* 17 (1954): 596–604.

Waugh, Patricia. "What Is Metafiction and Why Are They Saying Such Awful Things about It?" In *Metafiction*, edited by Mark Currie, 37–54. London and New York: Longman, 1995.

Weist, Jerry. "A Short History of Comic Fandom and Comic Book Collecting in America." In *The Overstreet Comic Book Price Guide*, 26th ed., compiled by Robert Overstreet, A104–5. New York: Avon, 1996.

Wertham, Fredric. "The Comics . . . Very Funny!" *Saturday Review of Literature*, May 29, 1948, 6–7, 27–29.

———. "Reading for the Innocent." *Wilson Library Bulletin* 29 (April 1955): 610–13.

———. *Seduction of the Innocent*. New York: Rinehart, 1954.

———. "What Parents Don't Know about Comic Books." *Ladies Home Journal*, November 1953, 50–53, 214–20.

———. *The World of Fanzines: A Special Form of Communication*. Carbondale: Southern Illinois University Press, 1973.

"What Is the Solution for Control of the Comics?" *Library Journal* 74 (February 1, 1949): 180.

Whitfield, Stephen J. *The Culture of the Cold War*. Baltimore and London: Johns Hopkins University Press, 1996.

Wiater, Stanley, and Stephen R. Bissette. *Comic Book Rebels: Conversations with the Creators of the New Comics*. New York: Donald I. Fine, 1993.

Witek, Joseph. *Comic Books as History: The Narrative Art of Jack Jackson, Art Spiegelman, and Harvey Pekar*. Jackson: University Press of Mississippi, 1989.

Wolf, Katherine M., and Marjorie Fiske. "The Children Talk about Comics." In *Communications Research*, 1948–1949, edited by Paul Lazarsfeld and Frank Stanton, 3–50. New York: Harper and Bros., 1949.

Yurkovich, David. "*Threshold*: The 31st Page" [column]. *Threshold* #1 (October 1996), Sleeping Giant Comics: 31.

Zorbaugh, Harvey. "The Comics—There They Stand!" *Journal of Educational Sociology* 18 (December 1944): 196–203.

———. "What Adults Think of Comics as Reading for Children." *Journal of Educational Sociology* 23 (December 1949): 225–35.

Index

DATE DUE

SEP 24